MODES OF COMPOSITION AND THE DURABILITY OF STYLE IN LITERATURE

Modes of Composition and the Durability of Style in Literature employs the tools and methods of computational stylistics to show that style is extremely resistant to changes in how texts are produced. Addressing an array of canonical writers, including William Faulkner, Joseph Conrad, Thomas Hardy, and Henry James, along with popular contemporary writers like Stephen King and Ian McEwan, this volume presents a systematic study of changes in mode of composition and writing technologies. Computational analysis of texts produced in multiple circumstances of composition, such as dictation, handwriting, typewriting, word processing, and translation, reveals the extraordinary durability of authorial style. *Modes of Composition and the Durability of Style in Literature* will be essential for readers interested in exploring the rapidly expanding field of digital approaches to literature.

David L. Hoover, Professor of English at New York University, holds a Ph.D. in English Language from Indiana University. He is Project Partner, "Quantitative Criticism," Universität Stuttgart; Co-Investigator, "Distant Reading for European Literary History" (COST); and Advisor, "The Riddle of Literary Quality" (Netherlands). He is the author of "Simulations and Difficult Problems" (2019) and "The Microanalysis of Style Variation" (2017) in *Digital Scholarship in the Humanities*, and *Digital Literary Studies* (with Culpeper and O'Halloran, Routledge, 2014).

MODES OF COMPOSITION AND THE DURABILITY OF STYLE IN LITERATURE

David L. Hoover

Routledge
Taylor & Francis Group
NEW YORK AND LONDON

First published 2021
by Routledge
52 Vanderbilt Avenue, New York, NY 10017

and by Routledge
2 Park Square, Milton Park, Abingdon, Oxon, OX14 4RN

Routledge is an imprint of the Taylor & Francis Group, an informa business

Library of Congress Cataloging-in-Publication Data
A catalog record for this book has been requested

ISBN: 978-0-367-36672-8 (hbk)
ISBN: 978-0-367-36670-4 (pbk)
ISBN: 978-0-429-34806-8 (ebk)

Typeset in Bembo
by Apex CoVantage, LLC

Dedicated to the memory of John F. Burrows

CONTENTS

FIGURES

TABLES

PREFACE

The origins of this project can be dated back to about 2005, when I became interested in the chronological changes in the style of Henry James and other authors. This interest was inspired, I believe, by John F. Burrows's "Not Unless You Ask Nicely: The Interpretative Nexus Between Analysis and Information," in which he discusses how different the original 1877 version of *The American* is from the 1907 revised version James included in his collected New York Edition. In 2006, my early investigations of the chronological development of James's style resulted in two conference presentations, "Stylometry, Chronology, and the Styles of Henry James" and "CaSTAing Breadth Upon the Waters," and a keynote address, "A Conversation Among Himselves," the last of which later became "Corpus Stylistics, Stylometry, and the Styles of Henry James," in a special issue of *Style* honoring *Style in Fiction*, that seminal text in stylistics by Michael Short and Geoffrey Leech.

I extended this interest in chronology to other authors and to how the literary vocabularies of various authors change over time ("Literary Style") and then turned to the intersection between genre and chronology ("Style Evolution"). By 2009, I had begun to work on the question of whether and how dictation might have affected James's style in a conference paper ("Modes"), and two years later, I broadened that work on dictation and style to an examination of Thomas Hardy, Joseph Conrad, and Walter Scott, in another conference paper, "Modes of Composition in Three Authors." By 2014, I had published a book, long in the making, *Digital Literary Studies* (with Jonathan Culpeper and Kieran O'Halloran), in which I approached the chronological changes in James's style in some different ways, and an article version of "Modes of Composition in Henry James," which had developed into a rigorous examination of and rejection of the widespread claim that James's adoption of dictation was responsible for the development of his late style. Much of my research since 2014 has focused on other projects on collaboration (Rybicki et al.; Hoover, "Cora Crane's Contribution"), on style variation ("Microanalysis"), on stylistics ("Metaphors" and "Mind-style"), and on general principles of evidence and argument in the digital humanities ("Simulations," "Argument," "Making," and "Starting").

Throughout the last decade, or so, however, I have continued to collect information and to do preliminary work on the relationship between modes of composition and style. In spite of the negative early experience investigating the possible effects of changes of mode of composition in Henry James, Thomas Hardy, Walter Scott, and Joseph Conrad, I expected to find authors whose styles showed a noticeable effect of a change in mode. This work has been painfully slow, largely because so little reliable and comprehensive information about how writers actually produce their texts is available. For example, the biographies of authors who are otherwise known to have used dictation for some of their writings often make no mention at all of this fact. For many authors, a single brief mention of a (change in) mode of composition was all that I was able to find. For example, a biography of Charles Kingsley simply quotes Mrs. Kingsley's comment that she took down every one of his compositions by dictation "for many years" (Thorp 58). In many other cases where some evidence about a change in mode of composition is available, it is too vague to allow a legitimate investigation. The writers themselves are often not very helpful either, even when they write about their own writing history and process. In Stephen King's well-known book *On Writing*, for example, there are only two references to "word processors," and neither is specific to his own use of them or to the Wang he bought in 1981.

Identifying cases of changes in mode of composition that *are* adequately described, however, is only the first step. It must be followed by an evaluation of the feasibility of each case. Unfortunately, the circumstances surrounding an author's change in mode are often such that no really legitimate investigation is possible. An example is Milton, whose blindness and use of dictation are duly famous, but for whom there is conflicting evidence (more than 350 years old) about what and why he dictated and when he began. Anne Rice, an author I considered in the early stages of my research, is another example, attractive because her first novel, *Interview With a Vampire* (1976), was typewritten but was followed by word-processed novels. The second of her vampire novels, *The Vampire Lestat*, did not appear until 1985, however, and the novels published between the two vary widely in genre. Finally, other books in her Vampire Chronicles were later interrupted by and inflected by her return to (and then re-abandonment of) the Catholicism of her youth. There is not enough typewritten fiction for an adequate investigation, and the issues of genre and religious conversion promise too much confusion for a legitimate study of Rice's modes of composition, in spite of her comments on the way she sees her new word processor affecting her writing: "things happen to your mind, I mean, you change as a writer" (qtd. in Kirschenbaum 50).

Isaac Asimov, whose adoption of word processing in 1981 (a change from typewriting) makes him one of the earliest major authors to take up word processing, is another author who initially seems very attractive for a study of the effects of a change in mode of composition. However, although he is known primarily for his science fiction, Asimov's last science fiction novel before the change to word processing was published nine years earlier, in 1972, and the works in the few years before and after his change in mode of composition include multiple collections of his "Black Widowers" mystery short stories and a series of novels about Norby the robot. I later discovered that, in his memoirs, Asimov also claimed that he initially used the word processor only for short works (see also Kirschenbaum 58). These complications make the difficulty of disentangling the various possible influences on his style almost insuperable.

Other attractive authors who could not be studied include Hamlin Garland, a very early adopter of the typewriter who typed some of his work on an all-upper-case typewriter as early as 1885 (Pizer 61n7), but he took up typewriting at the very beginning of his writing career. Michael Crichton, one candidate for the first author to have produced a published work of fiction on a word processor (Kirschenbaum 244), would also have been an interesting case, but his novels written just before and just after his change to word processing are too widely spaced and not numerous enough for a legitimate analysis. Similarly, Douglas Adams, another early adopter who bought his first word processor in 1982 (Kirschenbaum 111), initially seemed like a good prospect for analysis. Unfortunately, his five-novel series, *The Hitchhiker's Guide to the Galaxy*, published between 1979 and 1992, which would be the logical focus of analysis, has a confused composition history in which the three novels written before he bought the word processor were based on earlier radio scripts and film treatments (Simpson 204), and the two later word-processed novels were written under tremendous pressure with Adams essentially held captive in a London hotel (Simpson 204–6, 265–6). The eight-year gap between the fourth and fifth novels is also problematic.

Ford Madox Ford dictated most or all of his best known novel, *The Good Soldier* ("Note on the Text"), and also seems to have typed the last three of the four novels of his Parade's End tetralogy, which began with the 1924 *Some Do Not* (Meixner 222). These changes in mode, the fact that he collaborated with Joseph Conrad (who will be addressed in Chapter 3) on several works, and his comments on the effects on his writing that he perceived when typing or dictating seem to make him a good prospect for analysis. The case of Ford, however, suffers from insuperable difficulties. A quick test of the four Tietjens novels from the 1920s, however, shows no suggestion of a distinction between the first handwritten novel and the last three typed novels. This is in spite of a general view that the last three novels are substantially inferior (Meixner 222–32). An examination of the possible effects of dictation on *The Good Soldier* (1915) would also be quite problematic. The preceding novels from 1910 to 1913 are satires, a farce, a novelization of a play, and historical novels, and an eight-year gap separates *The Good*

Soldier from his next novel, *The Marsden Case*, a semi-autobiographical novel set during World War I (Harvey xxi–xxii).

Another possible author I had to abandon is Will Self, who says, in "My Writing Day," that he used a word processor regularly early in his career but later returned to the manual typewriter for his first draft. Unfortunately, he now apparently enters the first draft into a word processor for later drafts. His oeuvre is also very diverse. The novel before returning to the manual typewriter, *Dorian, An Imitation* (2002), is a modern take on Oscar Wilde's *The Picture of Dorian Gray*, and the previous novel had been narrated by a dead woman. The first novel after the change is a post-apocalypse novel narrated in both present time and a time more than five hundred years in the future, and the following one is a satiric allegory about the bizarre consequences of throwing a cigarette butt out of a window. As will become clear, some of the authors who are addressed in this book are also somewhat problematic, but none so problematic as those I have rejected.

Authors whose careers and changes in mode seem amenable to an investigation into the possible effects of the change in mode on their styles often present other practical and logistical problems. For example, Hoffman's *Fiction Writers on Fiction Writing* contains comments by more than one hundred writers about their writing methods. Unfortunately, even though the works of most of these authors are out of copyright, many of the authors are relatively unimportant and largely forgotten. As a consequence, for many of them, there is little or none of their writing easily available for analysis. In contrast, a large proportion of the works of Booth Tarkington, whose change from handwriting to dictation is analyzed in Chapter 3, are out of copyright and are available as electronic texts, including about twenty-five at Project Gutenberg, and a few more at *Wikisource*. However, the crucial period surrounding Tarkington's adoption of dictation is 1925 to 1935, and many of his stories from this period, all still in copyright, are available only in very poor quality PDF images from magazines, or, even worse, only available in microfilm or in hard-to-locate yellowing pages of paper copies of old magazines. In a broad study such as this, there is a limit to how many such problematic texts can be digitized and corrected: locating and transforming a single short story into an electronic text and correcting errors can take many hours.

The works of more recent authors like William Faulkner (see Chapter 4); Arthur Clarke, Octavia Butler, Stanley Elkin, and Ian McEwan (see Chapter 5); and Stephen King (see Chapter 7) are all still in copyright and are not typically legally available as editable, analyzable electronic texts. Buying e-books for these authors takes some of the pain out of creating analyzable texts, but the process of capturing the text of a single e-book and correcting the results of optical character recognition (which transforms the image into editable text) often takes much of a day of mind-numbing work. (I normally use ABBYY for this process.)

For some authors, care must be taken in selecting an edition for analysis. For example, Thomas Hardy's *A Laodicean* (see Chapter 3) was partly dictated while it was being serialized, so that analyzing the book version, which he created by revising the serial version after he had given up dictation, could be problematic. And it would be folly, knowing how radical a difference exists between Henry James's early and late style, to compare his late, dictated novels with the heavily revised versions of his early handwritten novels that he prepared for his New York Edition long after he began dictating, even though many of those revisions were handwritten (see Chapter 6).

Whatever the sources of the texts for analysis, they all call for additional editing—sometimes relatively minor and sometimes quite extensive. For example, a large proportion of electronic texts available online use the same character to represent the apostrophe and the single quotation mark. This might seem like a minor problem, but many texts, especially those very frequent ones that use a significant amount of dialect, contain hundreds of apostrophes at the beginnings of words like "'cause" for "because" and at the end of shortened words like "th'" for "the." Some text-analysis tools treat these all as if they were single quotation marks and therefore equate "'cause" with "cause." Others treat them all as apostrophes, and therefore fail to distinguish the reduced form of "because" from the word "cause" at the beginning of a quotation marked by single quotation marks. If an electronic text marks all quotations with single quotation marks, as many British texts do, and contains a great deal of dialect (think *Wuthering Heights*), thousands of errors in word-identification can result. My Excel Text-Analysis Tools website includes a program that streamlines the checking and correcting of the apostrophe problem, along with a series of other computational tools that I have developed and that will be applied to the question of the effects of changes in mode of composition ("Excel Text-Analysis").

My hope that this book will be of interest to literary scholars and general readers as well as those in the computational stylistics community has guided my approach to the computational analyses presented. My aim is to present enough detail and explanation for a general understanding of the methods and tools, and enough to allow the specialist to understand the methodology, without overloading the text with technical terminology and explanation. The question of what effect a change in mode of composition might have on an author's style is fortunately at a level where some of the more sophisticated machine learning tools are rarely appropriate. The important question for this study is whether a change in mode caused a *significant* or *important* variation in authorial style, or, in some cases, in the style of one or more texts, or even parts of texts, within an author's oeuvre. Pure classification tests based on minute effects that might allow texts to be identified as having been handwritten or typed, for example, are thus not particularly valuable for my purposes. In most of the cases examined here, the point at which the change occurred is already known. The question is how much the change in mode matters, and this question seems better approached through more exploratory methods and methods that are more intimately related to style and theme. This study will show that literary style is, in fact, very durable in the face of changes in mode of composition. Authorial style persists, largely unaffected by such changes. But that is to be demonstrated.

Without question, many other authors exist whose changes in mode of composition have escaped my notice and could be investigated. And it is of course possible that, for some authors, such changes had more significant effects than the extremely marginal ones suggested for some of the authors discussed here—that their styles were less durable in the face of changes in mode of composition than the styles of the authors I have investigated. Given the range and variety among the authors and the modes and circumstances of composition discussed here, however, I will be surprised if many such authors exist. Recognizing that surprise is more a normal expectation than an anomaly in the computational analysis of style, however, I am continuing my search for and analysis of more authors for whom an investigation of a change in mode is feasible.

References

ABBYY FineReader 14 Standard. ABBYY Production, LLC, 2017.

Burrows, John F. "Not Unless You Ask Nicely: The Interpretative Nexus Between Analysis and Information." *Literary and Linguistic Computing*, vol. 7, no. 2, 1992, pp. 91–109, doi.org/10.1093/llc/7.2.91.

Ford, Ford Madox. *The Good Soldier: A Tale of Passion*. Oxford World's Classics, edited by Thomas C. Moser, Oxford UP, 1990.

Harvey, David Dow. *Ford Madox Ford, 1873–1939: Bibliography of Works and Criticism*. Princeton UP, 1962.

Hoffman, Arthur S., editor. *Fiction Writers on Fiction Writing: Advice, Opinions and a Statement of Their Own Working Methods by More Than One Hundred Writers*. Bobbs-Merrill, 1923. archive.org/details/fictionwritersonO0indi.

Hoover, David L. "A Conversation Among Himselves: Change and the Styles of Henry James." *Style in Fiction International Symposium*, Lancaster University, 11 Mar. 2006.

———. "Argument, Evidence, and the Limits of Digital Literary Studies." *Debates in the Digital Humanities: 2016*, edited by Matthew Gold, U of Minnesota P, 2016, pp. 230–50. dhdebates.gc.cuny.edu/read/untitled/section/70f5261e-e268-4f56-928f-0c4ea30d254d.

———. "CaSTAing Breadth Upon the Waters." CaSTA 2006: Breadth of Text—A Joint Computer Science and Humanities Computing Conference, U of New Brunswick. Fredericton, NB, Canada, 13 Oct. 2006.

———. "Cora Crane's Contribution to Stephen Crane's Posthumous Fiction." *DH2015: Global Digital Humanities*, U of Western Sydney, 2 July 2015.

———. "Corpus Stylistics, Stylometry, and the Styles of Henry James." *Style*, vol. 41, no. 2, 2007, pp. 174–203.

———. *Excel Text-Analysis Tools*. wp.nyu.edu/exceltextanalysis/.

———. "Literary Style, Chronology, and Vocabulary: Problems of Stylistics and Classification." Joint Workshop on Data Analysis and Research in the Humanities. Digital Humanities and CSNA, Urbana-Champaign, 8 June 2007.

———. "Making Waves: Algorithmic Criticism Revisited." *Digital Humanities 2014*, Lausanne: EPFL-UNIL, 10 June 2014, pp. 202–4.

———. "Metaphors We May Not Live By." *International Journal of Literary Linguistics*, vol. 5, no. 1, 2016, pp. 1–16, doi.org/10.15462/ijll.v5i1.27.

———. "The Microanalysis of Style Variation." *Digital Scholarship in the Humanities*, vol. 32, suppl. 2, 2017, pp. ii17–ii30, doi.org/10.1093/llc/fqx022.

———. "Mind-Style." *The Bloomsbury Companion to Stylistics*, edited by Violeta Sotirova, Bloomsbury Academic, 2016, pp. 325–40.

———. "Modes of Composition in Henry James: Dictation, Style, and *What Maisie Knew*." *Digital Humanities 2009*, Maryland Institute for Technology in the Humanities, pp. 145–8.

———. "Modes of Composition in Henry James: Dictation, Style, and *What Maisie Knew*." *Henry James Review*, vol. 35, no. 3, 2014, pp. 257–77, doi:10.1353/hjr.2014.0024.

———. "Modes of Composition in Three Authors." *Digital Humanities 2011*, Stanford University Library, 2011, pp. 152–5.

———. "Simulations and Difficult Problems." *Digital Scholarship in the Humanities*, vol. 34, no. 4, 2019, pp. 874–92, doi.org/10.1093/llc/fqz034.

———. "Style Evolution in Henry James: Fiction, Short Fiction, Non-fiction, Drama." MLA Convention, San Francisco, 27 Dec. 2008.

———. "Stylometry, Chronology, and the Styles of Henry James." *Digital Humanities 2006*, Centre de Recherche Cultures Anglophones et Technologies de l'Information, 2006, pp. 78–80. www.allc-ach2006.colloques.paris-sorbonne.fr/DHs.pdf.

Hoover, David L., and Aaron Plasek. "Starting the Conversation: Literary Studies, Algorithmic Opacity, and Computer-Assisted Literary Insight." *Digital Humanities 2014*, EPFL-UNIL, 2014, pp. 305–7.

Hoover, David L. et al. *Digital Literary Studies: Corpus Approaches to Poetry, Prose, and Drama*. Routledge, 2014.

Kirschenbaum, Matthew G. *Track Changes: A Literary History of Word Processing*. Belknap Press, 2016.

Leech, Geoffrey, and Michael Short. *Style in Fiction*. 2nd ed. Addison-Wesley, 2007.

Meixner, John A. *Ford Madox Ford's Novels: A Critical Study*. U of Minnesota P, 1962. muse.jhu.edu/book/31799.

Pizer, Donald. "'John Boyle's Conclusion': An Unpublished Middle Border Story by Hamlin Garland." *American Literature*, vol. 31, no. 1, 1959, pp. 59–75. www.jstor.org/stable/2922652.

Project Gutenberg. Founded by Michael Hart, 1971. www.gutenberg.org.

Rybicki, Jan et al. "Collaborative Authorship: Conrad, Ford, and Rolling Delta." *Literary and Linguistic Computing*, vol. 29, no. 3, 2014, pp. 422–31, doi.org/10.1093/llc/fqu016.

Self, Will. "My Writing Day." *The Guardian*, 18 June 2016.

Simpson, M. J. *Hitchhiker: A Biography of Douglas Adams*. Justin, Charles and Co., 2005. archive.org/details/hitchhikerbiogra00simp.

Thorp, Margaret Farrand. *Charles Kingsley, 1819–1875, 1937*. Princeton UP, 2015. muse.jhu.edu/book/42948.

Wikisource contributors. "Main Page." *Wikisource*. en.wikisource.org/wiki/Main_Page.

ACKNOWLEDGMENTS

Without the inspiring, pioneering, and generative work of the late John F. Burrows, mentor and role model, this book would never have been written.

I am grateful to Hugh Craig for advice and counsel on the reframing of my argument and to Gabriel Egan for encouragement and support. I am also grateful to the whole community of scholars working on authorship attribution, computational stylistics, and digital humanities for stimulating and challenging discussions and conversations, with special thanks to Ray Siemens, Jan Rybicki, Maciej Eder, and Karina van Dalen-Oskam.

Thanks also to students in my classes at New York University and in my annual Out-of-the-Box Text Analysis for the Digital Humanities Seminar at the Digital Humanities Summer Institute at the University of Victoria for enlightening and productive discussions. Audiences and participants at the following conferences also deserve my thanks for questions, suggestions, challenges, and observations: MLA, Association for Computers and the Humanities/Association for Literary and Linguistic Computing, Digital Humanities, and Canadian Symposium on Textual Analysis.

I am grateful as well to Brianna Cregle, Special Collections Assistant, Public Services Division, Department of Rare Books and Special Collections, Princeton University Library, for checking the identity of the handwriting of some of the manuscripts of Booth Tarkington's fiction.

I would also like to express my gratitude for generous financial support provided by the Abraham and Rebecca Stein Faculty Publication Fund of the New York University Department of English.

Chapter 6 is a substantially revised version of "Modes of Composition in Henry James: Dictation, Style, and *What Maisie Knew*," Copyright © 2014, The Johns Hopkins University Press. This article first appeared in *The Henry James Review*, Volume 35, Issue 3, Fall, 2014, pages 257–77.

1

MODES OF COMPOSITION AND THE DURABILITY OF LITERARY STYLE

Introduction

> In every age since written language began, rhetorical forms have been to a considerable extent influenced by the writing materials and implements which were available for man's use. This is a familiar observation in studies of the past. Is it not, then, time that somebody inquired into the effects upon the form and substance of our present-day language of the veritable maze of devices which have come into widely extended use in recent years, such as the typewriter, with its invitation to the dictation practice; shorthand, and, most important of all, the telegraph? Certainly these agencies of expression cannot be without their marked and significant influences upon English style.
>
> *(O'Brien 464; qtd. in Seltzer 6–7)*

What should we expect to happen to the styles of authors who change from one mode of composition to another? This question seems relatively speculative, but the artistic and personal nature of literary composition suggests that a writer's style might well be affected by a change in the way the text is produced. More than a hundred years ago, when Robert Lincoln O'Brien wrote the quotation that begins this chapter, he obviously thought writing technology affected style. He immediately added, however, the prediction that "the saner and nobler literature of the world will always be written in more deliberate, and perhaps old-fashioned ways, by mechanical methods in which there has been little change from Chaucer to Kipling." When his prediction proved false, would he have expected the style of "nobler" literature to be affected by writing technology as well?

Writers' own perceptions that changes in mode affect their writing provide another justification for studying the question, even given the notorious inaccuracy of authorial opinions about their own texts and styles. The well-known differences between speech and writing, famously discussed by Walter Ong and others in terms of orality and literacy and more recently confirmed by corpus linguistics, suggest that producing a text by speaking rather than writing might cause significant and systematic differences in the resulting text. The differences between speech and writing also suggest the possibility that the use of dictation might affect dialogue and narrative in different ways or to different degrees. The fact that a handwritten (or typed or word-processed) text is immediately visible to the writer, while a text dictated to an amanuensis is not, might also have some effect. There is also evidence that handwriting and typing involve different mental processes and even different parts of the brain, and there has been some research suggesting that the ease of revision during composition with word processors facilitates the production of text and may affect the quality of writing, at least among young writers. These a priori grounds for thinking that style may be affected by mode of composition are sufficient for my purposes.

One complicating factor is that, for many of the writers known to have changed how they write, the reason for the change in mode of composition might itself also affect their styles. Henry James's wrist pain, Joseph Conrad's gout, the painful stomach problems of Walter Scott and Thomas Hardy, Stanley Elkin's finger pain because of multiple sclerosis, and Stephen King's pain following a car accident certainly cannot be ruled out as causes of stylistic change. Conrad's early use of dictation was also partly because of pressure to produce text more quickly, and Scott was hurrying, too, publishing three novels, a total of more than 370,000 words in 1819 alone, and speed of composition might also affect an author's style. Encroaching blindness might also have caused changes in Booth Tarkington's style, though its gradualness and the fact that he apparently began to dictate while his vision was still good enough that he could have handwritten his texts suggest that the cause of change of mode might not be as significant as the change itself.

William Faulkner's transition to typing most of his first drafts directly on the typewriter rather than writing them by hand about mid-career was apparently a matter of convenience, so that the cause of his change in mode seems much less likely to have altered his style than does the new mode of composition itself. This case is complicated by the fact that he had already been typing his initial handwritten drafts very shortly after writing them, so that editing, amplifying, and correcting at the typewriter were clearly very familiar by this time in his career. Similarly, the transitions from typewriter to word processor in the middle of a novel by both Arthur Clarke and Octavia Butler might seem relatively minor changes of mode, but the ease of immediate revision, and especially the ease of moving text from one part of the document to another, seems like differences significant enough for a possible stylistic effect. Clark and Butler, like Faulkner, switched voluntarily for convenience and speed, so that their cases present fairly pure tests of the effect of the change in mode.

Ian McEwan is another author for whom the change in mode was a voluntary one. After handwriting his first two novels, he switched to a word processor for later work. Stanley Elkin made the same change in mode, but not voluntarily. Instead, as noted earlier, he got a word processor because of finger pain caused by multiple sclerosis. Both McEwan and Elkin are attractive targets for analysis because they have also both written about their perceptions of how word processing changed their writing.

The case of Stephen King is exceptionally complex. King got a typewriter for Christmas when he was eleven (*On Writing* 13). Because he changed from handwriting to typing before the publication of his first book in 1974, his initial change in mode of composition is not testable. He switched to word processing in 1981 but went back to handwriting for two novels: *Bag of Bones* (1998) and *Dreamcatcher* (2001), with one word-processed novel between. After 2001, he returned to word processing. Intersecting with these seemingly promising changes of mode, however, is a complex history of alcohol and drug abuse that King has discussed openly. King reports that he wrote under the influence of alcohol or cocaine up to at least 1989, about six years after he began using a word processor. This seems to make the two late handwritten novels a good testing ground. In 1999, however, King was very seriously injured when he was hit by a van while taking a walk, and he wrote *Dreamcatcher*, the second late, handwritten novel, under the influence of Oxycontin because of severe pain. In spite of these difficulties, King's case presents a fascinating testing ground for the effects of both substance abuse and change of mode of composition on his writing style.

The question of revision also complicates the question of how a change in mode of composition might affect style. For most of these authors, the process of revision still involved handwritten changes, so that any unwanted effects of a change in mode could, if noticed, be removed or reduced in the revision process. Fortunately, the authors who will be studied here vary significantly in the amount and intensity of revision they practiced. James, Conrad, Tarkington, Faulkner, McEwan, and Elkin were extensive revisers, but Scott was notoriously not so, and Hardy and King seem to fall somewhere between. Editorial intervention has also often been suggested as a confounding or complicating factor in the study of literary style, but, as Chapter 2 will show, actual evidence for significant effects of editors on authors' styles is difficult to demonstrate.

Before turning to an examination of the possibility of stylistic changes caused by a change in mode of composition, the three elements of my title need some discussion: literary style, its relative durability, and the differences among the various modes themselves.

Literary Style, Authorial Style, and the Author

After some thousands of years of the study of the styles of individual authors, it seems peculiar to feel the need to begin a discussion of literary style, and especially authorial style, with a defense of the concepts themselves. The primary reason for this need is the immense influence, now perhaps waning somewhat, of ideas stemming from two essays originally published in the 1960s: Roland Barthes' "The Death of the Author" and Michel "What Is an Author?." These essays rightly emphasized the social construction of authorship and the problematic nature of a reliance on authorial intention (for an interesting collection of essays on authorship and intention, see Irwin). In some academic circles, however, an extreme version has taken root that claims to invalidate the entire idea of authorship attribution and denies the existence of authorial style. The extreme version is, however, what Bertrand Russell once referred to as "a Sunday truth, sacred and mystical, to be professed in awed tones, but not to be acted on in daily life" (125), and there is ample evidence that it has always attracted more lip-service than real belief (Farrell, *Varieties* 6–10 and "Why").

One source of the extreme form of the belief in "the death of the author" is undoubtedly Barthes' claim:

> We know that a text does not consist of a line of words, releasing a single "theological" meaning (the "message" of the Author-God), but is a space of many dimensions, in which are wedded and contested various kinds of writing, no one of which is original: the text is a tissue of citations, resulting from the thousand sources of culture.
>
> (6)

Although the rejection of a single essential and unchanging meaning of any text is now, justly, a commonplace, Barthes could not have known in 1967 that the claim that texts are tissues of unoriginal quotations would later become clearly and provably false.

Anyone who doubts my assertion is encouraged to do a web search for a sentence of eight or more words from a favorite novel, enclosed in quotation marks. Such a search almost invariably returns multiple copies of or quotations from the novel, but no hits from anywhere else. Searching similarly for sequences from Barthes's essay also (ironically) returns only multiple copies of or quotations from the essay itself. Conversely, searching for a sequence of eight or more words from a sentence in this paragraph, again enclosed in quotation marks, will almost certainly return no hits at all. This is true of quite ordinary-seeming sequences like "will almost certainly return no hits at all" and "searching for a sequence of eight or more." Perhaps Barthes did not mean that the actual wording of any text is not original (though "tissue of quotations" seems to refer to the wording itself), but it is useful to be reminded just how individual each person's language use is, even when that language is fairly straightforward and unexceptional.

The individuality of authorial style is, simply put, an irreducible fact that no theoretical argument can afford to deny, as Harold Love has persuasively argued in Chapter 1 of *Attributing Authorship,* his excellent general introduction to authorship and authorship attribution. This individuality is what makes plagiarism detectable and authorship attribution possible, as will be shown in the next chapter. (For a further exploration of the use of giant corpora and the web as sources of evidence for literary arguments, see my "The End of the Irrelevant Text: Electronic Texts, Linguistics, and Literary Theory." And for a critique of one extreme form of textual relativism, see my "Hot-Air Textuality: Literature after Jerome McGann.")

The social construction of reality and of the self, another related idea with many important and fruitful consequences, has also sometimes been propounded in an extreme form that suggests that all forms of human knowledge and even reality itself are equally constructed and contingent. It was this extreme form that led one postmodern journal to accept Alan Sokal's famous hoax argument that gravity is a social construct (see Hoover, "Argument" for discussion). Yet, surely John Guillory is right to point out that

> if positivism is a holistic or totalizing ideology that reserves the name of knowledge only for the results of the scientific method (narrowly defined), it does not follow that the critical disciplines must be based on a counter-holism in which everything is interpretation, in which the very possibility of a positive knowledge is called into question.
>
> *(Guillory 504)*

A strong form of social constructionism has also been taken by some critics as evidence that individual authorial styles cannot exit. The romantic individual subject, from whose genius the literary text flows, it is sometimes claimed, is an illusion because each self is constructed by society. If this claim were true, it would be impossible to use textual features to attribute texts to their authors. Yet there is an overwhelming amount of evidence that individual authorial styles *can* be distinguished computationally, and social constructionism does not really suggest otherwise. On the contrary, it can be seen as implying or even guaranteeing the existence of unique individual selves and styles, though we need not be committed to the overly romanticized individual genius. Ignoring the genetic uniqueness of each human being, if the self is constructed from environmental and social influences on the growing child, that self is necessarily unique because no two humans grow up in identical natural or social environments. There is thus every reason to believe that a socially constructed individual self will inevitably result in an individual and unique set of linguistic behaviors. Each person's idiolect is necessarily unique, and this allows for the possibility, at least, that each person's writing style is unique (see Love 8–10).

There is neither space for an extended discussion of these issues here, nor any need for such a discussion. Pending the demonstration of the effectiveness of computational methods of stylistic analysis in identifying variations in style in the next chapter, I will simply lay out my own views on literary style briefly and then turn to the durability of style and modes of composition.

In its broadest, simplest, and most basic sense, style is a way of doing something—here, an author's way of writing. Practically, however, the normal focus of a discussion or an analysis of style is actually the characteristics or features of texts. One recent discussion of style defines it as "a property of texts constituted by an ensemble of formal features which can be observed quantitatively or qualitatively" (Herrmann et al. 16). That this complex ensemble of characteristic features of any author's style together constitutes a unique "wordprint," analogous to a fingerprint, is a reasonable, if unprovable, assumption (Love 12; Burrows, "Not" 91).

Considering style to be a property of texts allows the term to apply to the style of a literary-historical period (Victorian, Romantic) or genre (Gothic, satire), of an author's complete oeuvre (Faulkner's style), of a chronological period within an author's oeuvre (Henry James's late style), of a single text (the style of *The Great Gatsby*), or even of part of a single text (Benjy's style in *The Sound and the Fury*, Holden Caulfield's style in *The Catcher in the Rye*, Elizabeth Bennet's style in *Pride and Prejudice*), among other possibilities. The question for this study is whether there are handwritten, typed, dictated, or word-processed sub-styles for authors who changed their modes of composition. For many of the authors, the question involves whether or not there are such sub-styles associated with two modes of composition within a single text.

Most discussions of literary style focus on linguistic features, although quasi-linguistic features like punctuation are also often relevant, and, for some writers who were able to control other characteristics of their texts, textual characteristics such as page size and layout and the color and thickness of the paper might be considered stylistic features. For example, Willa Cather specified heavy, cream-colored paper, wide margins, and large, dark type for her novels (*ix–x*). Some elements of style are obviously linguistic, such as grammar, vocabulary, morphology, phonology, figures of speech, cohesion, and collocation (for an excellent checklist of features, see Leech and Short 61–72). Other larger elements of style, such as the author's worldview, politics, themes, topics, plots, and characters are all, though not themselves linguistic, obviously expressed linguistically.

Style also normally involves repetition and pattern, and the way the stylistic elements are distributed is often crucial. Some striking stylistic effects are quite local, but a single isolated effect is likely to be difficult to interpret, and what we normally think of when we think of authorial style is a series of repeated characteristic features. All statements about style are essentially comparative, even if the comparison is not explicit. Any remark on a stylistic characteristic implies a comparison, even if it does not state one. Describing Faulkner's sentences as long and complex, for example, implicitly asserts that they are longer and more complex than "normal." If all writers' sentences were equally long and complex, there would hardly be a point in making the remark. In cases of a change in mode of composition, the comparison between the author's style before and after the change will necessarily be explicit.

The patterned, repeated, and distributed nature of literary style makes the use of computational methods both attractive and appropriate. I would not suggest that stylistic analysis *must* be computational, but it will become clear shortly why computational methods are necessary for an investigation of the possible stylistic effects of changes in mode of composition. I will normally concentrate on words in my analysis for both practical and principled reasons. Besides being very frequent, and thus appropriate for statistical analysis, words are also relatively easy to identify and count. In the analyses that follow, I will sometimes also examine the frequencies of sequences of words or sequences of characters, both of which have been shown to be more effective in distinguishing styles in some cases. Sequences capture some minimal elements of syntax, but I will not use syntactic parsers or study syntax explicitly. Changes in mode of composition might affect figures of speech, but figures of speech are neither frequent enough for statistical analysis nor feasible to identify automatically.

Words have been by far the most frequent focus of stylistics and authorship attribution and computational stylistics, but, as intuitively simple as the concept of "word" seems, different definitions are defensible in different circumstances and for different purposes. In the analyses in this book, I will define a word as a sequence of alphanumeric characters that are not broken by a space, with the additional proviso that the only punctuation marks allowed within a word are the hyphen and the apostrophe. It is important to distinguish between word types and word tokens: a *type* is a unique form and a *token* is an instance of a type. The previous sentence contains twenty-six word tokens, but only eighteen types because there are two or more tokens of many of the types. This definition treats contractions as single words. In some cases, one might be particularly interested in modal verbs or negatives and so might want to separate contractions; however, contracted forms are often stylistically significant, and it seems possible that their frequency might be affected by a change in mode of composition. I will also treat hyphenated compound words as single words. In some kinds of analyses it might be appropriate to separate compound words into their elements for analysis, but compounding, like contraction, seems potentially relevant to modes of composition, and compound words may have very different distributions from the single words that comprise them.

The amount of text to be dealt with here is so great that distinguishing homographs like the noun and verb meanings of *love* is not feasible. Fortunately, as the next chapter will show, the methods of analysis used here can easily cope with the resulting amount of error. For the same reason, the texts will not be lemmatized; that is, I will not count all of the inflected or variant forms of a word together. Rather, *go*, *goes*, *going*, *went*, and *gone* will be treated as different words, as separate types, as will *book* and *books*. Not only is this much simpler, but different forms of a single word sometimes show very different stylistic behaviors. For example, instances of the singular *eye* are very frequently figurative, as in "keep an eye out for him," "with an eye to publication," "a real eye opener," "an eye for detail," but this is not true of *eyes* (see Sinclair 167–72 for a discussion).[1]

The Durability of Style

This study will show that authorial style is remarkably durable in the face of changes in mode of composition. Like any other human behavior, however, style is not unchanging in any absolute sense. Not surprisingly, there is strong evidence that Alzheimer's disease and other forms of dementia have significant effects on authorial style. An early study of Iris Murdoch, whose Alzheimer's diagnosis was confirmed after her death, showed that her vocabulary declined significantly in her last novel (*Garrard*). Some of the limitations of that study were remedied in two later studies that found similar decreases in vocabulary and increased use of pronouns and of generic nouns and verbs in the late novels of both Murdock and Agatha Christie, who was also suspected of having Alzheimer's disease (Le et al.; Hirst and Feng). None of these studies, however, showed clear evidence of the decline in sentence complexity that has been found in the late stages of Alzheimer's disease, and this is consistent with previous research showing that syntax and grammar are more resistant to the effects of the disease than is vocabulary (Garrard 259).

Injuries and tumors that destroy parts of the language-processing areas of the brain can obviously also affect a person's language use in very serious ways, as can mental illnesses, such as some forms of schizophrenia. Similarly, extreme life experiences, such as religious conversions, political radicalization, or trauma—indeed, any experience that causes personality changes—can also affect a writer's style. (See King and Pennebaker on language and personality.)

Stylistic difference can also have less dramatic causes. For example, speech is very different from writing, a fact that has implications for the possibility of stylistic effects caused by dictation. Writing is more abstract and informational, with longer sentences and words, more nouns, a larger and more diverse vocabulary, while speech is more concrete and affective, more interactional, with more first- and second-person pronouns, more verbs expressing private feelings and emotions, and more emphatic forms (Biber 104–15). Writing in different major genres, such as fiction, nonfiction, poetry, letters, and drama, also has significant effects on style that are local and temporary (see Burrows, "Not").

Some authors also vary their styles intentionally through experimentation, innovation, imitation, disguise, parody, and pastiche. Consider Anthony Burgess's *A Clockwork Orange*, James Joyce's *Finnegan's Wake*, Russell Hoban's *Riddley Walker*, William Faulkner's *The Sound and the Fury*, or William Golding's *The Inheritors* in comparison to the rest of their work, for example. In the most extreme of these examples, such as *Finnegan's Wake* and *Riddley Walker*, the intentional distortions are great enough to disrupt an authorship attribution test. The same is likely to be true for writers associated with Oulipo, who voluntarily write under extreme constraints. It is difficult to imagine that writing a novel without the letter *e* would not radically affect an author's style, for example (the most famous case is Georges Perec's *La Disparition*).

Many authors' styles also change over time, often for no discernable reason. For example, Henry James's late style is very different from his early style, and the same is often said of writers as diverse as Ernest Hemingway, William Shakespeare, Charles Dickens, F. Scott Fitzgerald, W. B. Yeats, and Adrienne Rich. For writers like James, the chronological change is a regular development that follows a steady trajectory or drift. The works of other authors may divide into periods, but without a steady development. Some strike an early note and hold it. The styles of others vary over their careers, but without any clear chronological pattern (Willa Cather). The significance of the possibility of chronological change for this study is in its potential to mask or be confused with a stylistic effect caused by a change in mode of composition.

Modes of Composition and the Durability of Style

When asked what his daily work habits were like, J. G. Ballard responded:

> Every day, five days a week. Longhand now, it's less tiring than a typewriter. When I'm writing a novel or story I set myself a target of about seven hundred words a day, sometimes a little more. I do a first draft in longhand, then do a very careful longhand revision of the text, then type out the final manuscript. I used to type first and revise in longhand, but I find that modern fiber-tip pens are less effort than a typewriter. Perhaps I ought to try a seventeenth-century quill. I rewrite a great deal, so the word processor sounds like my dream. My neighbor is a BBC videotape editor and he offered to lend me his, but apart from the eye-aching glimmer, I found that the editing functions are terribly laborious. I'm told that already one can see the difference between fiction composed on the word processor and that on the typewriter. The word processor lends itself to a text that has great polish and clarity on a sentence-by-sentence and paragraph level, but has haywire overall chapter-by-chapter construction, because it's almost impossible to rifle through and do a quick scan of, say, twenty pages. Or so they say.
>
> (*"J. G. Ballard"*)

Nietzsche, after beginning to use a typewriter, famously opined, "Our writing instruments are also working on our thoughts" (qtd. in Kittler 200). In spite of the perceptions of writers, however, any stylistic effects caused by a change in mode of composition seem unlikely to be extreme. In a study unrelated to modes of composition, but suggestive, So and Piper tested hundreds of novels by authors who had attended MFA programs against hundreds written by authors who had not. They found very little difference in style, theme, vocabulary, or characters between the two groups. If active instruction does not have a discernable effect on style, perhaps mode of composition effects will be minor as well. This seems to be supported by a recent study of the relative strengths of variables that affect style, which suggests that the most powerful ones, in descending order, are Author, Text, Gender, Genre, and Decade (Jockers 79–81). If mode of composition seems likely to be low on this scale, controlling the other variables will be important.

Handwriting, Typing, and Word Processing

Writing a text with a pen or pencil is a fairly complex activity that involves quite precise and complex hand-eye coordination as well as mental acts of thinking, remembering, and invention.

> Writing by hand is a multi-sensory process involving areas of the brain that relate not only to sight but also to motor function and touch. Rather surprisingly, perhaps, it also calls upon the part of the brain responsible for sound, as we silently compose the words in our heads before writing them down.
>
> *(Warwick ii142)*

Handwriting is one-handed, and the hand typically shapes the letters while the eye concentrates on the point of the writing device. There is even evidence that alphabetic and logographic writing systems activate neural pathways differently (Mangen and Velay). It has also been shown that handwriting is controlled by very localized parts of the brain (Roux et al. 68–73).

Although three specific "writing centers" in the brain that are used in both handwriting and typing have been identified, at least one additional area has been shown to be used only in typing, at least in Japanese (Higashiyama et al. 13). Unlike handwriting, typing is (normally) a two-handed process in which the fingers play a much less intricate part, merely striking the appropriate keys, and the eye is not usually so closely focused on the point of impact of the key on the paper, or, for touch typist, on the keys. In some early typewriters, the typed text was not even immediately visible to the typist. Word processing allows the instant visibility of the text and involves very similar finger movements to typing, but with the potential addition of mouse actions. It also allows for immediate and normally untraceable revision and for the potential effects of spell-checkers and grammar-checkers (Mangen and Velay). These basic differences at least suggest the possibility that these different modes of composition might affect writing style.

A great deal of attention has been paid by media theorists to the changes in the technology of the writing process from handwriting to typewriting to word processing, most famously in the work of McLuhan and later Kittler (see also Wershler-Henry). A serious and valuable early study is Heim's *Electric Language:*

A Philosophical Study of Word Processing. A great deal of work has also been done by researchers in the field of composition, including a series of dissertations beginning in the 1980s in response to the burgeoning use of computers in freshman writing. Most of this work is not directly relevant to the question to be addressed here, except that it suggests the possibility of the effects of technology on style. Sudol, for example, suggests:

> The mechanical and linear modes of inscription characteristic of the Platonic tradition fostered contemplation, the stability of written forms, and the solitude of the culture of books. Word processing, on the other hand, fosters information exchange, the instability of the direct flow of oral discourse, and the culture of information management. Writing becomes digitized, fragmented, abstract, and writer-based. The psychic drama of the writer struggling with the resistant materials of writing, and forming language and thought as a result, succumbs to the easy flow and strict rationality of digital writing.
>
> (924)

Given the rather speculative nature of many of the discussions of the possible effects of technology and media, I turn very briefly, instead, to Matt Kirschenbaum's fascinating *Track Changes: A Literary History of Word Processing*. For my purposes, the main value of the book is as a source of cases for possible analysis and reports on when and how writers like Arthur Clarke, Octavia Butler, Ian McEwan, and Stanley Elkin (examined in Chapter 5) adopted word processing. In a later article, Kirschenbaum also addresses the issue of the possible effects of writing technology: "Not only do we write differently with a fountain pen than with a crayon because they each feel different in our hands, we write (and think) different kinds of things" ("Technology"). Kirschenbaum notes that many people he talked to about his book wanted to know what effect computers had on writers' styles:

> Style is at once something tangible—built up out of individual words and phrasings, with the academic specialization of stylometry devoted to its study—and elusive, associated with a writer's "voice" or the unique "feel" of their prose. Doubtless this is why it fascinates us, and why we're so concerned to know what computers are doing to it. And yet I think the question is misplaced.

He argues that it is the "sense of the text" that changes when a writer adopts word processing,

> the mental model of the words on the page (or screen) and how the writer perceives his or her relationship to them. Word processing, as the testimony

> of countless writers suggests, profoundly altered their sense of the text, both in terms of how they approached their writing and what they thought possible. But all of that is a far cry from "style," typically defined as an author's individual word choices and sentence structures or arrangements.

Kirschenbaum is rather dismissive of the kind of stylistic analysis proposed here in a passage that immediately follows the sentence just quoted:

> Which is not to say that kind of analysis couldn't be done. In fact, specialists have been doing it for decades. You would begin by choosing a writer like Isaac Asimov, someone who wrote a lot and for whom we happen to know the exact day on which he acquired his first computer. . . . You would want a digitized corpus of his books from before and after, and then you would see what you could find with your algorithms.
>
> Even then, though, the question would nag: What would those algorithms tell you? They might reveal some heretofore unimagined master key to Asimov's oeuvre. But you might also be left with something like stylometrist Louis Milic's contention about Jonathan Swift, famously demolished by literary theorist Stanley Fish: "The low frequency of initial determiners, taken together with the high frequency of initial connectives, makes [Swift] a writer who likes transitions and made much of connectives."

As I have pointed out in the preface, Asimov's case is actually not a very promising one for analysis because of the shape of his career, and Fish's famous "demolition" of stylistics is, as I have argued elsewhere, clever, but specious and unsound ("The End," *Language*). I would be wary, as Kirschenbaum is, of expecting a "master key" from a computational analysis, and I think he is right when he ends with the observation, "But we'll still be left with all the imponderables of hands on keyboards. Writing machines may be complicated, but writing itself is always infinitely more so." The question of whether authors' styles change when they put down a pen and put their hands on the keyboard, however, is a much simpler one. An author's "sense of the text" is subjective and impressionistic, but whether a change in mode of composition causes a change in style is a question that can be answered with a fair amount of objectivity and confidence, as I will show, using exactly the kind of before-and-after analysis he describes.

Dictation

A cogent, if impressionistic, early comment can begin a brief discussion of the possibility that dictation might cause stylistic changes:

> The invention of the typewriter has given a tremendous impetus to the dictating habit, especially among business men. The more ephemeral literary

> productions of the day are dictated, sometimes to a stenographer for transcription, and often directly to the machine. In either case the literary effects of the dictating habit are too manifest to need elaboration. The standards of spoken language, which in the days of the past stood out in marked contrast with the terseness and precision of written composition, giving rise to the saying that no good speech ever read well, have crossed over to the printed page. This means not only greater diffuseness, inevitable with any lessening of the tax on words which the labor of writing imposes, but it also brings forward the point of view of the one who speaks. There is the disposition on the part of the talker to explain, as if watching the facial expression of his hearers to see how far they are following. This attitude is not lost when his audience becomes merely a clicking typewriter. It is no uncommon thing in the typewriting booths at the Capitol in Washington to see Congressmen in dictating letters use the most vigorous gestures as if the oratorical methods of persuasion could be transmitted to the printed page.
>
> *(O'Brien 470–1)*

A study of typed long letters and similar letters dictated to voice-recognition software, however, found only relatively minor differences (Hartley et al.). The dictated letters had slightly shorter sentences and more first-person references, casual expressions, and references to the past (8–9). The authors' basic conclusion, which generally agrees with other studies they cite, is that "after practice, using a new technology makes writing physically easier for an experienced writer, but appears to have little effect on his or her actual productions" (12). Honeycutt reports similar minor effects in young writers ("Researching"). In a long article on the history of the use of dictation in Western culture that draws on Ong's concept of "secondary orality," he points out that, unlike the kind of dictation that will be dealt with in Chapter 3, voice-recognition technology allows the author "to draw instantaneously on previously produced text" ("Literacy" 314). He also suggests that the similarity of dictation to speech is only partial and that dictation may be "closer to writing than to speech, which has little in common with dictation in terms of context and purpose" (320).

The Following Chapters

Most of this book will focus on a variety of authors, modes of composition (including handwriting, typing, word processing, and dictation), and on changes in mode that were temporary or permanent and voluntary or involuntary. Any tools that will be used to test cases in which authors change their modes of composition for a change in style, however, must first be shown to be effective in detecting other kinds of style variation, including fairly subtle ones. Chapter 2 demonstrates the effectiveness of a series of computational tools and methods in detecting stylistic differences, beginning with differences that make authorship attribution possible and proceeding to more difficult tasks like distinguishing the voices of individual narrators or characters within a single text.

Chapter 3 discusses three authors who changed back and forth from handwriting to dictation: Thomas Hardy, Walter Scott, and Joseph Conrad. All of these authors changed their modes of composition within single texts. Chapter 4 examines the cases of William Faulkner and Booth Tarkington, both of whom made more permanent changes in mode—Tarkington from handwriting to dictation and Faulkner from handwriting to typing. They, too, changed modes within a single novel. Tarkington adopted dictation when he began losing his eyesight, while Faulkner seems to have begun composing on the typewriter as a matter of convenience. Chapter 5 explores the permanent changes from handwriting or typing to word processing of Arthur Clarke, Octavia Butler, Ian McEwan, and Stanley Elkin. The first three of these authors seem to have adopted word processing because of its perceived benefits in speed and convenience, while Elkin did so because of finger pain. Chapter 6 revisits the famous case of Henry James's adoption of dictation and the widespread idea that dictation caused the development of his radically different late style. Chapter 7 again treats a single author—in this case Stephen King—and his complex set of mode changes between typing, handwriting, and word processing, changes that overlap with his abuse of alcohol and cocaine and his recovery from that abuse. None of the authors studied in Chapters 2–7 presents a clear example of a significant change in style that can be attributed to the change in mode of composition. Chapter 8 focuses on the durability of authorial style to translation as a way of studying how and why mode of composition affects style in such a minor way.

Note

1. I am, of course, aware that automated methods exist for both syntactic analysis and part-of-speech tagging. It seems unlikely that parts of speech would be affected by mode of composition, however, and in tests of accuracy on well-respected taggers, I have seen literary texts with error rates nearing fifty percent. Errors in part-of-speech tagging produce errors in syntactic parsing as well. Previous work on authors whose styles have normally been discussed largely in terms of syntax has also shown that word frequencies alone are effective in identifying syntactic variations in style.

References

Barthes, Roland. "The Death of the Author." *The Death and Resurrection of the Author?* edited by William Irwin, Greenwood Press, 2002, pp. 3–7. Originally published in *Aspen*, vol. 5–6, no. 3, 1967. www.ubu.com/aspen/aspen5and6/threeEssays.html#barthes.

Biber, Douglas. *Variation Across Speech and Writing*. Cambridge UP, 1988, doi:10.1017/CBO9780511621024.

Burrows, John F. "Not Unless You Ask Nicely: The Interpretative Nexus Between Analysis and Information." *Literary and Linguistic Computing*, vol. 7, no. 2, 1992, pp. 91–109, doi:10.1093/llc/7.2.91.

Cather, Willa. *O Pioneers!* U of Nebraska P, 2003.

Farrell, John. *The Varieties of Authorial Intention: Literary Theory Beyond the Intentional Fallacy*. Palgrave Macmillan, 2017, doi:10.1007/978-3-319-48977-3.

———. "Why Literature Professors Turned Against Authors—Or Did They?" *Los Angeles Review of Books*, 13 Jan. 2019. lareviewofbooks.org/article/why-literature-professors-turned-against-authors-or-did-they.

Foucault, Michel. "What Is an Author." *The Death and Resurrection of the Author?* edited by William Irwin, Greenwood Press, 2002, pp. 9–22. Originally published as "Qu'est-ce qu'un Auteur?" *Bulletin de la Societe Française de Philosophie*, vol. 63, no. 3, 1969, pp. 73–104.

Garrard, Peter et al. "The Effects of Very Early Alzheimer's Disease on the Characteristics of Writing by a Renowned Author." *Brain*, vol. 128, no. 2, 2005, pp. 250–60.

Guillory, John. "The Sokal Affair and the History of Criticism." *Critical Inquiry*, vol. 28, no. 2, 2002, pp. 470–508.

Hartley, James et al. "Speaking Versus Typing: A Case-Study of the Effects of Using Voice-Recognition Software on Academic Correspondence." *British Journal of Educational Technology*, vol. 34, no. 1, 2003, pp. 5–16, doi.org/10.1111/1467-8535.d01-2.

Heim, Michael. *Electric Language: A Philosophical Study of Word Processing*. Yale UP, 1987. archive.org/details/electriclanguage00heim.

Herrmann, J. Berenike et al. "Revisiting Style, a Key Concept in Literary Studies." *Journal of Literary Theory*, vol. 9, no. 1, 2015, pp. 25–52.

Higashiyama, Y. et al. "The Neural Basis of Typewriting: A Functional MRI Study." *PLoS One*, vol. 10, no. 7, 2015, pp. 1–20, doi:10.1371/journal.pone.0134131.

Hirst, Graeme, and Vanessa Wei Feng. "Changes in Style in Authors with Alzheimer's Disease." *English Studies*, vol. 93, no. 3, 2012, pp. 357–70, doi:10.1080/0013838X.2012.668789.

Honeycutt, Lee. "Researching the Use of Voice Recognition Writing Software." *Computers and Composition*, vol. 20, 2003, pp. 77–95, doi:10.1016/S8755-4615(02)00174-3.

———. "Literacy and the Writing Voice: The Intersection of Culture and Technology in Dictation." *Journal of Business and Technical Communication*, vol. 18, 2004, pp. 294–327, doi:10.1177/1050651904264105.

Hoover, David L. "The End of the Irrelevant Text: Electronic Texts, Linguistics, and Literary Theory." *Digital Humanities Quarterly*, vol. 1, no. 2, 2007. www.digitalhumanities.org/dhq/vol/1/2/000012/000012.html.

———. "Hot-Air Textuality: Literature After Jerome McGann." *Text Technology*, vol. 14, no. 2, 2005, pp. 71–103.

———. *Language and Style in the Inheritors*. UP of America, 1999. archive.org/details/languagestyleint00hoov.

Irwin, William, editor. *The Death and Resurrection of the Author?* Greenwood Press, 2002.

"J. G. Ballard, The Art of Fiction No. 85." Interviewed by Thomas Frick, *The Paris Review*, vol. 94, 1984. theparisreview.org/interviews/2929/the-art-of-fiction-no-85-j-g-ballard.

Jockers, Matt. *Macroanalysis: Digital Methods and Literary History*. U of Illinois P, 2013, doi:10.5406/illinois/9780252037528.001.0001.

King, Laura A., and James W. Pennebaker. "Linguistic Styles: Language Use as an Individual Difference." *Journal of Personality and Social Psychology*, vol. 77, no. 6, 2000, pp. 1296–312, doi:10.1037//0022-3514.77.6.1296.

Kirschenbaum, Matthew G. *Track Changes: A Literary History of Word Processing*. Belknap Press, 2016.

———. "Technology Changes How Authors Write, but the Big Impact Isn't on Their Style." *The New Republic*, 26 July 2016. theconversation.com/technology-changes-how-authors-write-but-the-big-impact-isnt-on-their-style-61955.

Kittler, Friedrich A. *Gramaphone, Film, Typewriter*. Stanford UP, 1999.

Le, X. et al. "Longitudinal Detection of Dementia Through Lexical and Syntactic Changes in Writing: A Case Study of Three British Novelists." *Literary and Linguist Computing*, vol. 26, no. 4, 2011, pp. 435–61.

Leech, Geoffrey, and Michael Short. *Style in Fiction*. 2nd ed. Addison-Wesley, 2007.

Love, Harold. *Attributing Authorship*. Cambridge UP, 2002, doi:10.1017/CBO9780511483165.

Mangen, Anne, and Jean-Luc Velay. *Digitizing Literacy: Reflections on the Haptics of Writing, Advances in Haptics*, edited by Mehrdad Hosseini Zadeh, InTech, 2010.

McLuhan, Marshall. *Understanding Media: The Extensions of Man*. McGraw-Hill, 1964.

O'Brien, Robert Lincoln. "Machinery and English Style." *Atlantic Monthly*, vol. 94, 1 Oct. 1904, pp. 464–72.

Perec, Georges. *La Disparition: Roman*. Denoël, 1969.

Roux, Franck-Emmanuel et al. "The Neural Basis for Writing From Dictation in the Temporoparietal Cortex." *Cortex*, vol. 50, 2014, pp. 64–75, doi:10.1016/j.cortex.2013.09.012.

Russell, Bertrand. "An Outline of Intellectual Rubbish." *Unpopular Essays*, Allen and Unwin, 1921, pp. 95–145.

Seltzer, Mark. *Bodies and Machines*. Routledge, 1992.

Sinclair, John. *Reading Concordances: An Introduction*. Pearson Longman, 2003.

So, Richard Jean, and Andrew Piper. "How Has the MFA Changed the Contemporary Novel?" *The Atlantic*, 6 Mar. 2016. www.theatlantic.com/entertainment/archive/2016/03/mfa-creative-writing/462483/.

Sudol, Ronald A. "The Accumulative Rhetoric of Word Processing." *College English*, vol. 53, no. 8, 1991, pp. 920–32, doi:10.2307/377699.

Warwick, Claire. "Beauty Is Truth: Multi-sensory Input and the Challenge of Designing Aesthetically Pleasing Digital Resources." *Digital Scholarship in the Humanities*, vol. 32, Suppl._2, 2017, pp. ii135–ii150, doi:10.1093/llc/fqx036.

Wershler-Henry, Darren. *The Iron Whim: A Fragmented History of Typewriting*. Cornell UP, 2007.

2

A PROOF OF CONCEPT: IDENTIFYING DIFFERENCES IN STYLE

Introduction

> Given the information that makes nice questions possible and a nice enough formulation of those questions, literary statisticians can undoubtedly help to identify the authors of doubtful texts. They will usually rely on the analysis of stylistic resemblances, differences, and concomitant variations to adduce evidence of an inductive cast. Like anyone else who does that, from nomadic hunters to astronomers, they will sometimes be able to present a compelling argument but they will never be entitled to claim certainty. Whether or not they make use of computers in gathering their data, they need ask only one concession from their colleagues: that their evidence should not be treated with special deference or special scepticism but that it be taken, case by case, upon its merits.
>
> *(Burrows, "Not" 103)*

These comments from a seminal early article in 1992 put the task of this chapter into proper perspective. Determining whether or not a change in mode of composition alters an author's style is possible only if the methods of computational stylistics can be shown to be effective in detecting style variation. As Burrows put it ten years later, "The close reader sees things in a text—single moments and large amorphous movements—to which computer programs give no easy access. The computer, on the other hand, reveals hidden patterns and enables us to marshal hosts of instances too numerous for our unassisted powers" ("Englishing" 696).

The question is whether or not, as Burrows suggests, computational analysis can reveal the patterns that constitute such variations. Multiple methods and approaches will be introduced here and used in some of the following chapters:

exploratory methods, like cluster analysis and principal components analysis; methods that focus on characteristic vocabulary, such as topic modeling and Burrows's Zeta and Iota and variants of it ("All"); and machine learning techniques developed for authorship attribution, such as those implemented in Stylo (Eder et al.) and JGAAP (Juola, "JGAAP").

In the long history of authorship attribution, from which most methods of computational stylistics derive, the most popular textual features to analyze have been the most frequent function words, chosen because they are frequent enough for robust statistical analysis and because, as features that are inherently unlikely to be under the author's conscious control, they seem likely to produce reliable authorship markers. In the analyses in the following chapters, words will continue to be the most frequent focus, though not merely function words. Over the past fifteen years or so, analysts have been steadily increasing the numbers of words analyzed (see Hoover, "Statistical Stylistics" 424–36, for an early example), and it is increasingly clear that, as John F. Burrows nicely puts it, "evidence of authorship is indeed present in every frequency stratum" ("All" 46).

Although the theoretical argument for function words has seemed compelling to many scholars, it is easy to demonstrate that analyses based on larger numbers of words are almost invariably more accurate than those based on fewer words, unless the texts are very short. (For an examination of the effectiveness of authorship markers in various strata in various languages, see Rybicki and Eder 317–20.) Besides being frequent and easily counted, words have the benefit of being immediately meaningful and interpretable.

Recent work has suggested that analyzing n-grams—sequences of words or characters—sometimes produces more accurate results in authorship attribution (Clement and Sharp 433–44; Juola, "Authorship Attribution" 290–8; Antonia et al. 151–62), and n-grams will also be analyzed in some of the following chapters. (For an early argument for the effectiveness of the analysis of n-grams, there called sequences, see Hoover, "Frequent Word Sequences.") Word n-grams, like words, have the benefit of immediate meaningfulness and add some information about syntax that is present only obliquely in word frequencies, but they suffer from the fact that they are much less frequent than words. For example, the ten most frequent words in Charlotte Brontë's *Jane Eyre* range from *the*, with a frequency of 7,789, to *it*, with a frequency of 2,392, while the ten most frequent word three-grams (consecutive three-word sequences) range from *I could not*, with a frequency of 109, to *I had been*, with a frequency of thirty-four. Longer word n-grams are naturally even rarer. Character n-grams, which also capture some syntactic information, are very frequent but tend to be less readily interpretable (typically the most effective letter n-grams are those of three to five characters, including spaces and punctuation). Brian Vickers, who has championed the use of rare word n-grams in authorship attribution, has recently mounted a contrarian critique of the use of frequent words as inappropriate and faulty ("Shakespeare" 114–34 and "Misuse" 1–20), but his critique has been robustly and adequately answered, for example, by Burrows ("Second Opinion" 364–91), by Antonia et al. (151–62), and by me ("Simulations" 12–7), among others.[1]

Authorship Attribution

Decades of intensive research have shown that the differences between authors' styles are great enough that authorship attribution tests on English texts of known authorship typically achieve accuracy levels in the ninety-five to one hundred percent range for problems for which there are adequate numbers of texts of adequate type and length.[2] Just what counts as adequate is a matter of some debate, but the problems to be addressed in this study would all fall into the adequate class in the opinion of most researchers. (Special challenges in some of the problems will be addressed in context.) It seems unnecessary to demonstrate the reliability of authorship attribution extensively, as dozens of analyses of English novels in which many methods are completely accurate could easily be shown. Consider, however, a set of recent tests on some anonymous mid-nineteenth-century short stories, mainly from popular magazines, that have been suggested as possibly by Henry James (Horowitz; Hoover, "Simulations" 875–6). Many of these stories are as short as eight hundred to three thousand words, which is shorter than is ideal, but I have selected ninety-four of the stories by fifteen authors as known texts and have tested 116 additional stories by these authors as if they were anonymous, in order to evaluate the methods.

The machine learning, or "supervised" methods WEKA SMO, WEKA Multilayer Perceptron, and WEKA Linear Regression (Frank et al.), implemented in JGAAP (Juola, "JGAAP"), attributed ninety-seven to ninety-eight percent of the 116 texts to their correct authors. Given how difficult this task is, these are extraordinarily successful results. An explanation of these sophisticated methods is beyond the scope of this study and requires advanced mathematical understanding, but all of them work by analyzing the set of known texts for patterns of word frequencies (or the frequencies of other features) and using the information from that analysis to classify the texts of a test set. For some explanations of many of the algorithms (geared toward using the WEKA software tools), see the Weka Machine Learning Mini-Course (Brownlee).

It is an unfortunate fact of computational stylistics that no one method is the most accurate for every problem, and a method that is very effective on one set of texts may perform poorly on another. Other methods I tried on this set of texts possibly by Henry James achieved much poorer results of fifty-nine, seventy-six, and ninety percent. In practice, this means that initial testing of the sort I have just described must precede or be combined with any testing on texts of truly unknown authorship. In the case of the James apocrypha, the three methods with excellent accuracy on the known texts did not attribute any of the proposed apocrypha to Henry James, suggesting that the fascinating possibility of uncovering new James stories one hundred years after his death will have to be abandoned. Another limitation of these methods is that they are very much "black box" analyses in which the goal is an accurate classification rather than an increased understanding of the texts. Finally, compared to some more inductive and exploratory methods to be discussed shortly, these supervised methods require setting aside a significant proportion of the texts as a primary, or "training," set. Nevertheless, the high levels of attribution success make these methods indispensable in appropriate circumstances, and some of them will be used in later chapters of this study.

The high rate of accuracy of machine learning methods on the difficult James apocrypha problem shows their effectiveness, and the simplest application of authorship attribution to the problem of changes in mode of composition will be to treat the different modes as if they were different authors. Any effects of a change of mode seem likely to be less significant than the differences between authors, however, so it seems necessary to show that the methods are effective for subtler kinds of style variation.

Author Style, Text Style, and Genre

Multiple texts by the same author seem to provide a slightly more difficult challenge. Some authors seem to alter their styles, chameleon-like, from novel to novel, while others show a much more constant style across their entire oeuvre. The books of the chameleons are easy to distinguish, as an analysis of six of William Golding's novels, *Darkness Visible*, *Free Fall*, *Lord of the Flies*, *Rites of Passage*, *The Inheritors*, and *The Spire*, shows. A test of the whole novels would indicate only the similarities and differences among the novels, so I have divided them into sections of about fifteen thousand words, numbered consecutively. This creates the possibility of "errors" in which sections of different novels cluster together. Even an unsupervised exploratory method like cluster analysis groups all sections of all novels together in analyses based on the two hundred to one thousand most frequent words, and all but one section of *Darkness Visible* in the analysis based on the one hundred most frequent words.[3]

Custer analysis begins with the entire group of sections of Golding's texts and explores the relationships among them by comparing the frequencies of the most frequent words across all the sections. It clusters them hierarchically, meaning that it first finds the two sections that use the number of words being analyzed in the most similar way, and then looks for the next pair or trio or group that shows the next highest amount of similarity. In Figure 2.1, based on the seven hundred most frequent words, for example, the first two sections and the last two sections of *The Rites of Passage* appear to join together closest to the left side of the graph. The vertical proximity of *The Rites of Passage* (5) and *Lord of the Flies* (1) is not relevant; in fact, these two sections are very different from each other. The order of the texts and text-groups within each cluster of texts is alphabetic, so that the second and third sections of *Lord of the Flies* are placed below the first

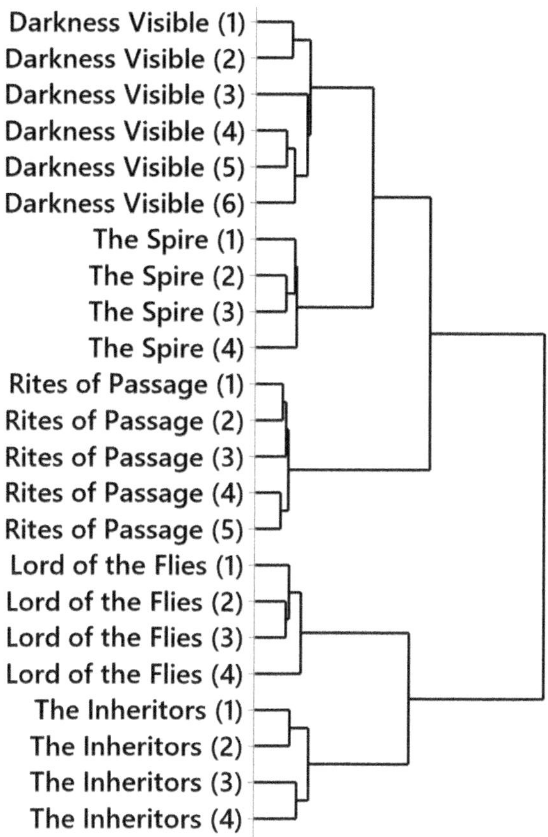

FIGURE 2.1 Cluster analysis of six novels by William Golding in sections of fifteen thousand words, based on the seven hundred most frequent words, with Ward linkage, squared Euclidean distance, pronouns deleted, and culled at eighty percent

section automatically. The graph would have the same interpretation if the *Lord of the Flies* cluster were in reverse order. Note that *Lord of the Flies* and *The Inheritors* form a group that is quite distinct from the other novels, as is indicated by how far to the right one must travel in the graph to get from them to a vertical line that leads to the other novels. This grouping makes sense, given that Golding has removed modern civilization in both novels—in *Lord of the Flies* by isolating a group of boys on an otherwise uninhabited island and in *The Inheritors* by imagining contact between Neanderthals and more modern humans in a prehistoric setting (see Hoover's *Language and Style* for a book-length study).

In this and most of the other analyses in this chapter, proper nouns and iconic vocabulary have been removed before performing the analysis. Other analysts have made principled arguments for the removal of some words from their analyses, including proper names (Burrows, "Not" 92) and personal pronouns (Binongo 269; Binongo and Smith 460). I normally also remove personal pronouns, to reduce the effect of point of view, but I have also long been removing from a word-frequency list any word for which a single text supplies a high proportion (typically sixty to eighty percent) of its occurrences (Hoover, "Frequent Word Sequences" 159). This automatic method, which I have called culling, assures that proper names and other peculiarly distributed words do not skew the analysis and simultaneously prevents shared proper names from speciously linking texts (Hoover, "Multivariate Analysis" 350–1).[4] Clearly, words like *Ralph*, *Piggy*, *Jack*, *conch*, *Roger*, and *littluns* might immediately identify *Lord of the Flies*, as *Lok*, *Fa*, *Ha*, *Mal*, *Liku*, *Tanakil*, *Marlan*, and *Tuami* might identify *The Inheritors*, so that they would function as good classification variables. From a stylistic point of view, however, it seems more important to know whether or not sections of Golding's novels can be grouped accurately without using such iconic vocabulary; therefore, the word list for Figure 2.1 has been culled at eighty percent. This marks an important distinction between the task of simple classification and that of stylistic analysis.

Edith Wharton is a more consistent writer than Golding, but her five novels published between 1912 and 1922, *The Reef* (1912), *The Custom of the Country* (1913), *Summer* (1917), *The Age of Innocence* (1920), and *The Glimpses of the Moon* (1922), divided into sections of about twenty thousand words, also cluster completely by novel in analyses based on the seven hundred most frequent words and the nine hundred to one thousand most frequent words; in the other analyses, the only "errors" are that the first two sections of *The Reef* cluster with *The Glimpses of the Moon*.

Consider also a cluster analysis of the six novels in Anthony Trollope's Barsetshire series: *The Warden* (1855), *Barchester Towers* (1857), *Doctor Thorne* (1858), *Framley Parsonage* (1861), *The Small House at Allington* (1864), and *The Last Chronicle of Barset* (1867). I have divided these novels into sections of about forty-five thousand words because they are very long. In spite of appearing in a series of related novels involving the same setting and many repeating characters, except for a single error in the analysis based on the two hundred most frequent words, all sections group by novel in analyses based on the one hundred to one thousand most frequent words. Textual identity is clearly more important here than series identity.

Finally, even Edith Nesbit's classic trilogy for children, *Five Children and It* (1902), *The Phoenix and the Carpet* (1904), and *The Story of the Amulet* (1906), generally cluster by book when analyzed in sections of approximately ten thousand words, with a maximum of one to three misplaced sections in analyses based on the two hundred to one thousand most frequent words. Even though cluster analysis is not optimized for classification, it is clearly able to detect sufficient differences among even related novels to distinguish among them and to group sections of the individual books together. Using Stylo (Eder et al. 115–17), a menu-driven stylistics tool for the statistical computing package R (R Core Team), I tested Nesbit's novels divided into the same sections, with the even-numbered sections treated as known and the odd-numbered sections tested for authorship. All of the supervised classification methods implemented in Stylo that I was able to test achieve one hundred percent accuracy over hundreds of tests.

Authors who write in more than one literary genre might also pose an interesting challenge to computational methods, and it has long been known that the major genres of nonfiction, fiction, poetry, and drama are quite different from each other. The classic corpus linguistics study is Biber's *Variation Across Speech and Writing*, and John F. Burrows showed both the diversity of the genres of fiction, letters, poetry, and drama and some ways of attributing authorship even across these significantly different genres in his classic article "Not Unless You Ask Nicely." But what about genre differences that might be less significant, such as that between fiction intended for adults and fiction intended for children? We can return to Edith Nesbit for a simple test. Along with her children's trilogy that has just been tested for coherence, Nesbit wrote many other children's books (short story collections as well as novels), including *The Magic City* (1910), *The Magic World* (stories) (1912), *The Enchanted Castle* (1907), and *The Railway Children* (1906). She also wrote fiction for adults, including *The Red House* (1902), *The Incredible Honeymoon* (1916), *The Incomplete Amorist* (1906), *Man and Maid* (stories) (1906), and *The Literary Sense* (stories) (1903). In a quick test of the seven books for children and the five books for adults, just listed, her two genres separate completely in all cluster analyses based on the one hundred and three hundred, and the five hundred to one thousand most frequent words (whole texts), with one error in the other two analyses.

Although I have been reporting the results of cluster analysis directly, in order to show where in the word-frequency spectrum any errors occur, it is also possible to determine the consistency of cluster analyses computationally. Stylo, the tool just used to test Nesbit's novels, includes an option called "Consensus Tree," which runs a series of cluster analyses and then graphs the results in a bootstrap consensus tree on the basis of the user's choice of what proportion of agreement there is among the analyses. Such a bootstrap consensus tree for the twelve Nesbit texts analyzed earlier, based on cluster analyses of the six hundred to twelve hundred most frequent words, in increments of one hundred words, is shown in Figure 2.2. The tree is based on a consensus of sixty percent, with pronouns removed, culled at ten to thirty percent in ten percent increments; the distance measure used for clustering is Eder's Simple distance, a version of John F. Burrows's popular Delta (Burrows, " 'Delta' "). (See Evert et al., for an excellent overview of the many versions of Delta.) In this tree, as in about half of the others, based on different distance measures, Nesbit's trilogy forms its own group within the children's book group.

The bootstrap consensus tree is an attractive visualization, but it must be used with caution. If the parameters chosen for the cluster analyses or the consensus

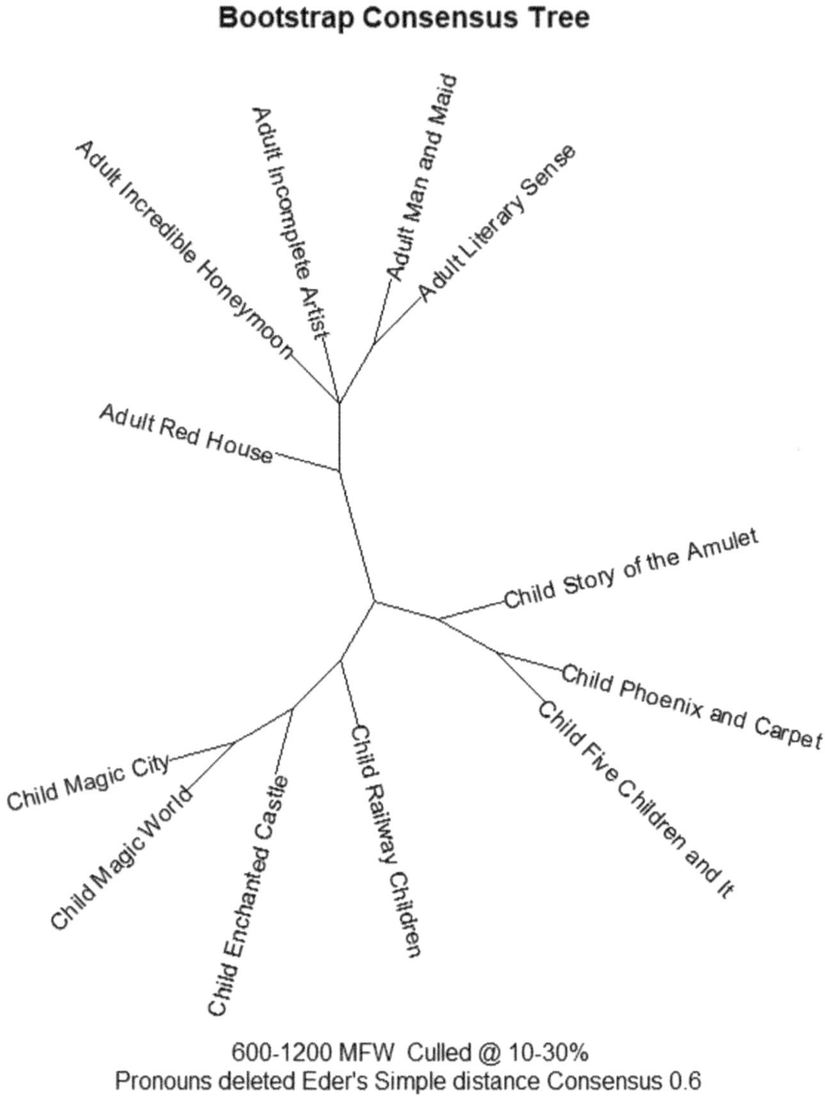

FIGURE 2.2 Bootstrap consensus analysis of seven Edith Nesbit books for adults and five for children, based on the six hundred to twelve hundred most frequent words, with Eder's Simple distance, pronouns deleted, culled at ten to thirty percent, and a consensus of sixty percent

analysis are not appropriate, it is possible to produce a consensus tree in which the consensus is wrong. This can be avoided by running a series of consensus trees with different parameters: in effect, testing the consistency of the consensus. I ran the previous analysis, for example, with eight different distance measures. (For a good discussion of these issues, and suggestions for other visualizations, see Eder, "Visualization" 55–62.) The interpretation of the tree in Figure 2.2 is relatively straightforward. Wherever two or more texts join at a point, there is sixty percent consensus of that grouping—those texts group together in sixty percent of the cluster analyses, as do the novels of Nesbit's trilogy. If the tree were based on a consensus of seventy percent, the points where texts join would mean that those texts cluster together at least seventy percent of the time, though they might cluster more consistently than that.

The genre difference between Nesbit's fiction for adults and her fiction for children can be tested with another method that has often been used in authorship attribution and computational stylistics: Student's *t*-test (for example, Jordan et al. 29–33; Hoover, "Authorial Style" 254–69; Craig and Kinney 28–39; a classic early discussion is Burrows, "Not" 97–103). Student's *t*-test is a well-studied method for testing how likely it is that the difference between two samples could have arisen by chance. Any introductory statistics text will provide a full explanation, but the test is based on how frequent and how evenly distributed a word is in the two samples.[5] For Nesbit, the goal is to identify words used so differently in her adult and children's books that those differences are unlikely to be a result of chance and are therefore likely to indicate real stylistic differences between the two genres. Student's *t*-tests done in Minitab on the three thousand most frequent words of four Nesbit books for adults and six for children identify 216 words that appear so much more frequently and consistently in the children's books than in the adult books that the probability of this distribution occurring by chance is less than five percent ($p < 0.05$). Conversely, 172 words are more frequently and consistently used in the books for adults at the same level of significance. Nearly one-third of the words in both groups are also significant at the one percent level ($p < 0.01$).

To test whether or not the differences among these ten books extend to some of Nesbit's other texts, I analyzed the individual stories of *Man and Maid*, a collection for adults, and *The Magic City*, a collection for children, using these 388 distinctively used words with another venerable exploratory method: principal components analysis (PCA) (an early and influential use is Burrows, *Computation* 98–106). PCA is a method that, like cluster analysis, can analyze the entire set of sections at once. Rather than hierarchically clustering the sections, however, PCA analyzes the frequencies of a specified number of words in the sections and combines as much of the information about the distributions of those frequencies as possible into a series of unrelated principal components. The texts are then graphed on the basis of the two principal components that explain the largest proportions of the variation in word frequencies. The more similar texts are, the closer together they appear in the graph.[6]

The PCA of Nesbit's stories produces a graph in which the stories are widely separated on the basis of audience, even though, it must be stressed, these stories had no part in creating the lists of distinctive words. The sensitivity of this test to a difference in genre and the relative consistency of Nesbit's two styles are nicely borne out by an additional test including the collection *These Little Ones* (1909), which is sometimes identified as for adults (Victorian Women Writers Project) and sometimes as for children (Worldcat). In this test, three of the stories group closely with the children's stories and one with the adult stories, but the other five group by themselves between the stories for adults and those for children.

The case of genre in the works of Louisa May Alcott is somewhat more complex. Alcott is primarily known for her hugely successful *Little Women*, normally considered a novel for young adults, but early in her career, she wrote sensational novels and stories, such as *A Modern Mephistopheles*, "A Whisper in the Dark," and "Pauline's Passion and Punishment," anonymously, and "Lost in a Pyramid," and "Perilous Play" under the initials L. M. A. (Eiselein and Phillips 187, 328). She published *Behind a Mask*, *The Abbot's Ghost*, *A Marble Woman*, and "V. V.: or, Plots and Counterplots" under the pseudonym A. M. Barnard. More rarely, such sensational stories, including "The Skeleton in the Closet" and "The Mysterious Key," appeared under her own name (Rostenberg 136n17).

I tested Alcott's A. M. Barnard texts *Behind a Mask* and *The Abbot's Ghost* (both republished in *Behind a Mask*) and the first three chapters of *A Marble Woman* (republished in *Plots and Counterplots*), against three stories not normally associated with them: "A Modern Cinderella," "Debbie's Debut," and "The Brothers," all published in Alcott's *A Modern Cinderella*. I ignored her children's fiction, which the analysis of Nesbit's fiction has just shown are likely to be quite different from her adult fiction (for more information about these texts, see Alcott's *Plots and Counterplots* 7–30).[7] Testing what seems likely to be a fairly subtle difference in genre gives fascinating results: "A Modern Cinderella" and "Debbie's Debut" cluster together as expected and separate nicely and consistently from the sensational stories over the whole range of analyses based on the one hundred to one thousand most frequent words. "The Brothers," however, consistently clusters with the Barnard stories in analyses based on the one hundred to four hundred most frequent words, before joining the other two "normal" stories in analyses based on larger numbers of words. In PCA analyses based on the same data, "The Brothers" shows more difference from the Barnard stories than the others on component one but is much more similar to the Barnard stories on the second component. Although t-testing of three Barnard texts and three nonsensational Alcott texts produces only sixty-three words significant at the $p < 0.05$ level, a PCA test of these words places "The Brothers" in the sensational Barnard group.

A little secondary research suggests a reason for this seeming misclassification. Eiselein and Phillips describe "The Brothers" (later published with the more controversial title "My Contraband") as a "tale of miscegenation, race relations, sexual rivalry, and revenge between half brothers of different races" (221). They go on to comment that it "represents an intersection of LMA's pseudonymous sensation fiction with her reform-minded fictions of moral development, and it thus invites critical investigation of the interactions between her overt and covert critiques of 19th-century social values" (222) (see also Patterson 159–62; McWilliam 53, 67–76). This unexpected but ultimately satisfying result is one of the benefits of more interpretive methods of computational analysis, a kind of distant reading that pushes the analyst back to the texts.

At first glance, the ability of computational methods to distinguish style variations within an author's work would seem to call the entire authorship attribution enterprise into question. I have argued, after all, that it is almost always possible to distinguish authors from each other, and this implies a consistency of style across all of the author's works. Yet an author's entire oeuvre can be consistent enough to be distinguished from work by other authors even if some of the texts display distinct sub-styles, or if sub-styles exist within the author's individual texts.

Imitation and Authorship

Imitative texts seem likely to pose more difficulty for computational methods than the kinds of stylistic variation just discussed. John F. Burrows asks the important question:

> Are our computational tests of authorship able to identify the author of an imitative text? The matter embraces serious imitations, where the intent is to deceive, as well as parodies, where the intent is to satirize. Texts revised or extended by a second author stand at the edge of the same territory.
>
> *(Burrows, "Who" 437)*

In the case of a text begun by one author and finished by another, the task of identifying the place where the change of authorship occurs intuitively seems as if it should be challenging. The second author is typically trying to imitate the style of the first; is using the setting, characters, and plot developed by the first author; and is often also working from notes, outlines, or partial drafts of the uncompleted text. Yet, even in such cases, the point at which the second author takes over is usually very easy to determine. This is true of Wilkie Collins's *Blind Love*, finished by Walter Besant (Hoover, "Authorial Style" 52–65); Stephen Crane's *The O'Ruddy*, finished by Robert Barr (Hoover, "Authorial Style" 65–70); Robert Louis Stevenson's *St. Ives*, finished by Arthur Quiller-Couch (Burrows, "Never" 14–7), and *Sanditon*, by Jane Austen and "another lady" (Burrows, *Computation*, especially 49–53). The only partial exception I know of is Lucas Malet's fairly successful copying of the style of her father, Charles Kingsley, in completing his unfinished novel *The Tutor's Story*. This case is complicated by the fact that the division of labor in the completed novel is known only from Malet's introduction to the novel and from her penciled notations in a first edition of the novel in the M. L. Parrish Collection of Victorian Novelists at Princeton University—notations that unfortunately leave off in the twenty-eighth of forty-one chapters (see Hoover, "*Tutor's Story*" 332–9 for more details).

In an interesting recent study, Jack Elliott tested another kind of imitation—the immensely popular Harlequin Romance series, in which the formulaic nature of the genre and the publisher's pressure on the authors to adhere to the expected characteristics of the series might be expected to mask the styles of the individual authors. Elliott used software imported from biology, where it was developed for analyzing genetic relationships, but he repurposed it to study style and theme. Among many interesting findings, he shows how the genre changed when a financial crisis hit the company and how various themes are typically distributed in the novels (71, 74, 77). Surprisingly, however, Elliott found that the force of authorship within the romances remains very powerful.

> Clustering by novel shows authorship is the elemental organizing principle of the genre. This is surprising given the centrifugal forces exerted on authorship, but these—heavy editorial intervention, mini-series that share settings between authors and sub-genres—fail to find traction in the face of this powerful tendency.
>
> *(66–7)*

A related case is that of the controversial Victorian weekly journal the *Saturday Review*, which was known for such a uniformity of its style and ideas that "[c]ontributors felt that they consciously changed their style when writing for the *Saturday Review*" (Craig and Antonia 67). Using PCA, Craig and Antonia first show that the journal's style is somewhat different from other contemporary journals. They are then able to show also that, although "differences in individual authorial style were greater than stylistic differences in the *Saturday Review* and its fellow periodicals, . . . each author indeed used words differently when writing for the *Saturday Review* than for other periodicals (75; see also Jordan et al. 22–9). Techniques that can detect the effect of "house style" on authorial style should also be useful in investigating the effects of a change in mode of composition.

The Pastiche: A Special Kind of Imitation

The pastiche, a conscious effort to mimic the style of an author, is another situation that might well challenge the accuracy of authorship attribution tools. As Frederic Jameson puts it, "Pastiche is, like parody, the imitation of a peculiar or unique, idiosyncratic style, the wearing of a linguistic mask, speech in a dead language. But it is a neutral practice of such mimicry, without any of parody's ulterior motives " (17).[8] Indeed, Sigelman and Jacoby include Robert B. Parker's completion of Raymond Chandler's *Poodle Springs* in their study of Chandler pastiches (14, 24–5). (For a good discussion of several studies of pastiches, see Somers and Tweedie.) This seems justified by the fact that, unlike Collins, Crane, and Stevenson (but more like Austen), Chandler's style is notoriously unusual and characteristic. As Sigelman and Jacoby point out,

> the very point of a pastiche is to appropriate the style of another author. Accordingly, the stylistician would need an extremely exacting set of methods and measures in order to distinguish between the work of Author A and deliberate imitations by other authors—far more exacting methods and measures than would be required to distinguish among various authors writing in their own individual styles.
>
> *(12)*

In spite of the difficulty of the task, however, by analyzing a series of characteristic features of Chandler's style, such as simple vocabulary, a great deal of action, a high proportion of dialogue, vivid language, frequent use of similes, and a low frequency of coordinating conjunctions (15–19), they show that, of the twenty-five pastiches they tested, none "has penetrated close to the stylistic core of Chandler's oeuvre. Most of his stories, and certainly all of what are acknowledged as his best stories, stand by themselves" (24). This focused analysis based on the target author's characteristic stylistic features seems appropriate and effective, but creating a pastiche by replicating a relatively small number of characteristic stylistic features should be easier than altering a whole authorial signature, so that their testing may make distinguishing the pastiche from the original easier than it would be using traditional authorship attribution tests. In any case, it seems worthwhile to do some further testing on a series of pastiches to see whether or not more traditional methods of computational stylistics can also reliably distinguish between originals and pastiches. The cases to be discussed in the following chapters all involve a single author, after all, so that they will focus on the question of whether or not a change in mode is accompanied by a style change where presumably none is intended. A pastiche involves a change in authorship with an active intention to *avoid* any change in style.

Consider, then, the style of Arthur Conan Doyle, whose Sherlock Holmes novels and stories have been the subject of hundreds of parodies and pastiches. Although the prolific Doyle wrote many other kinds of texts, including historical novels, poetry, and nonfiction works about war and spiritualism, he is known today almost entirely as the author of the Holmes stories and novels, which are the only ones that have generated large numbers of pastiches (the online resource *goodreads* listed 414 in May 2020). The first question is whether or not the Holmes style is distinct from the style of Doyle's other works. In a series of ten cluster analyses based on the one hundred to one thousand most frequent words (in increments of one hundred words), the two "genres" generally do separate. The Holmes stories almost never invade clusters of non-Holmes stories, and non-Holmes stories only rarely invade clusters of Holmes stories.

For these analyses, as in all of those discussed earlier, I have manually removed proper nouns and a few other words that are characteristic only of the Holmes stories (for example, *Holmes, Watson, Baker, Street, Hudson, 221, Lestrade*). (My automated method is not appropriate here, because much of this vocabulary runs through all of the Holmes stories.) As I have noted previously, it seems more appropriate to test whether or not the two groups of stories can be distinguished stylistically, rather than on the basis of such iconic vocabulary. It might make sense to classify a story as Holmesian because of the presence of such iconic vocabulary, and doing so might be an effective way to identify pastiches, yet many pastiches (and even more parodies) replace the iconic names, sometimes with humorous variants like Robert Barr's "Sherlaw Kombs" or more obscurely, August Derleth's "Solar Pons." Given the task of this study, it is important to determine whether or not we can detect subtle stylistic differences in the *absence* of iconic vocabulary because we cannot expect iconic vocabulary that distinguishes modes of composition.

These results of cluster analysis on Doyle's Holmes and non-Holmes stories can be augmented with those from PCA. Figure 2.3 shows a PCA score plot of the Holmes stories and non-Holmes stories based on the four hundred most frequent words (titles have been shortened to make the graph easier to read). One of the most obvious characteristics of this graph is the grouping of all the Holmes stories on the right side of the graph and the non-Holmes stories on the left. The first principal component, the artificial variable that combines the largest proportion of the variations in frequencies of the four hundred most frequent words in these stories, can be simply interpreted as "Holmesian." The Holmes stories appear on the right and the non-Holmes on the left, without any overlap. In this case, as often happens, the second principal component, graphed on the vertical axis, is not obviously interpretable, though it is tempting to see chronology as a possibility. There is a fairly strong tendency for the Holmes stories from Doyle's first two collections, *The Adventures of Sherlock Holmes* and *The Memoirs of Sherlock Holmes*, originally published in *The Strand* in 1891–92 and 1892–93, respectively, to appear toward the bottom of the graph and those from the next two collections, *The Return of Sherlock Holmes* and *His Last Bow*, published in *The Strand* in 1903–04 and 1908–17, to appear toward the top.

The orientation of the graph is not significant, and graphs based on different numbers of words might place the Holmes stories on the left. What *can* be interpreted is the distance between the texts on the graph. The further to the right a text falls, the more "Holmesian" it is, and the greater the distance between two texts, the less alike they are. It is important to distinguish similarity and difference on the two components, however. For example, the fourth section of "The Gully of Bluemansdyke" at the top left of the graph is very different from the third section of the same story at the bottom left on the second component, but both are about equally dissimilar to the Holmes stories.

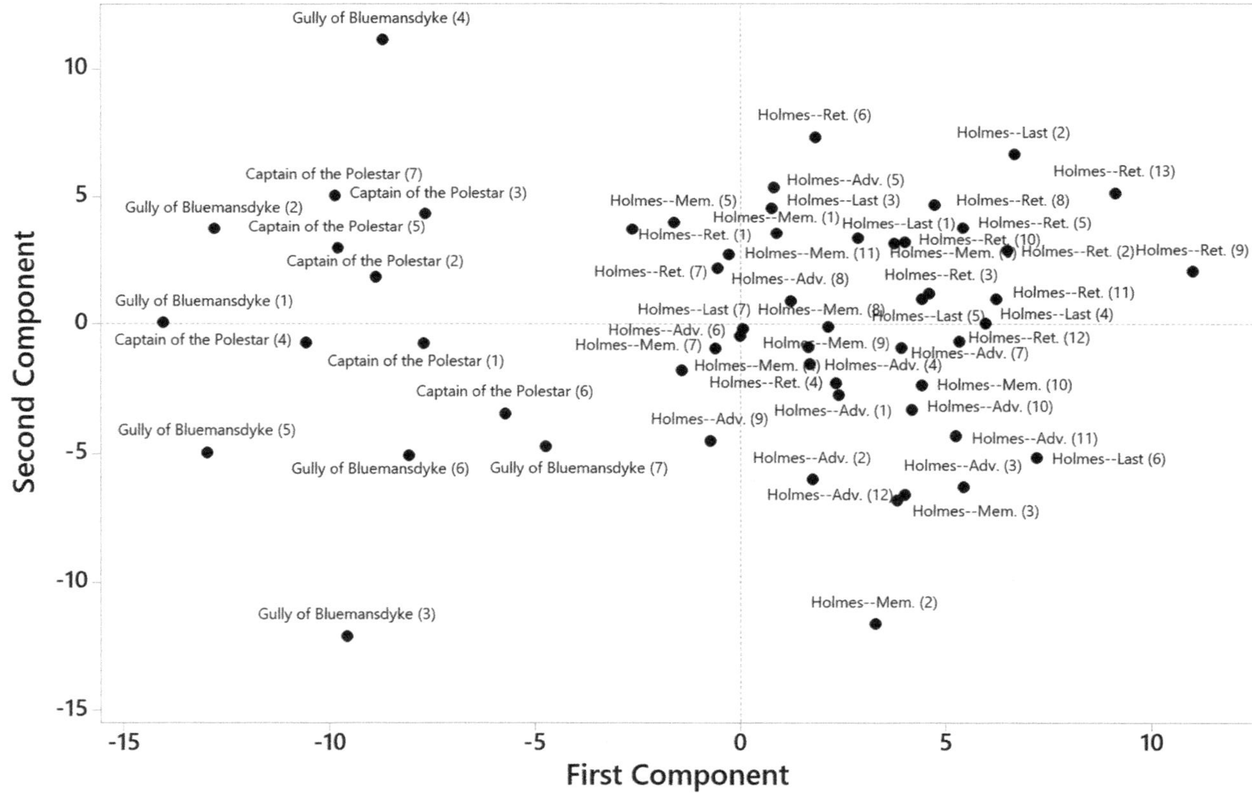

FIGURE 2.3 Principal components analysis score plot of Arthur Conan Doyle's Holmes and non-Holmes stories, based on the four hundred most frequent words, showing similarities and differences among the stories

One reason for the popularity of PCA is the fact that this method can also produce the loading plot in Figure 2.4 from the same data. In Figure 2.4, the variables that are most important in establishing the first two principal components appear in the same orientation as the previous graph, so that words that are most heavily used (loaded) in the Holmes stories appear on the far right, while those most heavily used in the non-Holmes stories appear on the far left. Although a high proportion of the four hundred most frequent words are function words, the presence of words like *crime, case, paper, papers, matter, ask, clear, think*, and *understand* on the right of the graph already suggests why the two kinds of stories can be distinguished. I have not read the non-Holmes stories, but some of the vocabulary on the left that would be worthy of investigation includes groups of prepositions and adverbs like *upon, by, among, through, behind, off, away, up, out, down, over, along*, and *towards* that suggest a possible emphasis on motion and action. Concrete vocabulary like *hard, white, head, heart, men, old, long, strong, body*, and *standing* would also be congruent with an emphasis on the physical rather than the mental.

PCA has usually been limited to the analysis of the most frequent words, but analyzing less frequent words, though it sometimes weakens the separation of the groups of texts, reveals the patterns of more meaningful words. For example, a graph of these same stories, based on the three hundred to seven hundred most frequent words (not shown), reveals much more significant Holmesian vocabulary, with words like *news, client, details, cases, crime, clue, affair, examined, facts, criminal, investigation, problem, points*, and *impossible* on the right. It also shows a more pronounced contrast between early and late stories on the second principal component, but this time with positions of the early and late stories reversed.

Initial testing of Holmes pastiches involves a corpus of detective fiction including the forty-three Holmes stories in Doyle's first four collections, *The Adventures of Sherlock Holmes, The Memoirs of Sherlock Holmes, The Return of Sherlock Holmes*, and *His Last Bow*, and twenty-seven pastiches by various authors, published between 1892 and 1976. Information about the pastiches was collected from various sources and online lists, including Ellery Queen's collection, *The Misadventures of Sherlock Holmes* (1944), the online *Arthur Conan Doyle Encyclopedia*, Peschel, and *goodreads*. I avoided very short pastiches and most parodies and focused mainly on relatively long, well-known works already available as electronic texts. In some cases, I had to capture desirable texts using OCR (optical character recognition), in which a computer program turns page images into editable texts. Although this process of collecting texts seems adequate for a relatively informal analysis like this one, a more serious study would need to be more systematic and more comprehensive.

The results of a series of cluster analyses show that only in those based on the one hundred to three hundred most frequent words do Doyle stories cluster with stories by others—in two of the three cases with a group of rather derivative stories written by Doyle's son Adrian (for a discussion of just how derivative they

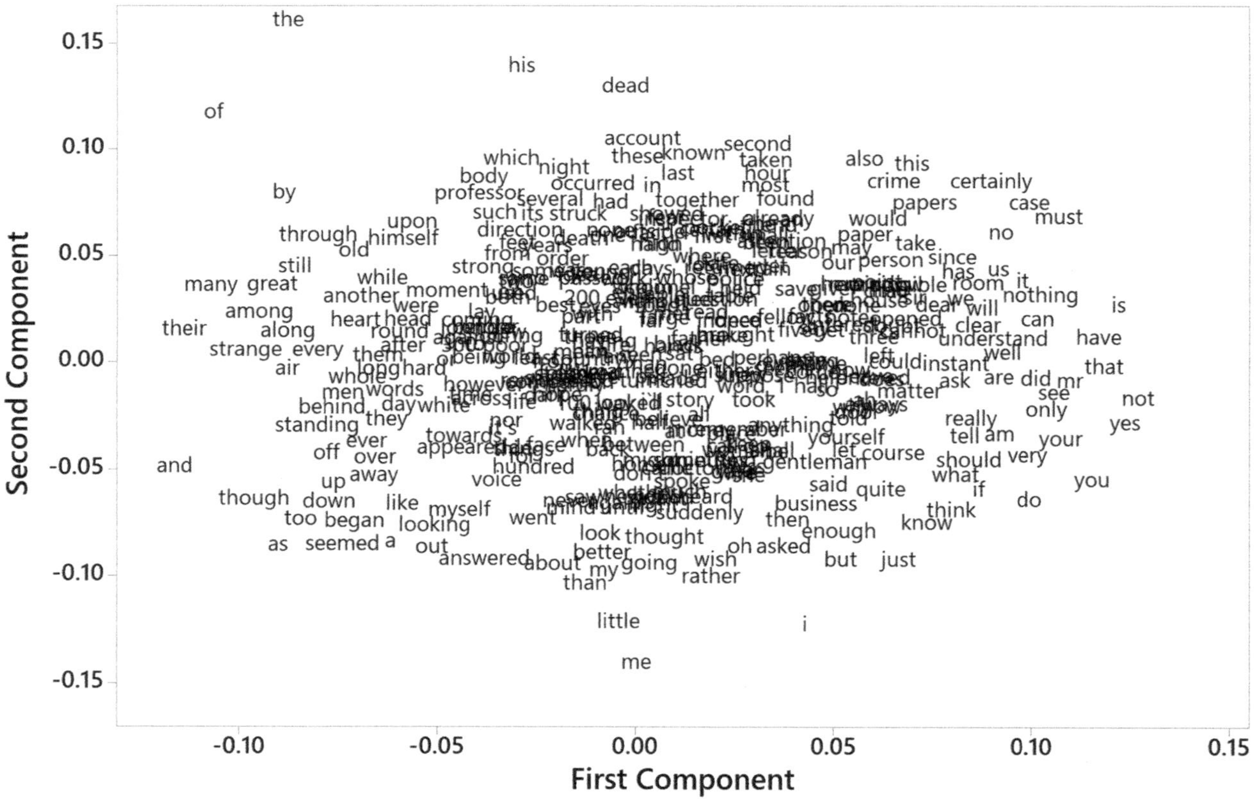

FIGURE 2.4 Principal components analysis loading plot of Arthur Conan Doyle's Holmes and non-Holmes stories, based on the four hundred most frequent words, showing the distribution of the words in the stories

are, see Nyqvist sec. 5). August Derleth's "The Adventure of the Circular Room," one of the most widely admired of the pastiches, clusters with Doyle's stories in analyses based on the one hundred to three hundred most frequent words and the five hundred to six hundred most frequent words. Arthur Whitaker's "The Man Who Was Wanted," which was first mistakenly published by Doyle's son as a genuine Holmes story (Tracy 299–301), clusters with Doyle in the analysis based on the two hundred most frequent words, but no pastiches cluster with Doyle in the analyses based on the seven hundred to the one thousand most frequent words.

Testing with PCA produces the same basic pattern, with minor mingling of the Doyle stories and pastiches in analyses based on small numbers of words but complete separation when larger numbers of words are used. The pastiches by Derleth and Whitaker are again most similar to those by Doyle, joined by Knox's "The Adventure of the First Class Carriage," another of the well-regarded pastiches. Analyzing a larger set of stories created by adding a few more pastiches and some other non-Holmes detective stories by the authors of the pastiches, while reducing the Doyle set to twenty-three of the longest Holmes stories, gives results in which no mixing of Doyle and the pastiches occurs at all.[9]

Two important consequences for the study of modes of composition flow from the results of these analyses: even exploratory methods are sensitive enough to detect the difference between Doyle's Holmes style and his non-Holmes style and to detect the difference between Doyle's Holmes style and pastiches of it. As so often, John F. Burrows puts it well in his discussion of *Shamela*, Fielding's parody of Richardson's *Pamela*: "Not quite like Fielding because his imitative attempt is successful enough to obscure his own signature. Not quite like Richardson because the attempt is not a complete success" (Burrows, "Who" 441).

Collaboration and Authorship

If completions and pastiches are problematic, the contributions of two collaborators to a single work are likely to be still more difficult to distinguish. In cases of very close collaboration involving each writer editing or revising the work of the other, indeed, it is often impossible to attribute parts of the finished work to either of the collaborators with any confidence, for the simple reason that the parts are effectively by neither of them. In such cases, the collaborative text often tests as unlike the style of either collaborator, producing a mixed third style. One example of this kind of collaboration is that of Robert Louis Stevenson and his son-in-law Lloyd Osbourne in *The Wrecker*, *The Wrong Box*, and *The Ebb Tide*. As I have shown, the sections of three artificially created simulations of collaborations comprising alternating sections of text by Stevenson and Osbourne can easily be attributed to the correct authors, but the actual collaborations give a confused picture that does not closely mirror the somewhat vague claims of the two authors but that does suggest an intimate collaboration (Hoover, "Simulations" 879–85).

When the collaboration is actually serial, however, with each author contributing continuous sections that alternate, the alternations are usually easily discernable, even with some cross-revising or editing. An interesting study of a collaboration mainly of the alternating kind, between D. H. Lawrence and Molly Skinner, on *The Boy in the Bush*, can be found in John F. Burrows's *Never Say Always Again: Reflections on the Numbers Game*. In the Skinner and Lawrence collaboration, most of the novel is strongly attributed either to Skinner or to Lawrence, including the parts that are known from external evidence to belong to each of them. Other parts of the novel, however, show both authors as about equally likely to be the author, suggesting a more thorough mixing of the two authors' styles in those parts, like that in the Stevenson and Osbourne collaboration.

In his analysis of *The Boy in the Bush* collaboration, Quiller-Couch's completion of Stevenson's *St. Ives*, and Sarah Fielding's *The History of Ophelia*, Burrows makes interesting use of what he calls "rolling segments," successive overlapping segments, each of which is tested for authorship. This process is intended to locate likely places where a continued or collaborative text changes authorship (for earlier work with overlapping sections of a Middle Dutch text, see van Dalen-Oskam and van Zundert 349–59). I used a tedious manual method of analyzing rolling segments in my study of *The Tutor's Story* (Hoover, "*Tutor's Story*" 331–2), but multiple types of rolling classification have recently been implemented in Stylo (Rybicki et al. 118; Eder, "Rolling Stylometry" 458–67). I also use rolling classify in my study of the collaborations of Stevenson and Osbourne, mentioned earlier (Hoover, "Simulations" 880–5).

The results of two new analyses of collaboration are shown in Figure 2.5. In the simpler one, at the bottom, rolling classify correctly identifies Stevenson as the author of the first thirty chapters of *St. Ives* and Quiller-Couch as the author of the last six chapters. This analysis uses SVM (support vector machine) based on the twelve hundred most frequent words to analyze rolling segments of four thousand words with an overlap of thirty-five hundred words. In the second, rolling classify is tested on *Stories by English Authors: England*, a collection of short fiction by Charles Reade, F. W. Robinson, Amelia Edwards, Angelo Lewis, Thomas Hardy, Wilkie Collins, and Anthony Hope. Rolling classify does a good job, correctly identifying all of the authors. This analysis uses Delta (cosine version) based on the fourteen hundred most frequent words and rolling segments of four thousand words with an overlap of thirty-five hundred words. Although rolling classify is still a relatively new technique that needs careful study, it seems an appropriate technique to consider applying to changes of mode, though it seems intuitively unlikely that a change in mode of composition will produce patterns as clear as those in Figure 2.5.

Chronological Style Variation

As I have suggested, any style variation caused by a change in mode of composition might be expected to be fairly subtle, so that the methods must also be proven on relatively minor variations in style. Fortunately, style variation

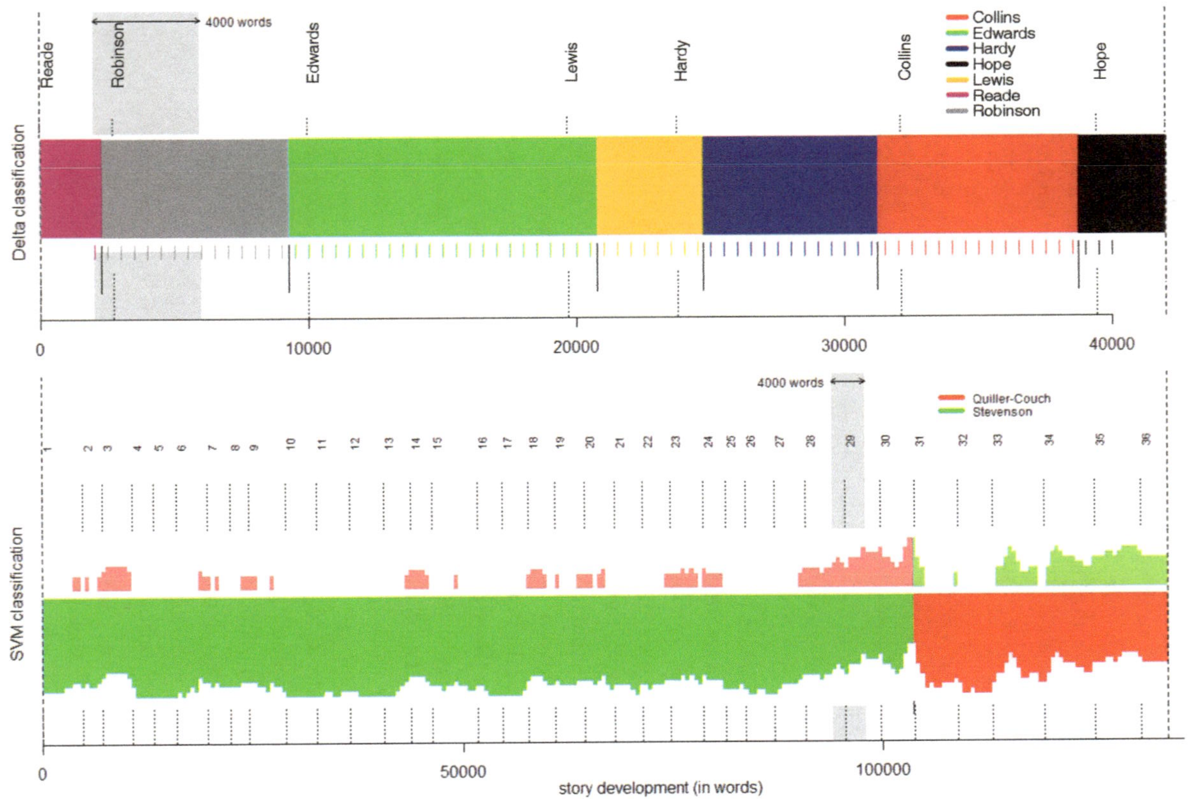

FIGURE 2.5 Two rolling classify analyses: Six authors and the collaborative collection, *Stories by English Authors: England* (top); Robert Louis Stevenson and Arthur Quiller-Couch and the authorship of *St. Ives* (bottom)

within a single author or within a single text can also generally be detected. As I have shown earlier, differences among an author's texts, including those caused by writing in different genres, are generally easily detectable. For differences between authors or texts, an objectively correct answer is also normally possible, but the detection of subtler kinds of stylistic variation is much more open-ended. Whether or not texts or sections of a text have different styles is typically a matter of judgment that may depend partly on critical consensus and common sense, as well as on computational analysis (for more discussion, see Hoover, "Multivariate Analysis" 341–50). For authors such as Henry James, Wilkie Collins, and George Meredith, for example, chronological style variation can be detected computationally. Critics overwhelmingly agree that Henry James's early and late styles are very different, and, as we will see, his early and late texts are as easy to distinguish computationally as texts by many pairs of authors. This is especially important because chronology is often implicated in a change in mode of composition, and a strong chronological effect could easily be misinterpreted as a change caused by the adoption of a new mode of composition or vice versa.

Earlier in this chapter, tests on Anthony Trollope's six Barchester novels showed that each novel has a style that is sufficiently unified that all sections of each novel form an individual group. Although that discussion ignored chronology, the twenty-five sections of these novels (about forty-five thousand words long) also divide nicely by date, with the novels from 1853 to 1860 in one group and those from 1863 to 1866 in another. Expanding this analysis to include Trollope's other series of six novels, these centered on the Palliser family, produces interesting results. The two series overlap in time, with the first Palliser novel, *Can You Forgive Her* (1864), published three years before the final Barchester novel, *The Last Chronicle of Barset* (1867). When the twelve novels are analyzed together, this time as whole novels, it is clear that, for Trollope, chronology is a more important variable than the series in which a novel appears. The twelve novels, like the six Barchester Towers, again form two groups, one containing the four Barchester novels from 1853 to 1860, and the other containing the Barchester and Palliser novels from 1863 to 1876. Even more interesting is the fact that the later novels form two subgroups, one containing one Palliser novel and two Barchester novels published from 1863 to 1866, and the other containing the remaining five Palliser novels published from 1867 to 1876.

The well-known and radical difference between Henry James's early and late styles deserves a more extended discussion. Consider the chronological pattern that results from a cluster analysis based on the seven hundred most frequent words, in which James's short fiction (eight thousand to twenty-six thousand words) forms four clear groups based on the date of publication: 1865–69, 1874–78, 1884–90, and 1900–10 (the gaps between the periods were created by leaving out any texts written in the missing years). Here the analysis agrees with the critical consensus, though it suggests not just a late and an early style but a continuous pattern of development, as will be seen in Chapter 6 (see also Hoover, "Corpus Stylistics" 178–93; Hoover et al. ch. 5).

Chronology can be tested in quite a different way that will illustrate the benefit of applying multiple methods to the same problem. Consider a group of twenty-five early and late short stories, plays, and literary criticism by Henry James tested against a wide selection of early and late James novels and short stories. The thirty-eight early novels and stories date from 1864 to 1881 and the thirty-one late ones from 1899 to 1917, approximately 1.25 million words for each period. The method to be applied is what I call "wide spectrum" analysis because it encompasses the entire word-frequency spectrum from the most frequent to the least frequent words (Hoover, "Text Analysis"). This method, which is a variant of Burrows's Zeta and Iota ("All" 30–45) as modified by Hugh Craig (Craig and Kinney 18–26), is implemented in an Excel spreadsheet available on my Excel Text-Analysis Tools website ("Excel Text-Analysis"). It departs from the usual emphasis on word frequency and tests consistency of use instead. Word-frequency lists for all of the texts are first created, the twenty-five texts to be tested are analyzed as whole texts, and the rest are analyzed in sections of three thousand words. Burrows's simple and elegant idea is to use consistency of use to measure the distributions of moderately frequent and rare words in samples of texts by two authors (or any two valid classes of texts). One benefit of this approach is that it can be applied to cases for which statistical analysis of frequencies might not be appropriate. Another is that it allows the analyst to compare the results of consistency analysis with those of frequency analysis. Finally, it has the attractive feature of producing lists of characteristic vocabulary for the two groups that are being tested.

Here, early James is treated as the primary author and late James as the secondary author. Wide spectrum analysis counts how many early James sections contain each word and how many late James sections do *not* contain the word. After converting these to decimals, it adds the early presence and late absence to create a distinctiveness score. The score theoretically ranges from two, for a word present in all the early sections but absent from all the late sections, to zero, for a word absent from all the early sections but present in all the late sections. In practice, however, scores above 1.7 and below 0.3 are unusual. The words are sorted on their distinctiveness scores, in order of distinctiveness, to create two lists of words—one characteristic of early James and the other characteristic of late James. In this set of texts, the most distinctively early word is *cried*, which is present in seventy-two percent of the 404 early James sections and absent from eighty-three percent of the 398 late James sections, with a distinctiveness score of 1.56. The most distinctive late word is *wasn't*, present in only ten percent of the early sections, and absent from only twenty-two percent of the late sections, with a distinctiveness score of 0.32. The fact that these scores are comparable to those found in comparisons of two different authors confirms just how different James's two styles are.

Studying the characteristic words reveals a great deal about the early and late verbal styles of Henry James, and James scholars would have little trouble identifying which list belongs to which period on the basis of the fifty most distinctive words alone. Wide spectrum analysis also produces the graph shown in Figure 2.6 (somewhat trimmed and with the titles of the early and late sections removed for clarity). In this graph, the horizontal axis records the proportion of the different words (word types) in each section or text that are words characteristic of early James. (The types are defined as unique spellings.) The vertical axis does the same for the words characteristic of late James. In the untrimmed graph, the section at the top left is from his great mature 1903 novel, *The Golden Bowl*, in which sixty-eight percent of the 882 different words are characteristic of late James, but only twenty-eight percent are characteristic of early James. The section at the bottom right is from the 1871 story "At Isella," with sixty-nine percent of its 1147 different words characteristically early words and twenty-eight percent characteristically late words.

The labeled texts on the graph identified in the legend as early and late "Ind. Sections" are short stories held out to test whether or not the distinction created by the texts designated as "Early James Sections" and "Late James Sections" attributes them to the correct period. Those identified as "Test Sections" are plays, criticism, and letters included to see whether or not James's stylistic development is detectable across multiple genres. It is clear that all the early and late stories, plays, letters, and criticism fall into their correct positions in the graph, in spite of the differences in genre and in spite of the fact that none of these texts had any part in creating the distinction upon which the graph is based. (Nonfiction titles end with "NF," play titles with "Dr," and letters with "Letters.") The 1903 story "Broken Wings," the 1909 play *The Outcry*, the 1913 critical article on Rupert Brook, and James's late handwritten letters appear toward the top left, and the corresponding early stories, plays, criticism, and letters appear toward the lower right. Because all of test sections contain words that are not in the texts on which the distinction is based, they appear only near to rather than within the clusters of early and late James sections.

Although wide spectrum analysis combines aspects of Burrows's Zeta and Iota, those two measures of difference are somewhat differently calculated, and each concentrates on a different part of the word spectrum. A quick test of the chronological change in Wilkie Collins's style using Zeta and Iota shows that, like wide spectrum analysis, both are effective in detecting chronological change. Like wide spectrum analysis, Zeta and Iota analyses are implemented in an Excel spreadsheet available on my Excel Text-Analysis Tools website. In these tests, six early (1852–62) and eight late (1879–89) Collins novels form the basis of the distinction, and three early (1852–53) and four late (1880–87) stories are tested. Both of these measures produce scores that are calculated as the rate of occurrence of characteristic early or late words per thousand words in each text. All the early stories have rates of occurrence of characteristically early rare words (the

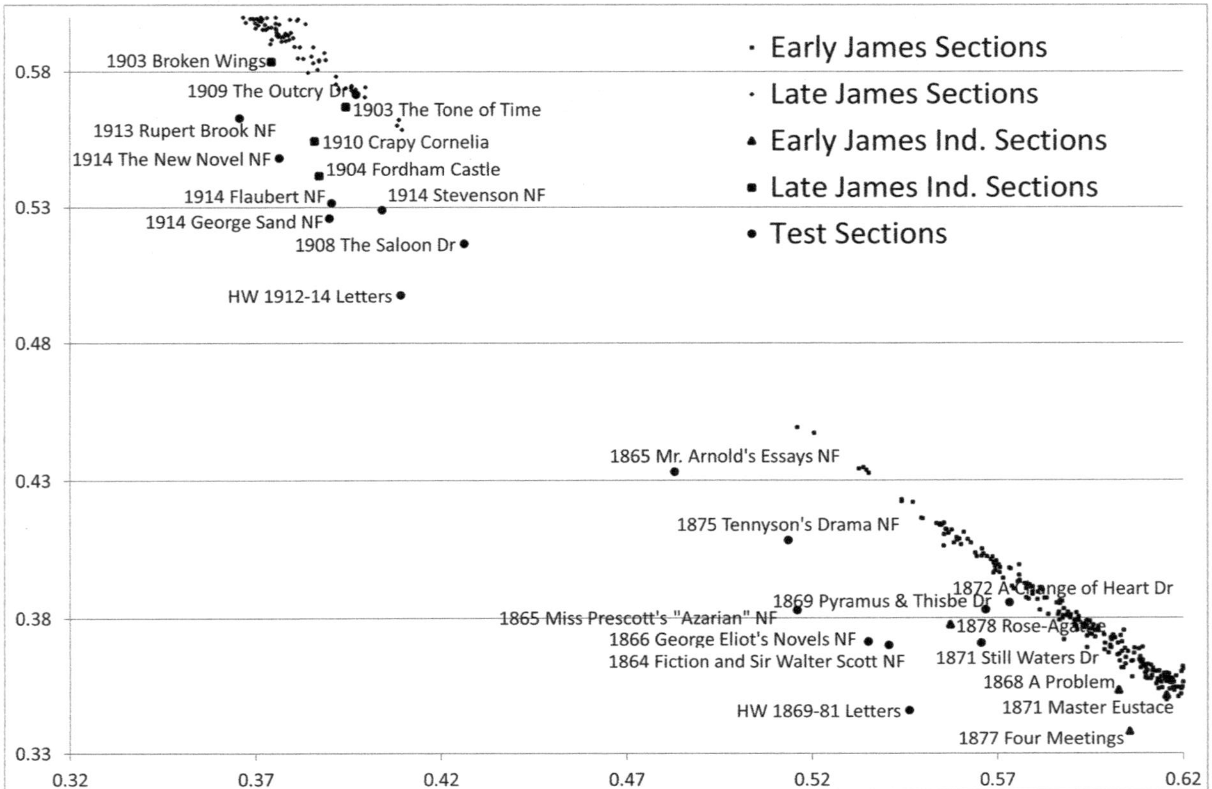

FIGURE 2.6 Wide spectrum analysis of genre and chronology in Henry James, showing the percentage of word types in each text that are characteristic of early James (horizontal axis) and late James (vertical axis)

Iota test) and moderately frequent words (the Zeta test) that surpass those of all the late texts in the analysis. The success of these tools across genres suggests that they should be sensitive enough to detect any style variation caused by a change in mode of composition.

Other Kinds of Intra-Authorial Style Variation

Even in the absence of a well-developed critical consensus like that around James's stylistic development, common sense can guide our reaction to a computationally detected style difference. That is, regular patterns of differentiation that are confirmed over a range of analyses, especially analyses of different kinds or based on different variables, demonstrate that the texts "really" are different. It remains for the analyst to connect such differences to an interpretation. As Hugh Craig puts it,

> Common sense suggests that if quantitative measures are reliable in telling authors apart, and if they offer access to new internal evidence genuinely independent of impressionistic criticism, then some among them ought also to be of use in the main business of literary study, the interpretation of texts.
>
> *(104)*

Consider the invented political treatise, *The Theory and Practice of Oligarchical Collectivism*, purportedly written by Emmanuel Goldstein, that Orwell inserts into *Nineteen Eighty-Four.* This section is trivially easy to distinguish from the rest of the novel, even using relatively uninteresting variables like word length, and even the twenty most frequent words are effective. It would be quite astonishing if this political treatise were indistinguishable from the rest of the novel computationally: it is clearly a different genre that common sense tells us should diverge from literary fiction. Yet demonstrating that it shows a huge increase in long, abstract words, for example, is reassuring. Equally reassuring is the fact that in a simple cluster analysis, Orwell's Appendix on Newspeak also separates well from the rest of the novel, but always joins loosely with Goldstein's book, and the fact that the final grim sections of the main novel always cluster separately from the rest (see Hoover, "Multivariate Analysis" 345–6, 354–6 for more discussion). These analytic divisions match our intuitions and fit sensibly into our understanding of the novel.

The final chapter of Margaret Atwood's dystopian novel, *The Handmaid's Tale* (1987), a report of an academic conference set about two hundred years after the rest of the novel, also seems like a clear instance of genre difference. In its optimistic view that Gilead no longer exists at the time of the conference, it is also an intentional echo of the appendix of Orwell's dystopia, according to Atwood herself (Ingersoll 71). This chapter, like Orwell's Appendix and Goldstein's book, is very easy to distinguish from the rest of the novel with a simple cluster analysis, and as purported nonfiction from so much later, its clear divergence is both expected and easily interpretable, though just how optimistically to read it remains a question (Westerman 377–9, 388–90). Here, as in the case of 1984, the analytic demonstration of difference is clearly an invitation to a fuller and more in-depth analysis of what makes it diverge.

A similar, but subtler, example is found in Stephen King's *Misery* (1987). (King's changes in mode of composition are the subject of Chapter 7.) In this novel, Paul Sheldon, a best-selling author who specializes in Victorian-era romance novels, has a serious automobile accident. Coincidentally, the accident happens very near the home of Annie Wilkes, a former nurse and an ardent (and psychotic) fan who takes him in and nurses him back to health. When Annie discovers that Sheldon has killed off the fictional Misery, her favorite heroine, in an attempt to branch out into more serious fiction, she forces him to write *Misery's Return*, a novel in which he resurrects Misery. King inserts several chapters of *Misery's Return* into the novel at various places, a total of almost nine thousand words. Removing *Misery's Return* and analyzing it and the rest of *Misery* in sections of about forty-five hundred words shows that King has made the partial romance novel within *Misery* different enough that its two sections separate very distinctly from the rest of the novel in cluster analyses based on the six hundred to one thousand most frequent words.

In spite of the lack of a definitive answer about whether or not two styles should be distinct, some other cases also seem fairly clear-cut: for example, the third-person omniscient narration of some chapters of Dickens's *Bleak House* and the first-person narration of other chapters by Esther Summerson. Surely, we can expect these two styles to be distinct and can expect that computational methods will confirm this (Hoover, "Some Approaches" 53–55). The same is true of the main narrators of Wilkie Collins's *The Moonstone*. Collins would hardly go to the trouble of separating the narration of the novel among several characters if he did not intend to make at least the main narrations distinct. Just as surely, the novel would have been unlikely to be successful if the narration of Betteredge, the good but obtuse old family servant with an obsession with *Robinson Crusoe*, were not distinct from that of the hypocritical poor relation, Miss Clack, with her "precious pamphlets" of religious inspiration and advice (see Hoover et al. 64–79 for more discussion). In both of these cases the multiple voices are fairly easy to distinguish, as we would expect. In a study on Early Modern drama, Burrows and Craig have shown that the ability to differentiate the speech of characters extends to drama as well. For example, in one test they extract the dialogue of multiple characters from multiple plays by Shakespeare and Fletcher and use PCA to show that the dialogue of Shakespeare's characters can be distinguished from the dialogue of Fletcher's characters (294–9).

More than thirty years ago, Burrows provocatively showed that the dialogue of Jane Austen's major characters can be distinguished even on the basis of the frequencies of the thirty most frequent words in the novels (*Computation*). The character speech of many other authors can also be distinguished computationally, though more recent work has used more variables and additional methods. For example, the voices of the characters of William Faulkner's *As I Lay Dying* and Doyle's *The Hound of the Baskervilles* (Hoover, "Microanalysis" ii18–ii22), Jack London's *The Sea Wolf* and Fanny Burney's *Evelina* (Hoover et al., ch. 4), and Virginia Woolf's *The Waves* (Balossi; Hoover, "Argument") can all be distinguished from one another computationally using many of the methods already discussed. The character voices in other novels are not as distinct. For example, the letters of the letter-writers in William Hill Brown's *The Power of Sympathy* and Hannah Foster Webster's *The Coquette*, both, like *Evelina*, late-eighteenth-century epistolary novels, fail to group well by writer, even when different addressees are taken into account (Hoover, "Microanalysis" ii22–ii24). The tedious difficulty of separating character dialogue has limited the number of such tests that have been performed.[10]

The Waves provides an opportunity for a brief exploration of the application of topic modeling to the study of style variation. Topic modeling has recently become a very popular method of analysis for collections of texts too large to read, but it can be used effectively on the micro level as well (for introductions, see Blei 77–83; Weingart; Graham et al.; Meeks and Weingart). There are many versions of topic modeling, but the one used here, implemented in MALLET (McCallum), is based on Latent Dirichlet Allocation, a kind of statistical analysis that creates its "topics" by identifying words that occur together in sections of text more often than they would be likely to do by chance. The topics are really statistical, not semantic, but they often seem very much like the kind of topics that humans might create when discussing texts they know (Jockers 122–53; Goldstone and Underwood 361–9; Rhody; Schmidt). Detecting style variation may seem an unlikely application for such a semantically oriented tool, but a look at a simple topic model of *The Waves* will suggest how it might be useful. Consider a seven-topic model based on just six sections of text, each containing all of the parts of one character's monologue, except that Bernard's section omits the final long summing-up chapter of the novel, all in Bernard's voice. That chapter would overweight the analysis toward him, and it is also removed in work on the novel by other researchers (Burrows, *Computation* 206; Ramsay personal communication; Balossi 84; Hoover, "Argument").

Among the seven topics is a single generic topic that is the heaviest topic in all six monologues, but each of the six voices of the novel shows a strong unique topic as the second heaviest. (To be clear, not all topic models with seven topics produce this precise pattern because each running of the program is based on a random number.) Micro topic modeling thus shows that the voices of *The Waves* are individualized and produces topics that make sense to human readers of the novel. The top thirty words of Susan's topic, for example, are easily recognized as hers: *fields, sleep, kitchen, winter, bury, hate, children, school, field, milk, dawn, higher, bread, limbs, summer, watch, kiss, bell, gate, escaped, blown, garden, window-pane, setter, washing, November, horses, clean, grass,* and *cart.* Susan becomes a housewife and lives in the country, and her concrete vocabulary marks her interest in her children and the farm. Louis—the Australian who is sensitive about his accent and about the fact that his father is a banker in Brisbane, and who often imagines he hears a beast stamping—also has a readily recognizable topic: *accent, passing, stamps, oak, Nile, boasting, grained, Australian, boy, steel, pitchers, beast, history, chained, city, rhythm, church, disorder, average, clerks, Brisbane, banker, grasses, stalk, sing, lived, wheel, names, hats,* and *vanity.* If the number of topics is increased to thirteen, a single generic topic that is heaviest in all six monologues again appears, and some of the characters have more than one topic associated with them. If topic modeling can distinguish the six speakers of *The Waves*, it should be able to detect any changes in the statistical distribution of words that might be caused by a change in mode of composition (see Chapter 5).

Conclusion

Authorship attribution tools and computational stylistics methods derived from or related to them are clearly capable of distinguishing authors from each other and sections of multiple texts by a single author from each other. They can do this even when one writer is trying to imitate another: for example, when completing a text begun by someone else, when writing in a restricted genre like the Harlequin Romance, or when writing for a journal with a rigid house style, like the Victorian *Saturday Review.* In the latter case, they can also detect a shift in the style of writers that brings them closer to the house style without obliterating their individual styles. In the specialized case of imitation represented by the pastiche, the same holds true: pastiches very rarely resemble the originals closely enough to erase authorial difference. Even in the difficult case of collaboration, these methods do a good job of distinguishing the individual styles of the collaborators, except in very close collaborations with substantial cowriting and rewriting of parts of the texts.

The methods of computational stylistics can also distinguish Edith Nesbit's fiction for children from her fiction for adults, Louisa May Alcott's sensational fiction from her more mainstream fiction, and Arthur Conan Doyle's Holmes stories from his other fiction. They can also detect variation in style within a single author's oeuvre, such as the chronological changes seen in the styles of Henry James and Wilkie Collins, and variations in style within a single text, such as the political tract inserted into *Nineteen Eighty-Four* and the imagined academic conference that concludes *The Handmaid's Tale.* They can detect differences among multiple narrators, like those of Charles Dickens's *Bleak House* and Wilkie Collins's *The Moonstone.* In many cases, they can distinguish the speech styles of multiple characters within a novel from each other, as if those characters were actual individual human beings.

The stage is now set for the rest of this study: an examination of what changes are discernable, if any, when writers change the way they produce their texts. If significant stylistic variations occur with a change in mode of composition, the methods of authorship attribution and computational stylistics will be able to detect them. If those methods do not detect systematic changes, either there are none or they are too subtle to be detected by these methods. Yet, given the demonstrated sensitivity of the methods and the relatively subtle changes they *can* identify, any changes so subtle as to escape detection are unlikely to be of much interest. What will emerge from the rest of this study is a picture of authorial style as surprisingly durable in circumstances that common sense would suggest might well alter it. Chapter 3 will explore one of the easiest scenarios to study: the temporary or occasional use of dictation by writers who otherwise wrote their texts by hand.

Notes

1. Other features that have been used in authorship attribution include, for example, word length, sentence length, vocabulary richness, syntactic complexity, the distribution of parts of speech, and hapax legomena and dislegomena (words appearing just once or just twice in a text); see Holmes for an authoritative discussion. Although these features may be useful in individual cases, they have not been shown to be broadly effective and will not be used widely here.
2. See Rybicki and Eder for a large series of tests on various languages, see Juola ("Authorship Attribution") for a comprehensive discussion, and see Love for an excellent general discussion of the history and nature of both traditional and computer-assisted authorship attribution.
3. For simplicity, throughout this study, I will report analyses in the range of the one hundred to one thousand most frequent words, though the actual upper limit for such analyses, imposed by my statistical software, Minitab, is between 992 and 996 words. The limit is not problematic because experience shows that the best results on texts of known authorship normally fall within this range. In this case, as in most others I have tested, the results based on the one hundred and two hundred most frequent words tend to be weaker than those based on more words. Except for analyses involving JGAAP and Stylo, or otherwise indicated, the word frequencies analyzed in this study are produced by the Intelligent Archive (Craig et al.), and all cluster analyses in this study are performed in Minitab, with standardized variables, Ward linkage, and squared Euclidean distance. Although cluster analysis can be performed in Stylo, I have used Minitab here because of the currently unexplained fact that Stylo (and presumably *R*, more generally) does not always produce the same results, even with exactly the same word frequencies. In some cases, the Minitab results are more accurate, rather than just different.
4. Recently, another kind of culling has been developed that limits the word-frequency list to words found in a specified minimum proportion of the texts being analyzed (Jockers et al. 470, 488n31; Rybicki and Heydel 711; Eder et al. 111). Depending on what proportion is chosen, this kind of culling can have an effect similar to that of my method. The practice of limiting an analysis to words that appear in every text (culling at one hundred percent) has a certain appeal but is unlikely to produce the most accurate results, and in hundreds of analyses, I have found that only rarely do culling rates above forty percent improve results. One reason for this is clearly that extreme culling percentages reduce the number of words available for analysis and so reduce the amount of information on which the analysis is based.

5. In a beautiful irony, this statistical test that has often been used in authorship attribution grew out of work that was originally published under the pseudonym "Student." Student was actually William S. Gosset, a mathematician working for the Guinness brewery, who developed the test as a way of selecting the best ingredients for making Guinness. The company considered Gosset's test as proprietary, so he was not allowed to publish under his own name or to mention the brewery (Sanyal; see Kopf for a much fuller account).
6. All principal components analyses in this chapter were performed in Minitab, using the correlation matrix (which prevents words with high frequencies from dominating the analysis). PCA is more typically used to analyze simple word frequency lists, rather than words that have been *t*-tested for significance, though Burrows uses the form described here to good effect ("Not" 97–103). The more typical PCA will be used frequently in this study and will be more fully explained in the discussion of Arthur Conan Doyle's stories, later in this chapter.
7. Only three chapters from *A Marble Woman* are included because I was unable to locate an e-text of this book and had to use OCR (optical character recognition) on *Plots and Counterplots*, to create it.
8. For a thorough and persuasive discussion of the related categories of parody, travesty, and pastiche (satiric or pure), see Chatman. I agree with Chatman's rejection of the notion (shared by Jameson) that pastiche is "the prototypical postmodern genre" (28).
9. Some of these detective stories are included in a discussion of my Delta spreadsheet, a tool implementing Burrows's Delta in Excel (Hoover, forthcoming), though the only pastiche analyzed there is Whitaker's.
10. For a partially automated tool for extracting character dialogue from texts, see my Analyze Textual Divisions Spreadsheet, available from my Excel Text-Analysis Tools website ("Excel Text-Analysis").

References

Alcott, Lousia May. *A Modern Cinderella: Or, The Little Old Shoe, And Other Stories*. Hurst, 1910. www.gutenberg.org/files/3806/3806-h/3806-h.htm.

———. *Behind a Mask: The Unknown Thrillers of Louisa May Alcott*. Edited by Madeleine B. Stern, William Morrow, 1975. archive.org/details/behindmaskunkno00alco.

———. *Plots and Counterplots: More Unknown Thrillers of Louisa May Alcott*. Edited by Madeleine B. Stern, William Morrow, 1976. archive.org/details/plotscounterplot00alco.

Antonia, Alexis et al. "Language Chunking, Data Sparseness, and the Value of a Long Marker List: Explorations With Word N-grams and Authorial Attribution." *Literary and Linguistic Computing*, vol. 29, no. 2, 2014, pp. 147–63, doi:10.1093/llc/fqt028.

The Arthur Conan Doyle Encyclopedia. www.arthur-conan-doyle.com/index.php?title=Main_Page; www.arthur-conan-doyle.com/index.php/Pastiches_&_Parodies.

Atwood, Margaret. *The Handmaid's Tale*. Fawcett Chrest, 1987.

Balossi, Giuseppina. *A Corpus Linguistic Approach to Literary Language and Characterization: Virginia Woolf's The Waves*. John Benjamins, 2014, doi:10.1075/lal.18.

Biber, Douglas. *Variation Across Speech and Writing*. Cambridge UP, 1988, doi:10.1017/CBO9780511621024.

Binongo, José Nilo G. "Joaquin's *Joaquinesquerie, Joaquinesquerie's* Joaquin: A Statistical Expression of a Filipino Writer's Style." *Literary and Linguistic Computing*, vol. 9, no. 4, 1994, pp. 267–79, doi:10.1093/llc/9.4.267.

Binongo, José Nilo G., and M. W. A. Smith. "The Application of Principal Component Analysis to Stylometry." *Literary and Linguistic Computing*, vol. 14, no. 4, 1999, pp. 445–65, doi:10.1093/llc/14.4.445.

Blei, David. "Probabilistic Topic Models." *Communications of the ACM*, vol. 55, no. 4, 2012, pp. 77–84, doi:10.1145/2133806.2133826.
Brownlee, Jason. *Weka Machine Learning Mini-Course*. 2016. machinelearningmastery.com/applied-machine-learning-weka-mini-course.
Burrows, John F. "All the Way Through: Testing for Authorship in Different Frequency Strata." *Literary and Linguistic Computing*, vol. 22, no. 1, 2006, pp. 27–47, doi:10.1093/llc/fqi067.
———. *Computation Into Criticism*. Clarendon Press, 1987.
———. "'Delta': A Measure of Stylistic Difference and a Guide to Likely Authorship." *Literary and Linguistic Computing*, vol. 17, no. 3, 2002, pp. 267–87, doi:10.1093/llc/17.3.267.
———. "The Englishing of Juvenal: Computational Stylistics and Translated Texts." *Style*, vol. 36, no. 4, 2002, pp. 677–99, doi:10.5325/style.36.4.677.
———. "Never Say Always Again: Reflections on the Numbers Game." *Text and Genre in Reconstruction. Effects of Digitalization on Ideas, Behaviours, Products and Institutions*, edited by Willard McCarty, Open Book Publishers, 2010, pp. 13–36. books.openedition.org/obp/646.
———. "Not Unless You Ask Nicely: The Interpretative Nexus Between Analysis and Information." *Literary and Linguistic Computing*, vol. 7, no. 2, 1992, pp. 91–109, doi:10.1093/llc/7.2.91.
———. "A Second Opinion on 'Shakespeare and Authorship Studies in the Twenty-First Century'." *Shakespeare Quarterly*, vol. 63, no. 3, 2012, pp. 355–92, doi:10.1353/shq.2012.0038.
———. "Who Wrote *Shamela?* Verifying the Authorship of a Parodic Text." *Literary and Linguistic Computing*, vol. 20, no. 4, 2005, pp. 437–50, doi:10.1093/llc/fqi049.
Burrows, John F., and Hugh Craig. "Authors and Characters." *English Studies*, vol. 93, no. 3, 2012, pp. 292–309, doi:10.1080/0013838X.2012.668786.
Chatman, Seymour Benjamin. "Parody and Style." *Poetics Today*, vol. 22, no. 1, 2001, pp. 25–39. muse.jhu.edu/article/27848.
Clement, Ross, and David Sharp. "Ngram and Bayesian Classification of Documents." *Literary and Linguistic Computing*, vol. 18, no. 4, 2003, pp. 423–47, doi:10.1093/llc/18.4.423.
Craig, Hugh. "Authorial Attribution and Computational Stylistics: If You Can Tell Authors Apart, Have You Learned Anything About Them?" *Literary and Linguistic Computing*, vol. 14, no. 1, 1999, pp. 103–13, doi:10.1093/llc/14.1.103.
Craig, Hugh, and Alexis Antonia. "Six Authors and the *Saturday Review*: A Quantitative Approach to Style." *Victorian Periodicals Review*, vol. 48, no. 1, 2015, pp. 67–86, doi:10.1353/vpr.2015.0004.
Craig, Hugh, and Arthur Kinney, editors. *Shakespeare, Computers, and the Mystery of Authorship*. Cambridge UP, 2009, doi:10.1017/CBO9780511605437.014.
Eder, Maciej. "Rolling Stylometry." *Digital Scholarship in the Humanities*, vol. 31, no. 3, 2016, pp. 457–69, doi:10.1093/llc/fqv010.
———. "Visualization in Stylometry: Cluster Analysis Using Networks." *Digital Scholarship in the Humanities*, vol. 32, no. 1, 2017, pp. 50–64, doi:10.1093/llc/fqv061.
Eder, Maciej et al. "Stylometry with *R:* A Package for Computational Text Analysis." *R Journal*, vol. 8, no. 1, 2016, pp. 107–21. journal.r-project.org/archive/2016/RJ-2016-007/RJ-2016-007.pdf.
Eiselein, Gregory K., and Anne Phillips, editors. *Louisa May Alcott Encyclopedia*. Greenwood Press, 2001.

Elliott, Jack. "Whole Genre Sequencing." *Digital Scholarship in the Humanities*, vol. 32, no. 1, 2017, pp. 65–79, doi:10.1093/llc/fqv034.

Evert, Stefan et al. "Understanding and Explaining Delta Measures for Authorship Attribution." *Digital Scholarship in the Humanities*, vol. 32, suppl. 2, 2017, pp. ii4–ii16, doi:10.1093/llc/fqx023.

Frank, Eibe et al. *The WEKA Workbench*. Online Appendix, *Data Mining: Practical Machine Learning Tools and Techniques*. 4th ed., Morgan Kaufmann, 2016. www.cs.waikato.ac.nz/ml/weka/index.html.

Goldstone, Andrew, and Ted Underwood. "The Quiet Transformations of Literary Studies: What Thirteen Thousand Scholars Could Tell Us." *New Literary History*, vol. 45, no. 3, 2014, pp. 359–84, doi:10.1353/nlh.2014.0025.

goodreads. www.goodreads.com.

Graham, Shawn et al. "Getting Started With Topic Modeling and *MALLET*." *The Programming Historian*, vol. 1, 2012. programminghistorian.org/en/lessons/topic-modeling-and-mallet.

Holmes, David I. "Authorship Attribution." *Computers and the Humanities*, vol. 28, no. 2, 1994, pp. 87–106, doi:10.1007/BF01830689.

Hoover, David L. "Argument, Evidence, and the Limits of Digital Literary Studies." *Debates in the Digital Humanities: 2016*, edited by Matthew Gold, U of Minnesota P, 2016, pp. 230–50. dhdebates.gc.cuny.edu/read/untitled/section/70f5261e-e268-4f56-928f-0c4ea30d254d.

———. "Authorial Style." *Language and Style: Essays in Honour of Mick Short*, edited by Dan McIntyre and Beatrix Busse, Palgrave Macmillan, 2010, pp. 250–71.

———. "Corpus Stylistics, Stylometry, and the Styles of Henry James." *Style*, vol. 41, no. 2, 2007, pp. 174–203, doi:10.5325/style.41.2.174.

———. *Excel Text-Analysis Tools*. 2019. wp.nyu.edu/exceltextanalysis.

———. "Frequent Word Sequences and Statistical Stylistics." *Literary and Linguistic Computing*, vol. 17, no. 2, 2002, pp. 157–80, doi:10.1093/llc/17.2.157.

———. *Language and Style in the Inheritors*. UP of America, 1999. archive.org/details/languagestyleint00hoov.

———. "The Microanalysis of Style Variation." *Digital Scholarship in the Humanities*, vol. 32, suppl. 2, 2017, pp. ii17–ii30, doi:10.1093/llc/fqx022.

———. "Modes of Composition in Henry James: Dictation, Style, and *What Maisie Knew*." *Henry James Review*, vol. 35, no. 3, 2014, pp. 257–77, doi:10.1353/hjr.2014.0024.

———. "Multivariate Analysis and the Study of Style Variation." *Literary and Linguistic Computing*, vol. 18, no. 4, 2003, pp. 341–60, doi:10.1093/llc/18.4.341.

———. "Simulations and Difficult Problems." *Digital Scholarship in the Humanities*, vol. 34, no. 4, 2019, pp. 874–92, doi:10.1093/llc/fqz034.

———. "Some Approaches to Corpus Stylistics." *Stylistics: Past, Present and Future*, edited by Yu Dongmin, Shanghai Foreign Language Education Press, 2010, pp. 40–63.

———. "Statistical Stylistics and Authorship Attribution: An Empirical Investigation." *Literary and Linguistic Computing*, vol. 16, no. 4, 2001, pp. 421–44, doi:10.1093/llc/16.4.421.

———. "Text Analysis." *Literary Studies in the Digital Age: An Evolving Anthology*, edited by Ken Price and Ray Siemens, MLA, 2013. dlsanthology.mla.hcommons.org/textual-analysis.

———. "Text-Analysis Tools in Excel." *Digital Humanities for Literary Studies: Theories, Methods, and Practices*, edited by James O'Sullivan, Texas A and MUP, forthcoming.

———. "*The Tutor's Story:* A Case Study of Mixed Authorship." *English Studies*, vol. 93, no. 3, 2012, pp. 324–39, doi:10.1080/0013838X.2012.668791.

Hoover, David L. et al. *Digital Literary Studies: Corpus Approaches to Poetry, Prose, and Drama.* Routledge, 2014.

Horowitz, Floyd R. *The Uncollected Henry James.* Garroll and Graf, 2004.

Ingersoll, Earl. "Margaret Atwood's *The Handmaid's Tale:* Echoes of Orwell." *Journal of the Fantastic in the Arts*, vol. 5, no. 4 (20), 1993, pp. 64–72. www.jstor.org/stable/43308174.

Jameson, Fredric. *Postmodernism, or, the Cultural Logic of Late Capitalism.* Duke UP, 1992, doi:10.1215/9780822378419.

Jockers, Matt. *Macroanalysis: Digital Methods and Literary History.* U of Illinois P, 2013, doi:10.5406/illinois/9780252037528.001.0001.

Jockers, Matt et al. "Reassessing Authorship of the *Book of Mormon* Using Delta and Nearest Shrunken Centroid Classification." *Literary and Linguistic Computing*, vol. 23, no. 4, 2008, pp. 465–91, doi:10.1093/llc/fqn040.

Jordan, Ellen et al. "The Brontë Sisters and the *Christian Remembrancer:* A Pilot Study in the Use of the 'Burrows Method' to Identify the Authorship of Unsigned Articles in the Nineteenth-Century Periodical Press." *Victorian Periodicals Review*, vol. 39, no. 1, 2006, pp. 21–45, doi:10.1353/vpr.2006.0024.

Juola, Patrick. "Authorship Attribution." *Foundations and Trends in Information Retrieval*, vol. 1, no. 3, 2008, pp. 233–334, doi:10.1561/1500000005.

———. "*JGAAP:* A System for Comparative Evaluation of Authorship Attribution." *Journal of the Chicago Colloquium on Digital Humanities and Computer Science*, vol. 1, no. 1, 2009, pp. 1–5, doi:10.6082/M1N29V4Z.

King, Stephen. *Misery.* Scribner, 1987.

Kopf, Dan. "The Guinness Brewer Who Revolutionized Statistics." *Pricenomics*, 11 Dec. 2015. priceonomics.com/the-guinness-brewer-who-revolutionized-statistics.

Love, Harold. *Attributing Authorship: An Introduction.* Cambridge UP, 2002, doi:10.1017/CBO9780511483165.

M. L. Parrish Collection of Victorian Novelists. Department of Rare Books and Special Collections, Princeton University Library.

McCallum, Andrew Kachites. "*MALLET:* A Machine Learning for Language Toolkit." 2002. mallet.cs.umass.edu.

McWilliam, Fiona. "Louisa May Alcott's 'My Contraband' and Discourse on Contraband Slaves in Popular Print Culture." *Studies in American Fiction*, vol. 42, no. 1, 2015, pp. 51–84, doi:10.1353/saf.2015.0001.

Meeks, Elijah, and Scott Weingart. "The Digital Humanities Contribution to Topic Modeling." *Journal of Digital Humanities*, vol. 2, no. 1, 2012. journalofdigitalhumanities.org/2-1/dh-contribution-to-topic-modeling.

Minitab Release 19, Minitab, Inc., State College, PA, 2019.

Nyqvist, Sanna. "Authorship and Authenticity in Sherlock Holmes Pastiches." *Transformative Works and Cultures*, vol. 23, 2017, doi:10.3983/twc.2017.0834.

Patterson, Mark. "Racial Sacrifice and Citizenship: The Construction of Masculinity in Louisa May Alcott's 'The Brothers'." *Studies in American Fiction*, vol. 25, no. 2, 1997, pp. 147–66, doi:10.1353/saf.1997.0000.

Peschel, Bill. *Sherlock Holmes Victorian Parodies and Pastiches: 1888–1899.* Peschel Press, 2015. peschelpress.com/sherlock-holmes-victorian-parodies-and-pastiches-1888-1899.

Queen, Ellery, editor. *The Misadventures of Sherlock Holmes.* Little, Brown, 1944. archive.org/details/scriblio_test_044.

R Core Team. "*R:* A Language and Environment for Statistical Computing." *R* Foundation for Statistical Computing, Vienna, Austria, 2019. www.R-project.org.

Ramsay, Stephen. *Reading Machines: Toward an Algorithmic Criticism*. U of Illinois P, 2011, doi:10.5406/illinois/9780252036415.001.0001.

Rhody, Lisa M. "Topic Modeling and Figurative Language." *Journal of Digital Humanities*, vol. 2, no. 1, 2012. journalofdigitalhumanities.org/2-1/topic-modeling-and-figurative-language-by-lisa-m-rhody.

Rostenberg, Leona. "Some Anonymous and Pseudonymous Thrillers of Louisa M. Alcott." *The Papers of the Bibliographical Society of America*, vol. 37, no. 2, 1943, pp. 131–40, doi:10.1086/pbsa.37.2.24293383.

Rybicki, Jan, and Maciej Eder. "Deeper Delta Across Genres and Languages: Do We Really Need the Most Frequent Words?" *Literary and Linguistic Computing*, vol. 26, no. 3, 2011, pp. 315–21, doi:10.1093/llc/fqr031.

Rybicki, Jan, and Magda Heydel. "The Stylistics and Stylometry of Collaborative Translation: Woolf's *Night and Day* in Polish." *Literary and Linguistic Computing*, vol. 28, no. 4, 2013, pp. 708–17, doi:10.1093/llc/fqt027.

Rybicki, Jan et al. "Collaborative Authorship: Conrad, Ford, and Rolling Delta." *Literary and Linguistic Computing*, vol. 29, no. 3, 2014, pp. 422–31, doi:10.1093/llc/fqu016.

Sanyal, Shourjya. "How a Brewer in Guinness Factory Secretly Discovered a Statistical Method." *Forbes*, 8 Jan. 2019. www.forbes.com/sites/shourjyasanyal/2019/01/08/how-a-brewer-in-guinness-factory-secretly-discovered-a-statistical-method/#29584cd5172f.

Schmidt, Benjamin M. "Words Alone: Dismantling Topic Models in the Humanities." *Journal of Digital Humanities*, vol. 2, no. 1, 2012. journalofdigitalhumanities.org/2-1/words-alone-by-benjamin-m-schmidt.

Sigelman, Lee, and William Jacoby. "The Not-So-Simple Art of Imitation: Pastiche, Literary Style, and Raymond Chandler." *Computers and the Humanities*, vol. 30, 1996, pp. 11–28, doi:10.1007/BF00054025.

Somers, Harold, and Fiona Tweedie. "Authorship Attribution and Pastiche." *Computers and the Humanities*, vol. 37, 2003, pp. 407–29, doi:10.1023/A:1025786724466.

Tracy, Jack, editor. *Sherlock Holmes: The Published Apocrypha, Sir Arthur Conan Doyle and Associated Hands*. Houghton Mifflin, 1980. archive.org/details/sherlockholmespu00doyl.

van Dalen-Oskam, Karina, and Joris van Zundert. "Delta for Middle Dutch: Author and Copyist Distinction in *Walewein*." *Literary and Linguistic Computing*, vol. 22, no. 3, 2007, pp. 345–62, doi:10.1093/llc/fqm012.

Vickers, Brian. "The Misuse of Function Words in Shakespeare Authorship Studies." *Göttingen Dialog in Digital Humanities*, 2016. www.etrap.eu/wp-content/uploads/2016/12/2016-11-30-vickers-misuse.pdf.

———. "Shakespeare and Authorship Studies in the Twenty-First Century." *Shakespeare Quarterly*, vol. 62, no. 1, 2011, pp. 106–42, doi:10.1353/shq.2011.0004.

Victorian Women Writers Project. Indiana University Digital Library Program, the Trustees of Indiana University, 2020. purl.dlib.indiana.edu/iudl/vwwp/VAB7166.

Weingart, Scott. "Topic Modeling in the Humanities." *The Scottbot Irregular*, 11 Apr. 2013. scottbot.net/tag/topic-modeling.

Westerman, Molly. "'Of Skulls or Spirits': The Haunting Space Between Fictional(ized) History and Historical Note." *CLIO: A Journal of Literature, History, and the Philosophy of History*, vol. 35, no. 3, 2006, pp. 369–93, 463.

Worldcat. OCLC Online Computer Library Center, Inc. www.worldcat.org.

3

CHANGING BACK AND FORTH FROM HANDWRITING TO DICTATION: THOMAS HARDY, WALTER SCOTT, AND JOSEPH CONRAD

Introduction

> Past literacy researchers tended to view speech and writing as dichotomous forms of communication, but many linguists today . . . instead see them as polar ends of a continuum of various genres exhibiting elements of both modes. Dictation seems best situated along such a continuum at a point closer to writing than to speech, which has little in common with dictation in terms of context and purpose. With the exception of public speaking, speech is primarily interactive orality in the presence of others whereas dictation, in its most frequent form, is autonomous writing produced via the spoken word. Some aspects of written voice may be influenced by the act of speech dictation, but for the most part, dictation is a distinct form of writing and not a form of speech, at least for mature writers. Dictation today emulates a strong legacy of written literacy.
>
> *(Honeycutt 320)*

In spite of Honeycutt's theoretical argument that dictation may best be considered more similar to writing than to normal speech, the intuitive plausibility and wide currency of the idea that changing from handwriting to dictating might result in a change in style suggests that the theory needs to be investigated systematically and objectively. Circumstances in which the new mode is temporary seem ideal for beginning such an investigation because they eliminate or at least reduce the possibility that a chronological effect might be mistaken for a change caused by a different mode of composition. Two of the cases to be examined in this chapter involve the temporary adoption of dictation by writers whose earlier and later books were handwritten: Thomas Hardy and Sir Walter Scott. Hardy dictated part of one novel, *A Laodicean*, over a period of about five months, and Scott dictated parts of three novels, *The Bride of Lammermoor*, *The Legend of Montrose*, and *Ivanhoe*, over a period of about fourteen months. In both cases, the change in mode was not voluntary but was, instead, caused by illness. The third author studied in this chapter, Joseph Conrad, switched back and forth from handwriting to dictation multiple times for multiple reasons over a period of nearly twenty years before he switched permanently to dictation, and he dictated at least parts of several of his novels, novellas, and reminiscences.

Under difficult circumstances, it seems entirely possible that changing back and forth from handwriting to dictation might cause changes in a writer's style (in the case of illness, possibly accompanied by further changes caused by the illness itself), whether these changes happened once or several times. The possibility that the effects of a change in mode of composition might increase over time is considered in later chapters, where long-term or permanent changes are examined.

Thomas Hardy and *A Laodicean:* Changing Back and Forth From Handwriting to Dictation

We know that Emma, Hardy's first wife, copied parts of some of the rough drafts of his novels and sometimes took down parts of them from his dictation. The extent of her contribution remains unclear, apparently at least partly because Hardy wanted it that way. Manford notes that Emma's handwriting is found suspiciously often at the ends of manuscript pages of *The Mayor of Casterbridge* that precede missing pages or at the beginning of pages that follow missing pages, and the same is true for places where the beginnings or ends of pages have been cut or torn off ("Who" 91–2). He concludes that "it seems abundantly clear that in the case of *The Mayor of Casterbridge* there was a deliberate and systematic attempt to suppress the fact of Emma Hardy's part in its manuscript" (92).

We know that Emma, then Emma Gifford, made a fair copy of the manuscript of Hardy's first novel, *Desperate Remedies* (1871), four years before they married (M. Millgate 120–1, 150). He later destroyed the original manuscript and possibly her copy as well (Purdy 4). Indeed, she had become "involved in Hardy's literary work from the beginning of their relationship" in 1870, and her handwriting appears on about one fourth of the pages of the fragmentary manuscript of *A Pair of Blue Eyes* (1873) (Ahmad 320–1). Although it is likely that Emma's contribution was limited to only a small portion of that novel, "[t]here are instances of additions . . . that, unless dictated by Hardy or copied from material not now extant, must be 'little emendations' by Emma" (Manford, "Who" 85). Her handwriting is more extensive in the manuscripts of *The Return of the Native* (1878) and *Two on a Tower* (1882) (Purdy 26, 43; Manford, "Who" 87–8, 89–91), and it is much more extensive in *The Woodlanders* (1887), in which more than one-fourth of the pages are wholly or partly in her hand (Manford, "Who" 92–94). Some of these pages show evidence of being taken from dictation, and some of

Emma's alterations and additions have at least a modest effect on the style, characterization, and plot of the novel (Manford, "Emma" 111–17). Finally, Hardy's biography, ostensibly written by his second wife, Florence, seems to have been essentially an autobiography couched in the third person and typed, possibly from Hardy's dictation, and then retyped to conceal any evidence of Hardy's participation (M. Millgate 476–9). The complexity and obscurity of the facts surrounding the contributions of both wives to the rest of Hardy's novels and "biography" fortunately do not extend to *A Laodicean*, written in 1880–81, which will thus necessarily be the focus of my investigation.

Florence (or Hardy himself?) describes the writing of *A Laodicean* as follows:

> Now he had already written the early chapters of a story for *Harper's Magazine—A Laodicean*. . . . This first part was already printed, and Du Maurier was illustrating it. . . . Its writer was, during the first few weeks, in considerable pain, and compelled to lie on an inclined plane with the lower part of his body higher than his head. Yet he felt determined to finish the novel, at whatever stress to himself—so as not to ruin the new venture of the publishers, and also in the interests of his wife, for whom as yet he had made but a poor provision in the event of his own decease. Accordingly from November onwards he began dictating it to her from the awkward position he occupied; and continued to do so—with greater ease as the pain and hemorrhage went off. She worked bravely both at writing and nursing, till at the beginning of the following May a rough draft was finished by one shift and another.
>
> *(Hardy 187–8)*

Some fifteen years before the brutal critical reception of the grim *Jude the Obscure* and his retreat from fiction to poetry, Thomas Hardy published *A Laodicean*. Although it is one of his less successful and less known novels, it provides an especially appropriate opportunity for beginning the investigation of whether or not, how, and to what extent a change in mode of composition might affect an author's style. Hardy's Preface to the 1896 edition of the novel lays out the basic facts:

> The writing of the tale was rendered memorable to two persons, at least, by a tedious illness of five months that laid hold of the author soon after the story was begun in a well-known magazine; during which period the narrative had to be strenuously continued by dictation to a predetermined cheerful ending.

The illness, the exact nature of which is not definitely known, seems to have involved internal bleeding. It began in late October of 1880 and quickly became severe. Initially, an operation was suggested, but the doctor decided that it could be avoided if Hardy were to lie in bed for months (Hardy 187). As Michael Millgate puts it:

> At the onset of his illness Hardy had already sent off to the printer the first thirteen chapters of *A Laodicean*, equivalent to the first three instalments and a little over, and was probably well advanced with the manuscript for the next few chapters, roughly corresponding to the fourth instalment. But there were still nine instalments left of the thirteen for which he had contracted. . . . His only recourse was to dictate the text to Emma, and in the event it was only her devoted assistance . . . that enabled him to keep up with the printer and so meet his obligations. . . . Hardy staved off any early crisis by putting the finishing touches to the fourth instalment and dispatching it to Bowker more or less on schedule.
>
> *(201)*

This description of the circumstances of Hardy's composition of the beginning of the novel provides a fairly clear point at which the change from handwriting to dictation took place. The first three instalments and at least part of the fourth were definitely handwritten, and the fifth and following instalments were dictated.

We are hindered somewhat in this case by the fact that "Hardy later destroyed the manuscript, largely because so much of it was in Emma's hand and because she was to claim, in years to come, that she had had much input to several of his novels" (Widdowson 94). The situation is further complicated by the fact that

> Hardy had somehow managed to correct the proofs in his own hand throughout his illness, and as time went on he became less and less dependent on dictation, writing the final sections of the manuscript in his own hand—the last page of all on 1 May 1881.
>
> *(M. Millgate 203–4)*

In a letter dated 6 April, Hardy reports,

> I am getting on pretty fairly, but don't go out yet—passing my days over the fire, with my feet on the mantelpiece, & a pen in my hand, which does not write as often as it should. . . . I am doing the 12th number of my story, & the nearness of the end prevents my attaining to it quickly—the consciousness that it can be done at any time causing dilatoriness. I should probably have gone out by this time if it had not been for the East wind. But patience is necessary.
>
> *(M. Millgate 204)*

This suggests that at least much and possibly all of part twelve and all of part thirteen were handwritten. Furthermore, given the difficult circumstances, it also seems unlikely that Hardy's revisions of the proofs could have been extensive enough to erase all traces of any significant effects of dictation. If dictation (or even the illness itself) changed Hardy's style, the handwritten beginning and ending of the novel should be different from the dictated middle.

It is well known that Hardy had a "seemingly irrepressible urge to tinker with a text at any opportunity" (Manford, "Emma" 111). Therefore, to avoid the possibility that Hardy might have removed any effects of dictation when he revised the novel for the book edition published later the same year, I will analyze the original *Harper's Magazine* version. A cluster analysis of the instalments of the novel based on the one hundred to one thousand most frequent words shows no significant evidence of an effect caused by dictation. (All cluster analyses in this chapter were performed in Minitab, with standardized variables, Ward linkage, and squared Euclidean distance.) The first instalment, consisting of the first four chapters, is an outlier in these analyses, as is often true of the beginnings of novels, probably because it is mostly scene-setting and because the first three chapters contain almost no dialogue. The handwritten second, third, and fourth instalments typically group together, but not with the fifth instalment, the first dictated instalment. This might seem significant if it were not for the fact that the fifth instalment almost always groups with instalment thirteen, which was definitely handwritten. It also seems significant that the first four instalments account for all of the first book, which takes place over a period of about one week (see Ireland for a narratological analysis of the novel).

There is some consistency of grouping in the analyses, but it is almost always a grouping of adjacent instalments, and almost all clusters that contain four or more instalments contain both handwritten and dictated instalments. If dictation had any significant effect, there should be evidence of a division between the fifth to eleventh instalments that were dictated and the first four and last two instalments that were handwritten, but there is no such evidence. The grouping patterns of sections of *A Laodicean* are similar to those for the three Hardy novels that precede it, *The Hand of Ethelberta* (1876), *The Return of the Native* (1878), and *The Trumpet-Major* (1880–81), and the three that follow it, *Two on a Tower* (1882), *The Mayor of Casterbridge* (1886), and *The Woodlanders* (1887). A quick check of statistics for vocabulary richness, sentence length, word length, and the frequencies of words of different lengths also gives no hint of a dictation effect in the middle of the novel.

In all analyses of these preceding and following novels, there is considerable grouping of consecutive sections, but the groupings are neither complete nor consistent, and beginnings sometimes group with endings. Bootstrap consensus trees performed in Stylo (Eder et al. 113–15), which are based on a wide range of numbers of the most frequent words, using multiple culling levels and several different methods, also show some grouping of consecutive instalments of *A Laodicean*, but even when a fifty percent consensus is selected (the weakest setting), the handwritten and dictated instalments fail to form separate groups. (All bootstrap consensus analyses in this chapter were produced in Stylo.)

The same is true of PCA. (All principal components analyses in this chapter were performed in Minitab, using the correlation matrix; this prevents words with high frequencies from dominating the analysis.) As with the cluster analyses, there is some evidence of the grouping of dictated instalments from the middle of the novel and some evidence of a divergence between the relatively cohesive second to fourth instalments and the rest of the novel. Yet, all the analyses show dictated and handwritten instalments toward both the left and right of the graph and toward both the top and the bottom. Neither principal component is clearly associated with mode of composition.

One peculiarity of the serial publication of the novel that should be addressed is that the relatively artificial division into instalments does not very closely match the division into books and chapters. A brief outline will illustrate the mismatch:

Book 1, "Somerset," instalments 1–4
Book 2, "Dare and Havill," instalments 4–6
Book 3, "De Stancy," instalments 6–8
Book 4, "Somerset, Dare and De Stancy," instalment 9
Book 5, "De Stancy and Paula," instalments 10–12
Book 6, "Paula," instalment 13

Cluster analysis of the novel divided into books rather than instalments and with the books divided into sections of about five thousand to six thousand words gives a confused picture in which the patterns that do exist suggest clustering by book rather than by mode of composition. (The books are divided into sections to allow for a finer-grained analysis.) In a few analyses there are clusters consisting of only handwritten sections or only dictated sections, but there are no analyses in which the handwritten beginning of the novel clusters with the handwritten end. The same is true of PCA, with similarly confused patterns. In none of the analyses does either of the first two principal components separate the handwritten and dictated sections.

t-Testing of the handwritten and dictated parts in sections of about eleven hundred words produces only ninety-one words significant at the $p < 0.05$ level, and such a small number of words with significantly different distributions shows that the distinction between the modes is very weak. It is clear that even this weak distinction is largely caused by the novel's structure. That is, most of the first handwritten part of the novel focuses on architecture and Somerset, while most of the dictated part focuses on other characters and on Paula's foreign travels, until the end of the novel (the last two chapters of the sixth book) when Paula and Somerset return to England after their honeymoon. Among the forty-six significant words characteristic of the handwritten part are *stone, old, age, Somerset, church, interior, chapel, drawing, sketch,* and *sketch-book*. Among the forty-five significant words characteristic of the dictated part are *Captain,*

Stancy, *de*, *Stancy's*, *Charlotte*, *Paula*, *hotel*, *journey*, *Charlotte's*, *Nice*, *return*, *spent*, and *met*. A PCA of sections of approximately six thousand words of the six books of the novel based on these ninety-one words, shown in Figure 3.1, confirms this. Although the first and sixth books cluster to the right, the fifth does not, even though we know that at least the fourth section was handwritten, and probably also the fifth section. (For a discussion of how to use information about *t*-tests to investigate style variation, see my "Simulations and Difficult Problems.")

Although the results so far do not suggest any significant effect of dictation, it seems important to press the analysis a bit further. It seems plausible, after all, that a change to dictation might affect narration and dialogue differently, though it is not clear whether the similarity of spoken dictation to spoken dialogue would be more or less likely to alter dictation than narration. This question can be tested by analyzing the narration and the dialogue separately, in spite of some problems that arise because of the distribution of the dialogue of the characters throughout the novel. Several of the characters, for example, have no dialogue, or almost none, in one or more instalments, and some characters have little or no dialogue in the dictated or handwritten parts. For example, Captain de Stancy,

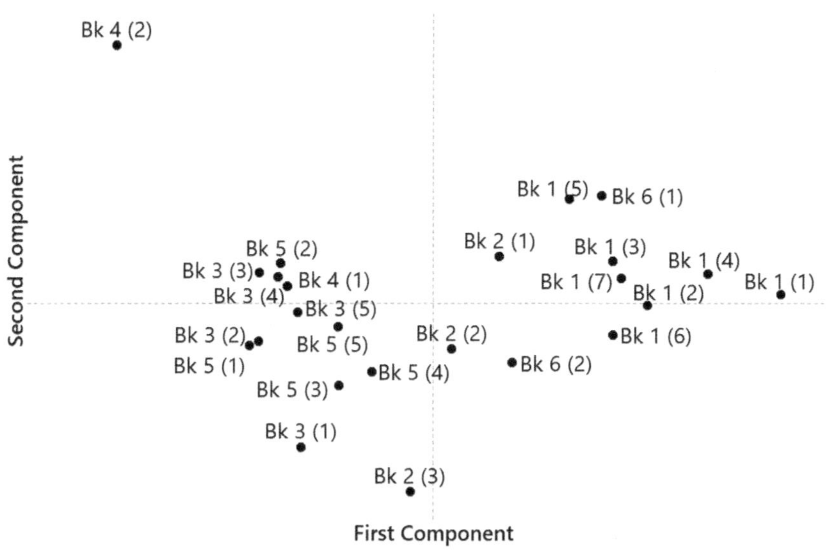

FIGURE 3.1 Principal components analysis of the six books of Thomas Hardy's *A Laodicean* in sections of six thousand words, based on the ninety-one *t*-tested words that are distributed significantly differently ($p < 0.05$) in handwriting and dictation

the character with the second-largest amount of dialogue (about seventy-eight hundred words), has only about seven hundred words of hand written dialogue, all in instalments twelve and thirteen, so that testing is not likely to produce reliable results. Nonetheless, a quick cluster analysis of his dialogue, divided into ten parts of about seven hundred words, in such a way that the handwritten dialogue is all of the tenth part, gives no evidence that dictation had an effect. The tenth part shows no tendency to diverge from the dictated parts. Cluster analysis of Dare's seventy-two hundred words of dialogue in sections of about seven hundred words also gives confused and inconclusive results. His handwritten dialogue from the twelfth and thirteenth instalments does cluster separately from the rest, but this dialogue is almost all from the twelfth instalment, from a long conversation with Abner Power, much of which is more like narrative. Furthermore, all analyses mix sections of his handwritten and dictated dialogue.

Paula, who has by far the largest speaking part, about 11,600 words of dialogue, is the only other character with sufficient dialogue appropriately spread among the handwritten and dictated parts of the novel to allow for analysis. She has thirty-three hundred words in the first four handwritten instalments, fifty-five hundred words in the dictated instalments in the middle of the novel, and twenty-eight hundred words in the last two handwritten instalments. Cluster analysis of Paula's dialogue, in sections of about nine hundred words, produces fairly strong clustering of the second to fifth dictated sections, but the handwritten final section of the novel also often joins this group. The other groupings are quite chaotic, and no analysis groups all of the handwritten sections separately from all of the dictated sections. Only in a single analysis (based on the four hundred most frequent words), shown in Figure 3.2, are all of the dictated sections of Paula's dialogue in a single cluster. This graph provides only very weak evidence of a dictation effect, however, because two handwritten sections invade the dictated cluster, because these results are not seen in any other analyses, and because the beginning and ending of the novel are also the parts of the novel set at the De Stancy castle.

Analyzing the narration separately from the dialogue also fails to suggest any significant effect of dictation. Cluster analyses of the narration in sections of about seven thousand words never group all of the handwritten sections separately from all of the dictated sections. Instead, there is some grouping of sections from the beginning of the novel, but overall, the groupings seem chaotic. The same is true of analyses of the narration in sections of four thousand words.

In the case of *A Laodicean*, then, it seems clear that neither Hardy's illness nor his switch from handwriting to dictation and back had any substantial effect on his style. None of the methods shown to be very effective in distinguishing even fairly subtle kinds of style variation in the works of Nesbit, Doyle, or Alcott in Chapter 2 provide any significant evidence for such an effect in *A Laodicean*.

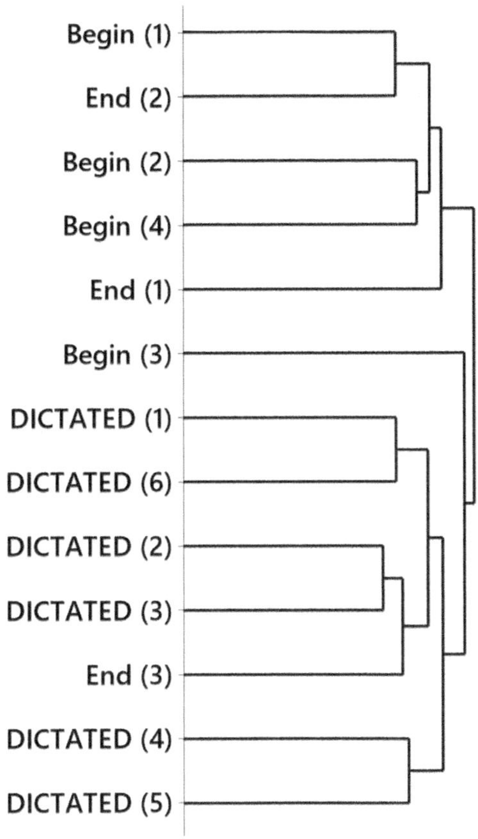

FIGURE 3.2 Cluster analysis of Paula's handwritten and dictated dialogue in Thomas Hardy's *A Laodicean* in sections of 825 to 925 words, based on the four hundred most frequent words

Sir Walter Scott and *The Bride of Lammermoor, The Legend of Montrose,* and *Ivanhoe:* Changing Back and Forth From Handwriting to Dictation

> Yet when his health was fairly reestablished, he disdained to avail himself of the power of dictation, which he had thus put to the sharpest test, but resumed, and for many years resolutely adhered to, the old plan of writing everything with his own hand. When I once, sometime afterwards, expressed my surprise that he did not consult his ease, and spare his eyesight at all events, by occasionally dictating, he answered—"I should as soon think of getting into a sedan-chair while I can use my legs."
>
> (Lockhart, *Memoirs,* vol. 2 134)

The question of whether or not a temporary change from handwriting to dictation changed Walter Scott's style is more complex for him than it was for Hardy. While writing *The Bride of Lammermoor* in 1818–19, Scott suffered from increasingly severe stomach pains from gallstone disease. These pains were so severe that they prevented him from sitting up to write. Lockhart's account of his suffering and of his use of amanuenses is justly famous:

> The *copy* (as MS. for the press is technically called) which Scott was thus dictating, was that of the *Bride of Lammermoor;* and his amanuenses were William Laidlaw and John Ballantyne; of whom he preferred the latter . . . on account of the superior rapidity of his pen; and also because John kept his pen to the paper without interruption, . . . whereas good Laidlaw entered with such keen zest into the interest of the story . . . that he could not suppress exclamations of surprise and delight. . . . I have often . . . heard both these secretaries describe the astonishment with which they were equally affected when Scott began this experiment. The affectionate Laidlaw beseeching him to stop dictating, when his audible suffering filled every pause, "Nay, Willie," he answered, "only see that the doors are fast. I would fain keep all the cry as well as all the wool to ourselves; but as to giving over work, that can only be when I am in woolen." John Ballantyne told me, that . . . he seated himself opposite to the sofa on which Scott lay, and that though he often turned himself on his pillow with a groan of torment, he usually continued the sentence in the same breath. But when dialogue of peculiar animation was in progress, spirit seemed to triumph altogether over matter—he arose from his couch and walked up and down the room, raising and lowering his voice, and as it were acting the parts. It was in this fashion that Scott produced the far greater portion of *The Bride of Lammermoor*—the whole of the *Legend of Montrose*—and almost the whole of *Ivanhoe*.
>
> (Memoirs, *vol. 2 133–4*)

Alexander confirms that dictation played a part in the three successive novels mentioned by Lockhart, all published in 1819, but reports that Lockhart exaggerated the proportions of the novels composed by dictation. He reports that, indeed, almost all of *The Legend of Montrose* was dictated but that only the end of *The Bride of Lammermoor* and only about the first half of *Ivanhoe* were dictated. Unfortunately, definite information about exactly what parts of what novels were dictated is sometimes difficult to determine. As Alexander explains:

> Scott expected his novels to appear in the form and format in which they did appear, but in practice what was done was not wholly satisfactory because of the complicated way in which the texts were processed. Until

1827, when Scott acknowledged his authorship, the novels were published anonymously.

(Bride xiii)

One reason for the anonymity is indicated in a letter from 1805, in which he comments on the composition of an early draft of *Waverley* as follows:

> Having proceeded . . . as far as I think the seventh chapter, I showed my work to a critical friend, whose opinion was unfavourable; and having then some poetical reputation, I was unwilling to risk the loss of it by attempting a new style of composition. I, therefore, then threw aside the work I had commenced.
>
> (Lockhart, *Memoirs*, vol. 1 255)

In a letter written in 1814, just after the publication of Waverley, he also suggests that novel-writing might not be considered "decorous" for a man in his position as a Clerk of Session (the highest court in Scotland) and that remaining anonymous allowed him "the freedom of writing trifles with less personal responsibility, and perhaps no more frequently than I otherwise might do" (Lockhart, *Memoirs*, vol. 1 480). One result of this desire for anonymity is that Scott's references to his novels in his letters are sometimes unclear. For example, in April of 1818, Scott says a novel is progressing and that his publisher will have a copy soon. It has long been assumed that the novel he was referring to was *The Bride of Lammermoor*, but the reference is not certain (Alexander, *Bride* 273).

A second consequence of the anonymous publication of Scott's novels adds some additional uncertainty to an analysis of possible stylistic variation introduced by a change in mode of composition. Scott was a partner, along with James and John Ballantyne, in the printing firm that printed much of his work:

> so that Scott's well-known handwriting should not be seen in the printing works the original manuscripts were copied, and it was these copies, not Scott's original manuscripts, which were used in the printing house. Not a single leaf is known to survive but the copyists probably began the tidying and regularising. The compositors worked from the copies, and, when typesetting, did not just follow what was before them, but supplied punctuation, normalised spelling, and corrected minor errors. Proofs were first read in-house against the transcripts, and in addition to the normal checking for mistakes these proofs were used to improve the punctuation and the spelling.
>
> (Alexander, *Bride* xiii)

Both the compositors and James Ballantyne (who also transcribed some of Scott's manuscripts) were also clearly expected and encouraged to correct punctuation, spelling, grammar, and other errors; to normalize spelling; and to remove verbal repetitions (Alexander, *Bride xiii*). Although it is possible that some stylistic variation caused by dictation might have been smoothed out by this process, the meticulously edited Edinburgh edition of Scott's novels does not suggest any greater level of intervention in these partially dictated novels than in the wholly handwritten ones.

It might seem logical to test these mainly consecutive dictated parts of the three novels together against the handwritten beginning of *The Bride of Lammermoor* and the handwritten end of *Ivanhoe*. However, the fact that sections of novels by a single author strongly tend to group by novel, as shown in Chapter 2, suggests that the handwritten and dictated parts of each novel will be more similar to each other than to the handwritten or dictated parts of two other novels, and thus that the novels should be studied individually.

A quick preliminary classification test in Stylo (Eder et al. 115–17), however, will test whether or not there is a simple and powerful correlation between style and mode of composition across the novels. For this test the nearly equal handwritten and dictated parts of *Ivanhoe* can be treated as known modes, so that the classification test treats them as if they were by different authors. The handwritten and dictated parts of *The Bride of Lammermoor* and *The Legend of Montrose* are then tested to see if they can be correctly identified by mode of composition. All the novels are divided into sections of about forty-five hundred words; all nineteen of the handwritten sections and nineteen of the twenty dictated sections of *Ivanhoe* are treated as known texts (to keep the numbers equal). That is, the classification test treats these sections as being known to be by either the handwritten or the dictated "author." The twenty-eight handwritten and sixteen dictated sections of *The Bride of Lammermoor* and *The Legend of Montrose* are then tested to see whether Stylo's classify function attributes the handwritten parts to the handwritten part of *Ivanhoe* and the dictated parts to the dictated part of *Ivanhoe*. In several tests using several different algorithms, various different numbers of words, and several different levels of culling, a maximum of fifty-six percent of the sections were attributed to the "correct" mode. In fact, most of the methods are less than fifty percent correct, some below forty percent—results that are worse than could be expected by chance. Because these are the same methods that identified which sections of Nesbit's novels came from each novel with an accuracy of one hundred percent in Chapter 2, any strong effect of mode of composition seems unlikely. Nevertheless, testing the three novels individually seems necessary.

The Bride of Lammermoor

It is true that, as Lockhart reports, Scott suffered from increasingly severe stomach pains from gallstone disease while writing *The Bride of Lammermoor* in 1818–19.

It is also true that the pain forced him to finish the novel by dictation (J. Millgate 170). According to Alexander, however:

> Lockhart's account of Scott's wrestling with excruciating stomach cramps while dictating the manuscript to William Laidlaw and John Ballantyne, and of his being unable to correct any proofs, is demonstrable romancing: most of the manuscript survives in Scott's hand, as do his corrected proofs from 240.28 to the end. There is a germ of truth in Lockhart, however: the last part of the manuscript was certainly dictated; the surviving proofs were probably preserved as evidence of authorship to complement the incomplete manuscript.
>
> *(Bride 274)*

The final extant MS leaf corresponds to chapter 26 (of 33). "And since it ends in a catchword and carries on its verso holograph corrections for a subsequent page now lost, it is clear that the part set down by Scott himself was originally even more extensive" (J. Millgate 170). There is no way to know, however, "whether the first leaf of the final portion of the novel was wholly or only partly in Scott's hand, or at what stage he began to dictate" (Alexander, *Bride* 274). We can be sure, however, that much, and probably most, of the last seven chapters were dictated, partly because of some peculiar errors in the proofs that Scott would have been unlikely to make if he had been writing the manuscript himself (Alexander, *Bride* 278).

Testing for a stylistic effect caused by Scott's use of dictation begins with a division of the novel into two parts. The first part corresponds to the MS and the second to the remaining and presumably dictated part. To allow for a finer-grained analysis and because the proportion of the novel that was dictated is not definitely known, I have further divided both parts into sections of about forty-three hundred words. This yields twenty-eight sections, the first twenty-five of which were handwritten and the last three of which were probably dictated. In the six cluster analyses based on the three hundred and on the six hundred to one thousand most frequent words, the final three sections group together; however, in the analyses based on the three hundred and the nine hundred to one thousand most frequent words, the final section corresponding to the manuscript joins this cluster. In the other four analyses, based on the one hundred to two hundred and the four hundred to five hundred most frequent words, the final manuscript section also joins with the first of the likely dictated sections. Dividing the handwritten and dictated parts into sections of sixty-four hundred words gives similar results. This suggests that the end of the novel tends to be coherent but does not support the idea that dictation significantly changed Scott's style. There is clearly more difference between the final handwritten section and the other handwritten sections that precede it than there is between the final handwritten section and the dictated sections that follow it.

In principal components analyses of sections of both forty-three hundred and sixty-four hundred words, there is also no hint of any grouping of the final sections separately from the rest of the novel. Finally, for sections of both sizes, bootstrap consensus trees based on various numbers of the most frequent words and on multiple culling percentages and distance measures also show some grouping of consecutive sections of the novel, but even when a fifty percent consensus is selected (the weakest setting), not a single analysis places all of the handwritten sections in a one group and all of the dictated sections in another. It seems safe to conclude that dictation did not significantly affect the style of *The Bride of Lammermoor*.

The Legend of Montrose

As with Lockhart's claim, quoted earlier, that "the greater portion" of *The Bride of Lammermoor* was dictated, his claim that "the whole of *The Legend of Montrose*" was dictated is clearly an exaggeration, "but it is likely that Scott did indeed dictate much of Montrose" (Alexander, *Legend* 187). The existing partial manuscript corresponds fairly closely to the eleventh to fourteenth chapters and accounts for about twenty percent of the twenty-three-chapter novel. Given that almost all of Scott's manuscripts from this period are extant (Sutherland 314), it seems fairly safe to assume that the partial manuscript of this novel represents most, at least, of the handwritten part. This is supported by the fact that the manuscript covers a substantial portion of the part of the novel missing from the extant second proofs, which, like those of *The Bride of Lammermoor*, contain errors of a kind that strongly suggest dictation (Alexander, *Legend* 188, 190). In any case, testing the novel in sections should uncover any substantial change in style caused by a change in mode of composition, wherever it exists, if it exists.

Cluster analysis in sections of about four thousand words gives fairly chaotic results, though the three manuscript sections normally group with the preceding section, for which no manuscript exists. This could suggest that the preceding section was also handwritten, but it is equally compatible with the tendency of consecutive sections of a novel to group together, and there is no other evidence that any manuscript has been lost. All three manuscript sections group together (along with the preceding section) in the five analyses based on the six hundred to one thousand most frequent words, and this could suggest style variation based on the mode of composition. All of those analyses, however, show greater differences between multiple groups of dictated sections than they do between the manuscript sections and dictated sections. The similarity between the manuscript sections and the preceding dictated section is confirmed in analyses of sections of about fifty-five hundred words, but the other manuscript sections never join this group. Finally, in the five analyses of sections of about seven thousand to eight thousand words based on the four hundred and on the seven hundred to one thousand most frequent words, the two manuscript sections group by themselves, but, again, they are more similar to other dictated sections than are the first two sections of the second dictated part, and the two sections do not group separately in any of the five other analyses. This is thus, at best, only very tentative evidence of a minor mode effect.

Principal components analyses of all three sizes of sections cast further doubt on a dictation effect. They never group the manuscript sections separately from the dictated ones. For sections of about four thousand words, bootstrap consensus trees based on various numbers of the most frequent words and on multiple culling percentages and distance measures also show some grouping of consecutive sections of the novel, but even at the weakest setting, there is no consensus that handwritten and dictated sections form separate groups. As with *The Bride of Lammermoor*, it seems that Scott's change in mode of composition did not significantly alter the style of *The Legend of Montrose*.

Ivanhoe

Soon after finishing *The Legend of Montrose* by dictation, Scott, still seriously ill, began dictating what is probably his most famous novel: *Ivanhoe*. When his health improved, however, he began writing again by hand, and, in spite of Lockhart's claim that almost all of *Ivanhoe* was dictated,

> the surviving fragment of the manuscript in Scott's hand contains almost half of the novel, 489 of the 1023 printed pages. It is probable that Lockhart, who had seen the manuscript and described it in his biography of Scott, was misled by the fact that it contains only one and a half chapters before apparently beginning Volume 3.
>
> (Tulloch 409)

Given Scott's rather scornful rejection of Lockhart's suggestion that he might like to continue dictating, and given the survival of almost all of Scott's manuscripts of his novels, it seems very likely that the manuscript contains all of what he wrote by hand (Tulloch 409).

When the novel is divided into handwritten and dictated sections of about ninety-five hundred words, cluster analysis provides no evidence of a significant shift in style when Scott's mode of composition changed, as with the other two novels. The last two dictated sections regularly cluster with the following manuscript sections, while the penultimate manuscript section clusters with dictated sections from much earlier in the novel. In all of the analyses there is some mixing of dictated and manuscript sections. Cluster analyses of sections of about seventy-five hundred words show a similar pattern, with the final sections of dictation grouping with the manuscript sections and the next-to-last manuscript section grouping with the earlier dictated sections. Principal components analysis of the sets of sections of both sizes presents a similar picture. The most reasonable interpretation of this behavior is that the last dictated sections are similar to the immediately following handwritten sections and that the important factor is again narrative structure rather than mode of composition.

Unlike *The Bride of Lammermoor*, which has only a small amount of dictated text at the end, and *The Legend of Montrose*, which has a relatively small amount of handwritten text near the middle, *Ivanhoe* is a long novel that is roughly half dictated and half handwritten. This allows the use of Stylo's rolling classify (Eder et al. 118) to test the effect of the change in mode. The first fifty thousand words of dictation from the beginning are treated as having dictation as their "author," and the final fifty thousand words of handwriting from the end are treated as having handwriting as their "author." The middle seventy-three thousand words of the novel, with the change from dictation to handwriting at the center, are then tested for authorship. I set the classification method to SVM and analyzed the nine hundred most frequent words, with a slice size of three thousand words and an overlap of twenty-six hundred words. These settings mean that the classifier moves through the text by classifying the first three thousand words using SVM based on the nine hundred most frequent words, then moving forward four hundred words and repeating the process. Although, as shown in Figure 3.3, rolling classify correctly identifies almost all of the handwritten part of *Ivanhoe* as handwritten, a substantial amount of the immediately preceding dictated part is also identified as handwritten. Using other classification measures, different numbers of the most frequent words, and other slice sizes generally confirms this result, though in many analyses, not only is a substantial proportion of the dictated section classified as handwritten but parts of the handwritten section are classified as dictated as well. Because both of these classifications are known to be false,

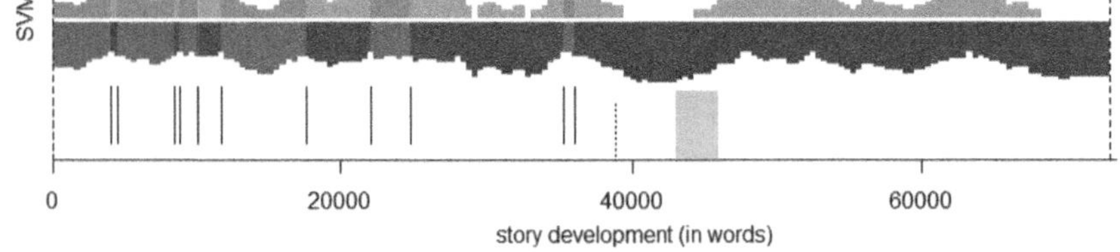

FIGURE 3.3 Rolling classify analysis of the handwritten and dictated parts of Walter Scott's *Ivanhoe*, based on the nine hundred most frequent words, with SVM classification, a slice size of three thousand words, and an overlap of twenty-six hundred words

rolling classify is thus consistent with the results of the other kinds of analysis in suggesting that narrative structure is far more important for Scott's style than is the mode of composition.

As with Hardy, then, mode of composition does not seem to have had any significant effect on Scott's style. Or, perhaps more accurately, any effect that the mode of composition might have is not great enough to disturb even the relatively weak tendency of consecutive sections of the novels to group together. The same is true of any possible effects of Scott's illness. Again as with Hardy, the possibility that revisions may have erased any effects of the changes in mode of composition (or illness) seems unlikely given Scott's practice of rapid and relatively modest changes in his proofs, most of which were additions (see "Essay on the Text" in Alexander, *Bride* for details).

In writing about Scott's alterations in his manuscript of his later novel, *Redgauntlet*, Wood and Hewitt suggest a possible reason that dictation might not have affected Scott's style very significantly:

> While the examination of the written words confirms that on the whole Scott did not discard whole passages, detailed consideration of the changes rather suggests that the discarding of imaginative material took place before it was committed to paper. His creating mind seems to have been oral, the narrative structure developing long before he wrote, and his revision providing details which confirm the implications of the story.
>
> *(Wood and Hewitt 386)*

Joseph Conrad: Changing Back and Forth From Handwriting to Dictation

> The next production [*The Shadow Line*] is a sort of autobiography—a personal experience—dramatised in the telling—the MS of which amounts to about 200 pp of pen and ink and a few (about 30) or so of type. That was when I could not hold the pen and tried to get on dictating to an operator who came from town for 3 days. From a literary point of view it will be curious for critics to compare my dictated to my written manner of expressing myself.
>
> (Conrad, *Collected Letters*, vol. 5 543)

The case of Joseph Conrad's use of dictation is more complicated than the cases of Hardy and Scott for several reasons. Unlike Hardy and Scott, Conrad was a heavy reviser (see Karl, "Significance"; Conrad, *Shadow-Line* 2013 "The Texts: An Essay" for details on revision in *Nostromo* and *The Shadow Line*, respectively). Conrad also dictated sporadically over a much longer period, between 1902 and his death in 1924, and dictation was involved to some degree in at least the following texts: *The Rescue* (1896–1919), *The End of the Tether* (1902), *Nostromo* (1903–04), *The Mirror of the Sea* (1904–05), *A Personal Record* (1908–09), *The*

Shadow Line (1915), and *The Arrow of Gold* (1917–18) (the dates are those of composition). *The Rover* (1922) and the posthumous *Suspense* (1925) were entirely dictated (Moore). It has been claimed that parts of *The Secret Agent* were also dictated (Halperin 787), but this claim seems difficult to accept because of the existence of an essentially complete autograph manuscript for the serial version (Conrad, *Secret Agent* 236–7). Although "no really comparable text exists in either MS or S [serialization]" for the substantial expansions and additions Conrad made to the end of the novel in the preparation of the book editions, many errors and differences between the English and American editions seem to have arisen from the misreading of Conrad's handwriting (Conrad, *Secret Agent* 265–7). It is possible that "Prince Roman," a reminiscence that exists only in typescript (Moore), was dictated, but there is insufficient information about it for analysis.

Again unlike Hardy and Scott, Conrad also dictated for more than one reason. He suffered from painful gout in his hand over much of his career, but he also suffered periodically from depression (see Karl, *Joseph Conrad* 310, 343, 498–500, 591–2, 681–3, 839; Najder 167–8, 277–8, 411; Knowles and Moore, "health"; Mizener 86). He also suffered what we might now call writer's block, perhaps a side-effect of the depression (Knowles and Moore, "collaborations" and "Pinker, James Brand"). Dictation had the added benefit that he could produce text more quickly than he could by handwriting. This was especially true for less serious texts that would bring quick payment, a consideration that was important because he struggled financially for most of his life. As he wrote to H. G. Wells of his *The Mirror of the Sea:*

> I've started a series of sea sketches and have sent out P [Pinker] on the hunt to place them. This must save me. I've discovered that I can dictate that sort of bosh without effort at the rate of 3,000 words in four hours. Fact! The only thing now is to sell it to a paper and then make a book of the rubbish. Hang!
>
> So in the day Nostromo and from 11 pm to 1 am dictation. No more just now.
>
> (Collected Letters, *vol. 3 112*)

The fact that the American collector John Quinn began buying all of Conrad's manuscripts in 1911, including those of early works, makes Conrad's use of dictation fairly easy to determine (see Karl, *Joseph Conrad* 701–3; Conrad, *Collected Letters*, vol. 5 475). His constant money worries and Quinn's willingness to pay well made Conrad eager to sell his manuscripts. For example, Conrad asked Quinn for £100 for the manuscript of *The Secret Agent*, even though he received only £200 for the book publication of *Lord Jim* (Karl, *Joseph Conrad* 836, 629). The result is that Quinn's collection is remarkably complete, especially for autograph manuscripts up to 1918. (For a detailed account of the manuscripts and typescripts of Conrad's work, see Moore.)

An initial test for any significant chronological variation in Conrad's style, using bootstrap consensus analysis based on various numbers of the most frequent words and on multiple culling percentages and distance measures, shows that Conrad's sixteen novels and novellas, published between 1894 and 1925, strongly tend to divide into early and late periods, with the division point after either *Nostromo* (1904) or *The Secret Agent* (1906). Additional testing in which only the handwritten or only the dictated part of each of the partially dictated novels is included shows that the parts of the novels continue to group by date rather than by mode of composition. An apparent exception is that, when only the dictated part of *The Rescue* (1919) is included, it groups with the later novels, including the last, dictated ones, but when only the handwritten part (1896) is included, it groups with the early handwritten novels. Yet this is actually a grouping by date, as the late handwritten novels also join this group. The dictated part of the early *Nostromo* consistently groups with other early handwritten novels, and the handwritten part of the late *The Shadow Line* consistently groups with the other late novels, both dictated and handwritten. Although this initial testing does not suggest that mode of composition has any significant effect on Conrad's style, the problem of chronology can be dealt with by treating the texts separately, proceeding roughly in order of increasing tractability.

The End of the Tether, A Personal Record, The Mirror of the Sea, The Rescue, and The Arrow of Gold

When, under the time pressure of serial publication, Conrad had to recreate part of *The End of the Tether* that was burnt in an accident with a lamp, he dictated some of the burnt material to Ford Madox Ford (Najder 323–5; Karl, *Joseph Conrad* 536). Unfortunately, the details of the dictation and of the delivery of the manuscript and typescript of the novella are confused, not least because of Ford's unreliable account of his part in it (Najder 325). Conrad's account of what was lost and what had to be recreated is also unreliable. As Knowles puts it:

> Further, in his letter to Blackwood of 24 June explaining the recent fire, Conrad still clung to the pre-accident estimate of the story's length as a work of three instalments and at most 28,000 words, whereas the version finally delivered ran to six instalments and 53,500 words. Although it is just conceivable that the story might have expanded by 25,500 words during its "reconstruction", it seems more likely that the accidental fire rescued Conrad from the pain of having to confess to his publisher just how far behind schedule he was.
>
> (Conrad, *Youth* 284)

Apparently, the long conclusion of the book was completed under tremendous time pressure with Ford's help. "Given that it consisted of some 19,000 words, with composition continuing right up to the mid-October deadline, it is almost certain that a fair proportion must have been in manuscript form" (Conrad, *Youth* 290). The confusion and uncertainty surrounding this text and the fact that all of the late preprint documents have been lost suggest that any analysis is unlikely to be productive.

Conrad's nonfiction reminiscences, *A Personal Record* (1912), present almost insuperable problems: "The scarcity of pre-print material for *A Personal Record* and the disappearance of the *English Review*'s files means that the genesis and transmission of the work must be reconstructed almost exclusively from Conrad's surviving letters to Ford and to Pinker" (Conrad, *Personal Record xxvi*). Ford's claims to have taken down most of the book from dictation have now been replaced by the view that "Ford took down very little—not most—of *A Personal Record;* he is likely to have typed up hardly any of it" (Conrad, *Personal Record* 134). Clearly, Conrad "wrote out at least part of the second series, published [in serial form] from April to June 1909, in longhand, though precisely how much cannot now be known," though the evidence of the numbering of the surviving leaf suggests that all of the sixth chapter was likely handwritten (Conrad, *Personal Record* 127, 130). Analyzing this text with cluster analysis and PCA (in sections of about thirty-two hundred words, roughly half the size of the chapters) gives some hints of a division critics see between the first four and the last three chapters, but there is no suggestion that either the sixth chapter or the fifth to seventh were handwritten: the late chapters always group with parts of the first and second.

The same kinds of confusion and unreliable reports from Ford plague the case of Conrad's memoirs, *The Mirror of the Sea* (1904–05), some of which he dictated while working on *Nostromo* (Najder 340–1). Conrad also claims *Mirror* was mostly dictated, in this case because he was under financial pressure and could produce copy more rapidly by dictating (*Collected Letters*, vol. 3 112), substantial partial manuscripts of the eleventh to fourteenth parts of the fifteen-part text exist, so that some testing is possible. Cluster analysis of the fifteen parts in sections of three thousand words (only three parts are long enough for two sections) yields some clustering patterns that are consistent, but in all of them, parts of the text known to be dictated cluster with those for which a substantial part of the manuscript exists. Principal components analyses are not as easy to interpret, but they also show a consistent mixing of dictated and handwritten parts.

As already noted, *The Rescue* is unusual in that Conrad began the novel twenty-five years before completing it. In a 1920 letter to Thomas J. Wise, who had by then replaced Quinn as the main collector of his manuscripts, Conrad suggested the possibility that his style might have undergone a significant evolution:

> The comparison of the pen and ink text which you have got with the final text of the book would be a curious experience as showing how severe an author may be in his more mature period with the work of his early days.
>
> *(Collected Letters, vol. 7 100)*

Some testing of the handwritten and dictated parts in sections of five thousand and seven thousand words with cluster analysis confirms that, in spite of some substantial revision of the early parts when the book was finally published, the sections tend to group by date, and, therefore, by mode. However, in nearly all analyses, either the first or the first and second of the late, dictated sections group with the preceding handwritten sections, typically most closely with the final handwritten sections. This mixing of mode and date clearly suggests that the narrative structure is more important than either date or mode and that Conrad has patched the joint between the parts quite effectively. It also confirms Jean-Aubry's intuitive statement that "there is no perceptible break between the first part, which he left unchanged, and the second, which was added so much later" (174). It also validates Karl's rejection of Conrad's suggestion of a difference between his early and late styles: "Conrad's style from 1896 to 1918–19 did not evolve in a linear fashion. On the contrary, he returned to his early style, and his work on *The Rescue* is homogeneous" (*Joseph Conrad* 816).

Except for the first chapter, *The Arrow of Gold* (1917–18) was entirely dictated (Moore). Analyzing the novel in sections of about four thousand words (the first chapter is 3,883 words long) using cluster analysis and PCA produces patterns that are quite consistent. The handwritten first chapter groups with the following four sections, typically along with the thirteenth and fourteenth. Bootstrap consensus analysis based on various numbers of the most frequent words and on multiple culling percentages and distance measures confirms these findings. The nature of this case means that any significant stylistic difference caused by dictation would result in a separation of the dictated first chapter from the immediately following dictated ones, something never seen in any of these analyses.

The Shadow Line

The Shadow Line (1915) provides a more promising opportunity for testing for the influence of mode of composition than did the five texts just discussed. As in Hardy's *A Laodicean*, a dictated section of this novella separates the beginning and ending handwritten sections. The first handwritten section is about eleven thousand words long, the dictated section about twenty-two thousand words long, and the final handwritten section about seven thousand words long. (For a precise account of the division between the handwritten and dictated parts of the novel, see Conrad, *The Shadow-Line 2003* [xxxv]). Furthermore, this novella seems especially important because here, as in the case of *The Rescue*, Conrad himself mused about the effects of the mode of its composition on his style, suggesting that critics might want to compare the handwritten and dictated parts of *The Shadow Line* (*Collected Letters*, vol. 5 543; quoted earlier).

Cluster analysis of the three parts of the novella in sections of about thirty-five hundred words gives very consistent results in which the sections group sequentially rather than by mode. One very consistent group contains the first four of the six handwritten sections of the opening of the novel, and the other contains the remaining two opening handwritten sections, the three dictated middle sections, and the two handwritten ending sections. Within the second group, the initial dictated section very consistently forms a subgroup with the fifth and sixth sections of the handwritten beginning. PCA gives generally similar results but also places the two handwritten final sections of the novel in a group of their own. None of these analyses show any tendency for the handwritten opening and closing sections to group together separately from the dictated middle. These results are confirmed by bootstrap consensus analysis based on various numbers of the most frequent words and on multiple culling percentages and distance measures and reconfirmed in an especially telling way when the dialogue and narration are analyzed separately, as can be seen in Figure 3.4. Note how the eight initial

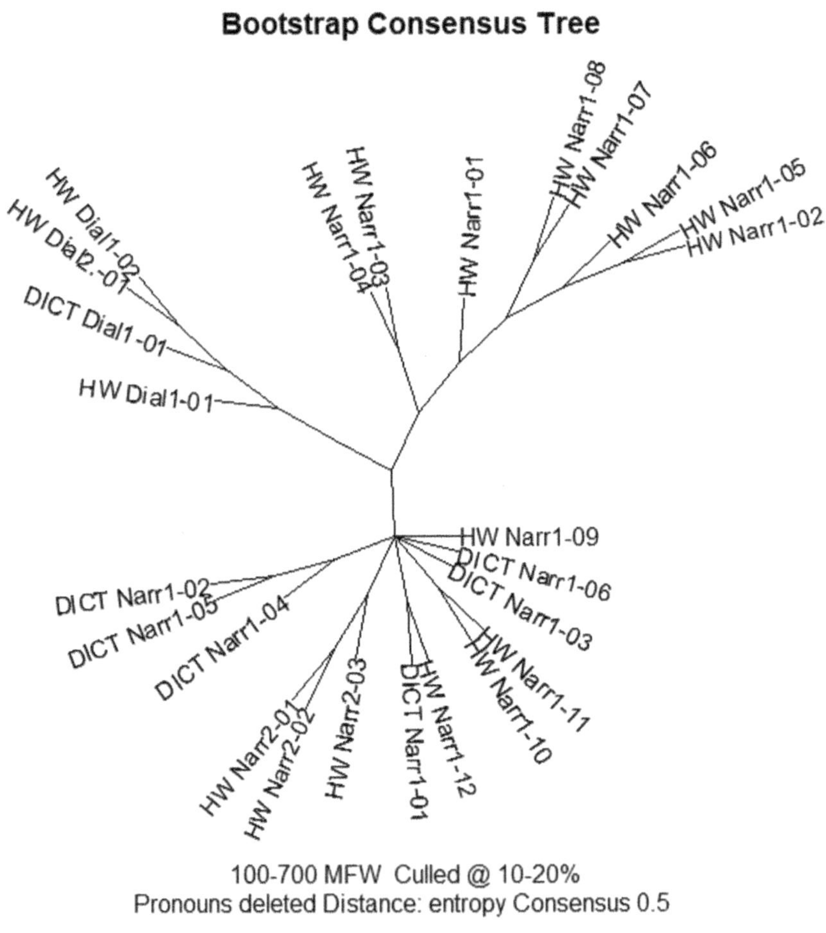

FIGURE 3.4 Bootstrap consensus analysis of the handwritten and dictated parts of Joseph Conrad's *The Shadow Line* in sections of thirty-five hundred words, based on the one hundred to seven hundred most frequent words, with pronouns deleted, culled at ten to twenty percent, entropy distance, and a consensus of fifty percent

handwritten narrative sections group together at the upper right without any of the joining of the final handwritten narrative sections that would be expected if mode of composition were an important variable. The group of handwritten and dictated dialogue on the upper left also shows no grouping by mode. Finally note how the first dictated narrative section groups with the last of the handwritten narrative sections at the bottom center of the graph. Again, narrative structure is a much stronger factor than mode of composition.

Nostromo

The circumstances surrounding the composition of *Nostromo* (1904), though complex, now seem fairly clear, and both the dictated and the manuscript parts of this longest of Conrad's novels are themselves ample for analysis. The writing of *Nostromo* took Conrad all of 1903 and until September of 1904, with the last month dedicated to revising and expanding the serial version for book publication. This was a period during which he was collaborating with Ford Madox Ford on *Romance* and also working on *The Mirror of the Sea*. As with *Mirror*, Ford made some famous, if dubious and contradictory, claims about his help with *Nostromo*. While ostensibly debunking the idea that he had written a great deal of the novel, about twenty years later he nevertheless claimed, "I may have written ten thousand words that I remember and could place my finger on fairly substantial passages and perhaps another twenty thousand that I remember only faintly and should find difficult to trace" (qtd. in Brice 79).

The occasion of these claims was his being shown a copy of part of the manuscript of the novel (about thirty-three hundred words) in his own hand, and the existence of these pages has sometimes been accepted as proof of Ford's claims. The arguments in favor of Ford's composition by Mizener (89–91) and Harvey (107) are based largely upon Morey's unpublished 1960 dissertation, but Carabine, in the World Classics edition published by Oxford UP in 1984, also sees some traces of Ford's style in the part of the text corresponding to the manuscript in his hand. He then points out that "when Conrad revised the serial for the book publication he cut out over 100 words which remind me of Ford at his most facile" (Conrad, *Nostromo* [Carabine] 583). More recently, however, research has shown that, "On balance, Ford's claims are not exaggerations but are simply false, a piece with his claims to have played a significant role in composing *A Personal Record*. Far from writing some 30,000 words, he appears to have taken down Conrad's dictation for, at most, twenty-three pages, amounting approximately to 4,500 words" (Brice 92; Najder concurs 340–2). Curiously, there is no discussion of the possibility of Ford's composition of part of *Nostromo* in the 2009 Oxford University Press edition of the novel (Conrad, *Nostromo* [Berthoud and Kalnins]).

Despite the direction of the current critical winds, it seems prudent to separate the portion of the novel in Ford's hand for analysis and to begin by determining whether or not Ford's style can be distinguished from Conrad's. Initial testing of a series of novels, novellas, and long stories by Conrad and Ford from about

1900 to 1915, overlapping with the date of *Nostromo*, shows that the two authors are, in fact, very easy to distinguish. This suggests that the question of Ford's true part in *Nostromo* should be fairly easy to determine by testing the text from the manuscript in his hand against surrounding sections of text in Conrad's own handwriting.

One of the clearest statements of the relationship between the existing partial manuscript of the novel and the parts that exist only in typescript, and therefore assumed to be dictated, is Frederick Karl's. He compares the autograph manuscript to the 566-page Doubleday collected edition of 1925, and reports that the autograph manuscript ends on page 505. He also reports that it is missing pages 195 to 415, and is also missing thirty-seven manuscript pages between pages 136 and 235 ("Significance" 130–1). The most recent edition of the Conrad Manuscript Register generally agrees with this account (Moore), as does the account of Brice (78), though Brice notes that several manuscript pages that would have immediately followed the Ford dictation are missing, so that that portion of the novel may well have also been dictated. I have seen no explicit indication of exactly where Conrad's handwriting begins again, but the situation is clear enough for a test of the two places in the novel that show a definite change in mode.

In a simple cluster analysis of the novel in sections of about thirty-three hundred words (the size of the Ford dictation), there is a lot of grouping by novel section, and therefore by mode as well. The picture is quite chaotic over all, however: except for one cluster containing only manuscript sections from the beginning of the book, all clusters mix handwritten and dictated sections. There is no evidence of a change in style at the points at which one mode replaces the other. Furthermore, the handwritten section preceding the one in Ford's handwriting always groups with Ford's section and the two sections following it, strongly confirming both that Ford was taking dictation rather than composing and that the narrative sequencing is a much stronger signal than the mode.

To reduce the effect of the narrative structure, it seems worthwhile to test just substantial sections of the novel that surround the three changes of mode at pages 174, 415, and 505 in the collected edition. Conrad's autograph manuscript exists for pages 1 to 174, and Ford's dictation follows, from pages 174 to 185. The status of pages 185 to 195, which are also missing from the manuscript, is uncertain, but they may have been on missing pages dictated to Ford. Pages 195 to 415 are also missing from the manuscript, but Conrad's handwriting begins again on page 415, only to disappear again at page 505. Testing sections of thirty-three hundred words that precede and follow the changes of mode, along with the Ford manuscript and the following short passage missing from the manuscript with Stylo's bootstrap consensus analysis based on various numbers of the most frequent words and on multiple culling percentages and distance measures universally produces patterns in which handwritten and dictated sections group together. In the great majority of these, Ford's manuscript is grouped with the preceding Conrad manuscript and with the following dictated sections. A representative analysis is shown in Figure 3.5, in which the only clusters of sections in the same mode are also consecutive sections, and the clustering of the first three dictated sections of the end of the novel seems more likely to be a result of Conrad's extensive expansion of the serial ending, to which he added about fourteen thousand words (Conrad, *Nostromo xxxiii*). (In Figure 3.5, sections 13–15 are the final handwritten sections of about thirty-three hundred words before section 16, the Ford manuscript, and section 17, the following section of the novel not found in the manuscript. Sections 18–23 are the first three and the last three sections of dictation that precede the next change in mode at page 415, sections 24–30 are

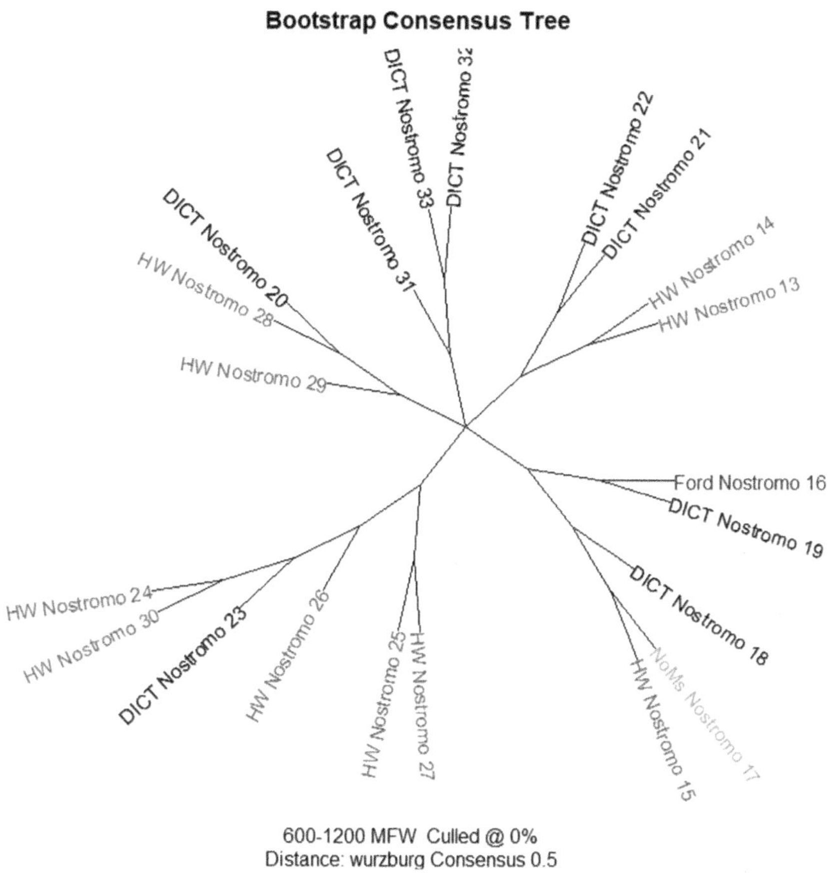

FIGURE 3.5 Bootstrap consensus analysis of the handwritten and dictated parts of Joseph Conrad's *Nostromo* in sections of thirty-three hundred words, based on the six hundred to twelve hundred most frequent words, with pronouns deleted, not culled, Wurzburg Delta distance, and a consensus of fifty percent

the handwritten sections corresponding to pages 415–505, and sections 31–33 are the first dictated sections of the end of the novel.)

The parts of this long novel written in the different modes are long enough that it is possible to test dialogue and narration separately. In cluster analyses of both dialogue and narration, in sections of about fourteen hundred words, handwriting and dictation continue to mix together and the Ford manuscript continues to group with the preceding manuscript in Conrad's handwriting.

Finally, as noted in Chapter 2, the *t*-test is a well-known way of testing whether or not the distributions of the words in sections of texts could have happened by chance. Here we can test the dialogue and the narration separately in the dictated and handwritten parts of *Nostromo* for significant differences in the distribution of vocabulary between the modes. The tests examine the most frequent words and determine what the likelihood is that all the sections are "really" part of a single sample. That is, what are the chances that the distribution of each word across the three handwritten and the three dictated sections of dialogue and narration could have happened by chance. In this case, the total amount of dialogue is only about forty-one thousand words, so that many of the words are too rare for their distribution to be significant.

For *t*-testing, the dialogue is first divided into sections. The border sections are held out for testing, along with the sections before and after a change of mode, the Ford dictation, and the small portion for which evidence is unclear. Student's *t*-tests are done on the one thousand most frequent words of all of the remaining manuscript sections and an equal number of dictated sections (selected at random). Only twenty-two words have a probability of less than five percent of being distributed as they are by chance. Compare this to artificially created sections of the dialogue of Henry James's *The Ambassadors* of exactly the same size. All of this dialogue was dictated, so there is no actual variation in mode of composition, and James's vocabulary is significantly smaller than Conrad's. Nevertheless, thirty-two of James's words have *p*-values of 0.05 or below. This suggests that the distribution of the most frequent words of the dialogue of *Nostromo* is essentially the same whether it was handwritten or dictated. As for those words identified as having statistically significant distributions, it is well to remember that a ninety-five percent chance that the distribution is meaningful is also a five percent chance that it is not (see Burrows, "Not" 97).

An even clearer indication that the distinction between modes of composition is not really valid is the fact that principal components analysis of the sections that were held out and the dictated sections that were not used for the *t*-test shows poor separation of manuscript and dictated sections. The most that can be suggested concerning a distinction by mode is that the three manuscript sections are on one side of the graph. The fact that nearly half of the dictated sections join the manuscript sections on the same side of the graph shows that any distinction by mode is, at best, very minor. Cluster analysis shows even less grouping by mode.

There is more than three times as much narrative as dialogue in *Nostromo*, and the *t*-test (conducted in the same way as for dialogue, though with longer sections) identifies 142 words that are significant at the $p < 0.05$ level. Yet when the border sections, the Ford dictation, the section of unknown mode, and the remaining dictated sections not used for the *t*-test are tested with PCA and cluster analysis, they show no tendency to group by modes of composition.

Conclusion

Aside from a possible slight difference between handwritten and dictated dialogue in *Nostromo*, then, Conrad's style, like those of Hardy and Scott, shows no significant effect caused by changes in mode of composition. The idea that revision might have removed some stylistic effects of dictation for these three authors cannot be entirely ruled out. However, what we learned in Chapter 2 about the sensitivity of the tests used here and the relatively minor effects observed in the case of the restrictive house style of Victorian periodicals suggests that such an erasure is unlikely. This is especially true for Hardy and Scott, whose revisions were less extensive than Conrad's, and it is only Conrad's style that shows even a hint of the effect of changes in mode. The question for Chapter 4 is whether a more permanent change in mode, rather than the temporary or sporadic changes seen in Hardy, Scott, and Conrad, might have a more significant effect on literary style.

References

Ahmad, Suleiman M. "Emma Hardy and the Ms. of *a Pair of Blue Eyes*." *Notes and Queries*, vol. 26, no. 4, 1979, pp. 320–2, doi:10.1093/nq/26-4-320.

Alexander, J. H., editor. *The Bride of Lammermoor*. 1995. The Edinburgh Edition of the Waverley Novels, vol. 7 [A], Edinburgh UP, 2017, doi:10.1093/actrade/9780748605712.book.1.

———. *A Legend of the Wars of Montrose*. 1995. The Edinburgh Edition of the Waverley Novels, vol. 7 [B], Edinburgh UP, 2017, doi:10.1093/actrade/9780748605729.book.1.

Brice, Xavier. "Ford Madox Ford and the Composition of *Nostromo*." *The Conradian*, vol. 29, no. 2, 2004, pp. 75–95. www.jstor.org/stable/20873529.

Conrad, Joseph. *The Collected Letters of Joseph Conrad*. Vol. 3, edited by Frederic Karl and Laurence Davies. Cambridge UP, 1988. books.google.com/books?id=zJBklzxB5BEC.

———. *The Collected Letters of Joseph Conrad*. Vol. 5, edited by Frederic Karl and Laurence Davies. Cambridge UP, 1996. archive.org/details/collectedletters0005conr/mode/2up.

———. *The Collected Letters of Joseph Conrad*. Vol. 7, edited by Laurence Davies and J. H. Stape. Cambridge UP, 2005. books.google.com/books?id=UVzMFTPFP9MC.

———. *Nostromo: A Tale of the Seaboard*. Oxford World's Classics, edited by Jacques Berthoud, and Mara Kalnins, Oxford UP, 2009.

———. *Nostromo: A Tale of the Seaboard*. The World's Classics, edited by Keith Carabine, Oxford UP, 1984. archive.org/details/nostromotaleofse00conr_0.

———. *A Personal Record*. The Cambridge Edition of the Works of Joseph Conrad, edited by Zdzisław Najder and J. H. Stape, Cambridge UP, 2008, doi:10.1017/CBO9781107341012.

———. *The Secret Agent: A Simple Tale*. The Cambridge Edition of the Works of Joseph Conrad, edited by Bruce Harkness and S. W. Reid, Cambridge UP, 1990. books.google.com/books?id=kp9uRMboUDMC.

———. *The Shadow-Line: A Confession*. The Cambridge Edition of the Works of Joseph Conrad, edited by J. H. Stape and Allan H. Simmons, introduction and explanatory notes by Owen Knowles, Cambridge UP, 2013. books.google.com/books?id=uocPAQAAQBAJ.

———. *The Shadow-Line: A Confession*. Oxford World's Classics, edited with an introduction and notes by Jeremy Hawthorn, Oxford UP, 2003. books.google.com/books?id=o4ceZwmWHGIC.

———. *Youth, Heart of Darkness, The End of the Tether*. The Cambridge Edition of the Works of Joseph Conrad, edited by Owen Knowles, Cambridge UP, 2010. books.google.com/books?id=Kle9WnHV_IsC.

Eder, Maciej et al. "Stylometry with *R:* A Package for Computational Text Analysis." *R Journal*, vol. 8, no. 1, 2016, pp. 107–21. journal.r-project.org/archive/2016/RJ-2016-007/RJ-2016-007.pdf.

Halperin, John. Review of *The Collected Letters of Joseph Conrad*, Vol. 3, edited by Frederick Karl and Laurence Davies. *Modern Fiction Studies*, vol. 35, no. 4, 1989, pp. 786–8. JSTOR. www.jstor.org/stable/26283401.

Hardy, Florence Emily. *The Early Life of Thomas Hardy*. Palgrave Macmillan, 1928. archive.org/details/earlylifeofthoma00hard.

Harvey, David Dow. *Ford Madox Ford, 1873–1939: Bibliography of Works and Criticism*. Princeton UP, 1962.

Honeycutt, Lee. "Literacy and the Writing Voice: The Intersection of Culture and Technology in Dictation." *Journal of Business and Technical Communication*, vol. 18, no. 3, 2004, pp. 294–327, doi:10.1177/1050651904264105.

Hoover, David L. "Simulations and Difficult Problems." *Digital Scholarship in the Humanities*, vol. 34, no. 4, 2019, pp. 874–92, doi:10.1093/llc/fqz034.

Ireland, Ken. *Thomas Hardy, Time and Narrative: A Narratological Approach to His Novels*. Palgrave Macmillan, 2014.

Jean-Aubry, Gérard. *The Sea Dreamer: A Definitive Biography of Joseph Cornrad*. Translated by Helen Sebba, Doubleday, 1957. archive.org/details/seadreamerdefini0000jean.

Karl, Frederick R. *Joseph Conrad: The Three Lives, a Biography*. Farrar, Straus and Giroux, 1979. archive.org/details/josephconradthre00karl.

———. "The Significance of the Revisions in the Early Versions of *Nostromo*." *Modern Fiction Studies*, vol. 5, no. 2, 1959, pp. 129–44. www.jstor.org/stable/26277114.

Knowles, Owen, and Gene M. Moore, editors. *Oxford Reader's Companion to Conrad*. Oxford UP, 2011.

Lockhart, John G. *Memoirs of the Life of Sir Walter Scott, Bart*. Vol. 1, Carey, Lea, and Blanchard, 1837. archive.org/details/memoirslifesirw01lockgoog/mode/2up.

———. *Memoirs of the Life of Sir Walter Scott, Bart*. Vol. 2, Carey, Lea, and Blanchard, 1837. archive.org/details/memoirslifesirw83lockgoog/mode/2up.

Manford, Alan. "Emma Hardy's Helping Hand." *Critical Essays on Thomas Hardy: The Novels*, edited by Dale Kramer, assisted by Nancy Marck, G. K. Hall, 1990, pp. 100–21.

———. "Who Wrote Thomas Hardy's Novels? A Survey of Emma Hardy's Contribution to the Manuscripts of Her Husband's Novels." *The Thomas Hardy Journal*, vol. 6, no. 2, 1990, pp. 84–97.

Millgate, Jane. *Walter Scott: The Making of the Novelist*. 1987. U of Toronto P, 2015, doi:10.3138/9781442683211.

Millgate, Michael. *Thomas Hardy: A Biography Revisited*. Oxford UP, 2006.

Minitab Release 19, Minitab, Inc., State College, PA, 2019.

Mizener, Arthur. *The Saddest Story: A Biography of Ford Madox Ford*. Bodley Head, 1971. archive.org/details/saddeststorybiog00mize.

Moore, Gene M. *A Descriptive Location Register of Joseph Conrad's Literary Manuscripts*. 2016. www.josephconradsociety.org/02MSS_register.pdf.

Morey, John H. "Joseph Conrad and Ford Madox Ford: A Study in Collaboration." Unpublished Ph.D. dissertation, Cornell University, 1960.

Najder, Zdzisław. *Joseph Conrad: A Life*. Translated by Halina Najder, Camden House, 2007.

Purdy, Richard Little. *Thomas Hardy: A Bibliographical Study*. Oxford UP, 1954. archive.org/details/thomashardybibli0000purd.

Sutherland, Kathryn. "Made in Scotland: 'The Edinburgh Edition of the Waverley Novels'." *Text*, vol. 14, 2002, pp. 305–23. www.jstor.org/stable/30228002.

Tulloch, Graham, editor. *Ivanhoe*. 1998. The Edinburgh Edition of the Waverley Novels, vol. 8, Edinburgh UP, 2017, doi:10.1093/actrade/9780748605736.book.1.

Widdowson, Peter. *On Thomas Hardy: Late Essays and Earlier*. Palgrave Macmillan, 2016.

Wood, G. A. M., and D. Hewitt, editors. *Redgauntlet*. 1997. The Edinburgh Edition of the Waverley Novels, vol. 17, Edinburgh UP, 2017, doi:10.1093/actrade/9780748605804.book.1.

4

CHANGING OVER FROM HANDWRITING TO DICTATION OR TYPING: BOOTH TARKINGTON AND WILLIAM FAULKNER

> For myself I dislike writing with a pen. My writer's cramp has never completely left me, and every word I write is accompanied by a little pain. Towards the end of my morning's work it will be a very severe pain running from the knuckle of my third finger to my elbow. But for me, it is worth while. . . . After the volume I began at St. Jean Cap Ferrat [*Some Do Not*] the cramp became so severe that I could not hold a pen at all. I took to writing with a machine and then, worst of all, to dictating! I am not to that extent machinophobe—or even a hater of stenographers—that I consider the one or the other below my dignity. It is that the one—and still more the other!—make me become too fluid. It is as if they waited for me to write, and write I do. Whereas if I have to go to a table and face pretty considerable pain I wait until I have something worth saying to say and say it in the fewest possible words.
>
> *(Ford 218–19)*

Introduction

As I have noted in my preface, the nature and circumstances of Ford Madox Ford's changes in mode of composition make him unsuitable for inclusion in this study, yet his perception of the effects of dictation and typing on his writing seems relevant here. They form a bridge between the demonstration in Chapter 3 that changing back and forth from handwriting to dictation had no strong effect on the styles of Thomas Hardy, Sir Walter Scott, or Joseph Conrad and this chapter's exploration of the possible effects of permanent changes in mode of composition from handwriting to dictation or typing.

Unlike Hardy and Scott, who dictated for brief periods in their careers, and unlike Conrad, who changed back and forth from handwriting to dictation sporadically for nearly twenty years before switching to dictation permanently for his last two novels, Booth Tarkington (1869–1946) and William Faulkner (1897–1962) made essentially unidirectional changes in their modes of composition. Both also commented explicitly on their own writing processes. Tarkington abandoned handwriting for dictation because of severe vision problems that left him almost completely blind for a time. Faulkner switched from handwriting his first drafts and then retyping them to composing directly on the typewriter in the middle of a novel, apparently as a matter of convenience. These authors thus provide two different perspectives: they changed to and from different modes and for different reasons.

William Faulkner was only two years old when Booth Tarkington published his first novel, but the two authors share the distinction (along with John Updike) of being the only authors to win two Pulitzer prizes for fiction. Tarkington won for novels that are universally agreed to be among his best: *The Magnificent Ambersons* in 1919 and *Alice Adams* in 1922. Faulkner won for *A Fable* in 1955 and *The Reivers* in 1963, novels that few would regard as equal to his great early novels, *The Sound and the Fury* (1929), *As I Lay Dying* (1930), or *Light in August* (1932). In other ways, however, Tarkington and Faulkner were very different. Along with his two Pulitzers, Faulkner won the Nobel Prize for Literature in 1950 and is considered among the greatest authors writing in English, while Tarkington is rarely read and largely forgotten, in spite of receiving "in 1933 from the National Institute of Arts and Letters the gold medal previously awarded only to Howells and Wharton, and in 1945 from the American Academy of Arts and Letters the William Dean Howells medal awarded only once in five years" (Woodress, *Booth Tarkington* 251; see also Gottlieb). On the other hand, Faulkner's sometimes radically experimental style and his often unpleasant subject matter kept him from becoming a popular writer, left him struggling financially throughout much of his life, and forced him to work as a screen-writer to make ends meet. Tarkington, in contrast, was immensely popular, both as a fiction writer and as a playwright (with multiple plays on Broadway at once). He was wealthy enough that he once asked *The Saturday Evening Post* to reduce what they were paying him for stories, and he could afford to "buy an impressive number of works by Reynolds, Gainsborough, Lawrence, Lely, Stuart, Romney, Dobson, Raeburn, and even a Titian, a Velasquez, and a Goya" (Woodress, *Booth Tarkington* 286, 296).

Booth Tarkington: Blindness and Changing Over From Handwriting to Dictation

> I have discovered that it is a great relief to be freed of the hard, purely mechanical task of writing by hand.
>
> (Tarkington, qtd. in MacDonald 15)

Conflicting newspaper accounts and biographies make it impossible to construct a completely consistent account of Booth Tarkington's problems with his sight, but the broad outlines are fairly clear. He suffered from eye problems as early as 1917 (Kunitz 399) and was told to avoid straining his eyes during treatment for cataracts in 1922 (Woodress, *Booth Tarkington* 202, 272). In spite of his increasing vision problems in 1927, Tarkington frequently denied that he was threatened with blindness (Woodress, *Booth Tarkington* 272) and rejected the idea of dictating his work to a secretary ("Blindness Menaces" 1) or taking up typing (MacDougall 5). As late as October of 1928, he was refusing to consider surgery (Woodress, *Booth Tarkington* 272), but in December of 1928, Mrs. Tarkington mentioned in an interview that he had begun dictating some of his work to rest his eyes ("Mrs. Tarkington Denies" 26). Although he tried dictating to other secretaries briefly, Elizabeth Trotter, who had already been a close family friend, quickly became so valuable and indispensable that she lived with the Tarkingtons for the rest of Booth's life (Mayberry 76; Woodress, *Booth Tarkington* 272; Hallet WM7). Indeed, "Betty was almost in a literal sense Uncle Booth's eyes" (Mayberry 75).

Beginning in early 1929, Tarkington underwent several operations for cataracts that provided brief improvements in vision ("Tarkington Blind" 29; "Booth Tarkington Cheered" 6; "Booth Tarkington Better" 6; "Tarkington Is Gaining" 4), but the problems always returned, and a detached retina left him completely blind for about five months after August of 1930. Although a successful operation in January of 1931 restored good vision in one eye, he continued to dictate almost all of his literary work from 1929 until his death in 1946 (Woodress, *Booth Tarkington* 273–4; MacDonald 15; Morehouse 10; Barron 2; "Booth Tarkington Still Writes" 9). Blindness itself might also conceivably cause stylistic changes, but its onset was gradual, Tarkington began to dictate while his vision was still good enough that he could have handwritten his texts, and he continued dictating even after his vision was largely restored. Under these circumstances, the change in his mode of composition seems more likely to have caused a change in style than the vision problems themselves.

The Booth Tarkington Papers, 1812–1956, at Princeton University, where Tarkington studied for two years, contains manuscripts of most of Tarkington's work. In fact the collection "is certainly one of the most completely preserved records of any significant American author" (Woodress, "The Tarkington Papers" 46). The finding aid for the collection indicates for each item whether it is a typescript or manuscript. Unfortunately, however, some items labeled manuscript or autograph manuscript are in Tarkington's handwriting and some are in the handwriting of his secretary, Elizabeth Trotter. A trip to Princeton and an examination of many of the manuscripts in the collection allowed me to confirm the mode of composition and the identity of the handwriting for a large selection of Tarkington's novels and stories from 1924 to 1936. In most cases, the folder that contains the manuscript has been labeled by the archivist to indicate whose handwriting is involved, but Tarkington's and Trotter's handwriting are so distinctively different that no one would be likely to confuse them.[1]

Before proceeding with testing for a dictation effect, however, it is worth commenting on Tarkington's own attitude toward dictation. According to his niece, Susanah Mayberry,

> Uncle Booth told me once that the hardest thing he ever had to do—and he had had to do some hard things—was to learn how to dictate to a secretary instead of writing down his thoughts in long-hand. He said that he had tried several very competent secretaries but was always uncomfortably aware of their waiting presence. Betty [Trotter], he said, had the quality of seeming to absent herself entirely, so that his concentration was not spoiled by the consciousness of another person. Betty told me once he would be silent for as much as an hour while he searched for just the right word.
>
> *(Mayberry 76)*

In spite of the difficulty of learning to dictate, Tarkington later came to believe that dictation improved his writing. Three years after his sight was restored, for example, a reporter

> asked him if he thought he could do as good work by dictation as when he wrote in his own hand. "Yes, better work," he replied. "I have discovered that it is a great relief to be freed of the hard, purely mechanical task of writing by hand. I can lean back, eyes shut, hands and my whole body at rest, and dictate my stories, and I get many letters telling me that I am doing the best work of my life now."
>
> *(MacDonald 15)*

Tarkington's biographer, speaking of the first novel that was partly dictated, claims:

> The slightness of *Young Mrs. Greeley* is understandable in light of biographical fact, and the real wonder is that the novel was finished at all. During its composition Tarkington suffered the physical blow that made him a semi-invalid for years and seriously impaired his activities for the rest of his life: blindness. In the midst of the novel he had to alter radically his entire procedure of literary composition, and while facing the bleak prospect of blindness, he had to learn to write by dictating. By sheer force of will he made the abrupt transition, accomplishing it so smoothly that *Young Mrs. Greeley* contains neither rough joinery nor noticeable variations in style.
>
> *(Woodress, "The Tarkington Papers" 272)*

The manuscript of that first partly dictated 1929 novel in the Booth Tarkington Papers provides an important starting point for testing for any effects of dictation on Tarkington's style. The first five chapters of the manuscript of the novel (about thirty percent) are in Tarkington's handwriting, and the remaining twelve chapters are in Elizabeth Trotter's handwriting, taken from Tarkington's Dictation. Because of this division, initial testing will compare the handwritten and dictated parts of *Young Mrs. Greeley* with his handwritten novels and stories from the years before the change to dictation in 1929 and the dictated novels and stories that followed the change.

Because of Tarkington's long publishing career (1899–1945), however, any possible effect caused by dictation must first be distinguished carefully from any ongoing chronological drift in his style. Initial cluster analysis testing on Tarkington's handwritten short fiction from 1900 to 1928 shows a fairly strong tendency for texts from 1900 to 1918 to group separately from the later texts, and for those from 1925 to 1928 to group separately from earlier texts (electronic texts of much of this short fiction had to be created by OCR from magazine PDFs, located using the Russo and Sullivan bibliography). (All cluster analyses in this chapter were performed in Minitab, with standardized variables, Ward linkage, and squared Euclidean distance.) PCA shows a similar, though weaker, pattern. (All principal components analyses in this chapter were performed in Minitab, using the correlation matrix; this prevents words with high frequencies from dominating the analysis.) Given this tendency for a chronological drift in Tarkington's style, I will restrict my testing for a possible effect of his change in mode of composition to texts written between 1925, four years before his first eye operation, and 1936, five years after a final operation restored good vision to his left eye. This should prevent any chronological drift from masking a dictation effect.

I begin with a series of bootstrap consensus analyses in Stylo (Eder et al. 113–15) of *Women* (1925), *The Plutocrat* (1927), and *Claire Ambler* (1928), the three handwritten novels that precede the change, and *Mary's Neck* (1932), *Presenting Lily Mars* (1933), and *The Lorenzo Bunch* (1936), the three dictated novels that follow it. The tests are based on multiple different distance measures, culling percentages, and various numbers of the most frequent words, word n-grams, and character n-grams. (For an early argument for the effectiveness of the analysis of n-grams, there called "sequences," see Hoover, "Frequent Sequences"; all bootstrap consensus analyses in this chapter were performed in Stylo.) There is a strong tendency for the pre-1929 and the post-1929 to group separately in these analyses, which at first seems to suggest a dictation effect. Unfortunately, the chronological drift that was evident in the novels before 1929, just discussed, would also explain these groupings.

This possibility can be explored further using classification tests in Stylo (Eder et al. 115–17). For these tests, the six novels used in the bootstrap consensus tests are designated as training texts and the handwritten and dictated parts of *Young Mrs. Greeley* and eight other handwritten and ten other dictated stories and novels published between 1925 and 1936 are designated as test texts. These tests show a maximum success rate of about seventy-five percent. However, most analyses (using several versions of Delta, Support Vector Machine, K Nearest Neighbors, and Nearest Shrunken Centroid, with various numbers of words and word and character n-grams, and various culling percentages) give correct results in the fifty-five to sixty-five percent range. The average success rate of several hundred tests is about sixty-three percent. Although most tests correctly classify the first part of *Young Mrs. Greeley* as handwritten and the second as dictated, the overall results do not suggest a significant dictation effect, especially as most errors miss-classify dictated texts as handwritten. This is impossible to reconcile with a strong dictation effect. Furthermore, when the primary texts are selected from just before and just after the change in mode, rather than from throughout the handwritten and dictated periods, the accuracy of the classification drops below fifty percent for many analyses. This suggests that chronological drift may be inflating even the relatively weak initial results and casts further doubt on any dictation effect. This possibility will be addressed shortly in analyses of *Young Mrs. Greeley* alone.

The results of the classification tests are supported by another series of bootstrap consensus analyses, expanded to include the same texts used in the classification tests. These tests, which are again based on multiple different distance measures, culling percentages, and consensus strengths, and various numbers of the most frequent words, word n-grams, and character n-grams, give similar results. There is some grouping of handwritten and dictated texts, but nothing to suggest a strong or consistent dictation effect. Many of these tests show most of the novels grouping together separately from the short fiction, suggesting the possibility that variations in text length may be masking a dictation effect. When the tests are repeated with the short fiction tested along with a single section of ninety-five hundred words of each of the novels selected at random (roughly matching the length of the shorter texts), the results are quite similar. There is no suggestion that the dictated texts are significantly different from the handwritten ones.

The handwritten and dictated parts of *Young Mrs. Greeley* do not form a pair at the fifty percent consensus level in these analyses, but they both do group with both handwritten and dictated texts. Handwritten or dictated texts that tend to form consistent groups in these analyses also tend to be chronologically close, which suggests that a tighter chronological focus might be appropriate. Yet, testing texts from narrower time spans, such as 1927 to 1931 or 1928 to 1930, still fails to produce results in which the texts are consistently grouped by mode of composition.

To see just how compelling this failure is, consider three analyses that give the best possible chance for a dictation effect to appear. For these analyses, I have selected only the following texts from 1928 to 1930 (for information on the publication of Tarkington's fiction, including the publication dates of these stories, the bibliography by Russo and Sullivan has been invaluable):

1928 What You Want in Life (January)
1928 Claire Ambler (January)
1929 Young Mrs. Greeley (handwritten part)

1929 Young Mrs. Greeley (dictated part)
1929 Pansy Dale and Patsy Dorker (August)
1929 Belinda Interferes (December)
1930 Carola's Causes (August)

Besides *Young Mrs. Greeley*, among these, *Claire Ambler* is the only novel, so I have taken a nine-thousand-word section from it at random. I have tested these texts with bootstrap consensus analysis, based on cluster analyses of the six hundred to twelve hundred most frequent words, in increments of one hundred words, culled at ten, twenty, thirty, and forty percent, with pronouns deleted, and using eight different distance measures, and then repeated the same tests based on word two-grams, and on character three-grams, four-grams, and five-grams. These stipulations produce forty different consensus trees for each test. In the first set of forty tests, with both the handwritten and dictated parts of *Young Mrs. Greeley* included, the two parts of the novel always group together separately from any other text, so that neither part ever groups with the previous handwritten or the following dictated texts. This is perhaps not surprising, given the strong tendency (demonstrated in Chapter 2) of sections of a text to be similar.

For the next two sets of forty tests, either the handwritten or the dictated part of *Young Mrs. Greeley* is included, but not both. These tests effectively remove the issue of chronology from serious consideration, as well as the issue of textual identity, so that the similarities and differences among just six texts are responsible for the groupings. When the dictated part of the novel is tested, two handwritten texts and four dictated texts are compared. When the handwritten part is tested, three handwritten texts and three dictated texts are compared. The results of the tests, eighty bootstrap consensus trees, show that the six texts never group by mode of composition. In fact, it is fairly rare for even two of the three handwritten texts to pair, and many trees show three pairs of texts, each consisting of one handwritten and one dictated text. One of the most common patterns of grouping is shown in Figure 4.1.

Focusing on *Young Mrs. Greeley* alone will address the possibility of a chronological influence on the results of the classification tests just discussed. At the same time, it will eliminate any possibility that the initial change to dictation had an effect that later dissipated. (If the change in mode had a cumulative effect, however, it would presumably have been revealed by the classification tests.) *Young Mrs. Greeley* can first be tested for a dictation effect by dividing the handwritten and dictated parts into chapters and using cluster analysis, PCA, and bootstrap consensus analysis. (Because the second chapter is only about 630 words long, it has been combined with the first chapter.) In dozens of analyses based on multiple different distance measures, culling percentages, and various numbers of words, word n-grams, and character n-grams of various lengths, the four handwritten chapters never group separately from the twelve dictated chapters.

When the handwritten and dictated parts of the novel are divided into equal sections of about three thousand words, the results are the same: in none of the

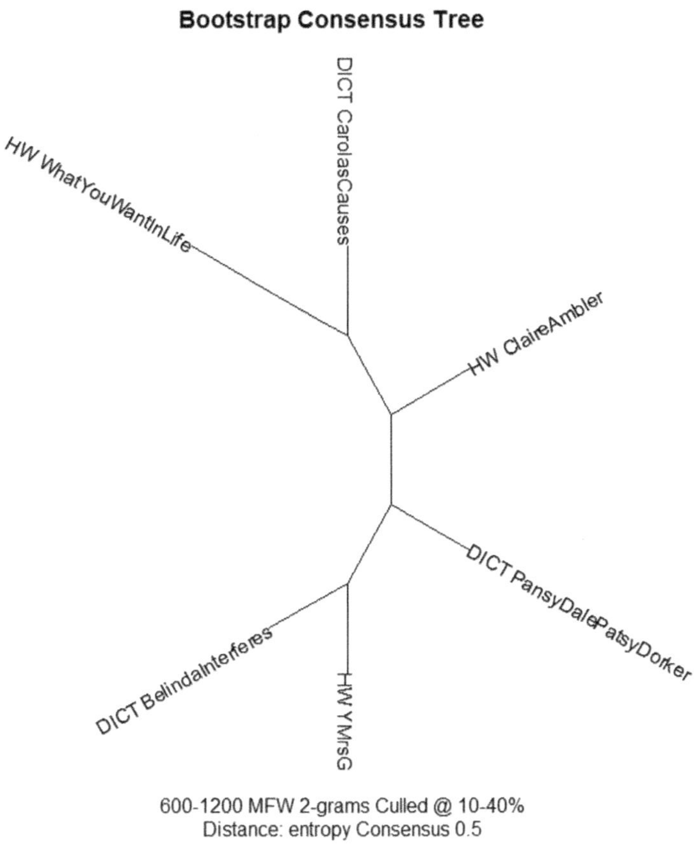

FIGURE 4.1 Bootstrap consensus analysis of the handwritten part of Booth Tarkington's *Young Mrs. Greeley*, two other handwritten texts, and three dictated texts, based on the six hundred to twelve hundred most frequent word two-grams, culled at ten to forty percent, with entropy distance and a consensus of fifty percent

analyses do the handwritten and dictated sections group separately. In a majority of these analyses, the first two handwritten parts (chapters or sections) form one group with some dictated parts and the third and fourth handwritten parts form another group with some dictated parts. Although these results show that any effect of dictation is not very significant, the fact that the final handwritten parts almost never group with the first of the dictated parts suggests the possibility of a minor and temporary effect.

Separate analysis of the dialogue and the narration of the handwritten and dictated parts of *Young Mrs. Greeley* is one way to address this possibility. It seems plausible, after all, that dictating might have a different effect on dialogue than on narration, though one could imagine that the effect on dialogue might be either more or less significant because of the similarity of dialogue to speech.

Performing the same kinds of analyses on sections of about twenty-five hundred words of handwritten and dictated dialogue and narration as were performed on the handwritten and dictated texts written just before and after *Young Mrs. Greeley*, however, gives very little evidence of any effect of the change in mode of composition.

In most of the dozens of analyses, all of the sections of dialogue form one group and all of the sections of narration form another, as might be expected, given the well-known differences between speech and narrative (Biber). Crucially, however, the handwritten and dictated sections of dialogue or narration never divide neatly by mode of composition in any analysis. A representative analysis is shown in Figure 4.2. In fact, in only three of forty analyses do the

FIGURE 4.2 Bootstrap consensus analysis of handwritten and dictated dialogue and narration of Booth Tarkington's *Young Mrs. Greeley* in sections of twenty-five hundred words, based on the two hundred to eight hundred most frequent words, with pronouns deleted, culled at ten to twenty percent, entropy distance, and a consensus of fifty percent

three handwritten sections of narration form a single group within the sections of narration. In the other thirty-seven analyses, these three sections all fall into one of two large groups: one of mixed handwritten and dictated sections and the other of dictated sections (there are only five handwritten sections but twelve dictated sections). The two handwritten sections of dialogue sometimes also form a pair within the dictated sections of dialogue. Although this might be seen as equivocal evidence of a minor effect of dictation, it seems more likely a result of the fact that the handwritten sections comprise the dialogue of the beginning of the novel. In no analysis do the handwritten and dictated sections of dialogue form two separate groups. Furthermore, if switching to dictation significantly affected the style of Tarkington's dialogue, the dictated sections should be the ones that group together separately from the handwritten ones.

In spite of Tarkington's resistance to the idea of dictation, then, and in spite of his statement that learning to dictate was the hardest thing he had ever done, it seems clear that his adoption of dictation had no very significant effect on his style. The equivocal results of multiple kinds of tests do not entirely preclude the possibility that dictation had some effect, but they clearly do preclude any strong or lasting effect, for, as shown in Chapter 2, these tests are capable of distinguishing quite subtle variations in style. The lack of a clear distinction between handwritten and dictated texts necessarily also constitutes a lack of a clear distinction between early and late texts from 1924 to 1936. Given the clear tendency of a chronological drift in style in Tarkington's earlier career, this suggests the intriguing but untestable possibility that dictation might have stabilized his style rather than altering it.

William Faulkner: Changing Over From Handwriting to Typing

> About three o'clock that afternoon, Faulkner unrolled the last sheet of the story from the machine. Then he sat for another half hour, making changes in the manuscript with a pen.
>
> "What're you going to call it?" asked the young man as Faulkner arranged the manuscript into a neat pile.
>
> "'Go Down, Moses,'" said Faulkner. "Do you like the title?"
>
> (Meriwether and Millgate 48, "Interview with Dan Brennen, 1940")

> Having shaken hands with Commins and Faulkner, we retreated to a corner of the office and watched the sole owner and proprietor of Yoknapatawpha County bring forth prose. He typed very, very slowly, mostly with the middle finger of his right hand, but with an occasional assist from the index finger of his left.
>
> (Meriwether and Millgate 75, "Interview in *The New Yorker*, 1953")

The preservation of a very large number of manuscripts, typescripts, galleys, and other pre-publication material relating to William Faulkner's works makes it possible to form a fairly clear picture of his writing practices. The largest single repository of these materials is The William Faulkner Collection in the Albert and Shirley Small Special Collections Library at the University of Virginia. This collection has been described as follows: "In scope, magnitude, and depth, the Faulkner Collections described in these pages can hardly be equaled elsewhere; altogether they constitute one of the largest and most important assemblages of works by and relating to any single modern author" (*William Faulkner* Introduction). Most of the important materials for my purposes have been printed in facsimile in the twenty-five volumes of the *William Faulkner Manuscripts* (Blotner et al.).

The earliest forms of most of Faulkner's novels are handwritten manuscripts, but it was long believed that Faulkner composed his first two novels, *Soldiers' Pay* (1926) and *Mosquitoes* (1927), directly on the typewriter, partly because the earliest known versions of these novels were typescripts. The 1987 sale by a private collector of the partial holograph manuscript of *Mosquitoes* to the University of Virginia's Alderman Library, however, cast some doubt on this view of Faulkner's composing process (Mcdowell 15; Crane 1+). It is also significant that the holograph manuscript of Faulkner's abandoned novel, *Father Abraham*, which was the origin of some of the material that was much later incorporated into *The Hamlet*, also dates from 1926 or 1927. On the other hand, another abandoned novel (from 1925), *Elmer*, also exists only in typescript and is assumed to have been composed at the typewriter (*William Faulkner: Novels 1936–1940* 1112; Blotner et al., vol. 1: 1; Crane 1+). Whatever Faulkner's very early practice was, however, "[f]rom *Sartoris* to *The Hamlet* the collection affords ample manuscript evidence . . . that Faulkner habitually wrote first in ink, revising as he went along, and not using the typewriter until he was ready to prepare a final typescript for the publisher" (Meriwether 61). In a 1937 interview, Faulkner claims "that his method is always to write his first draft in longhand, then make revisions, finally to rewrite when typing out his manuscript for the publisher" (Karl 599).

This practice changed during the composition of *The Hamlet* (1940), which James Kibler describes as follows (see Kibler, "Study" 270–89 for a more detailed chronology):

> Faulkner, with what he had written of his manuscript before him, began typing his first draft, quit after page 62 and revised, reworked, and added new material to some of these pages, then picked up where he had broken off and continued expanding from his manuscript. Reaching typescript page 104, he again stopped, revised, expanded, and rearranged some of these sheets, and then continued typing from his manuscript until completing typescript page 208. Once again he stopped, reread what he had

> written and made some revisions and expansions before going on and typing the remainder of the novel in the final phase.
>
> *(Kibler, "Review" 316–17)*

Michael Millgate notes that the manuscript of *The Hamlet* is "practically complete up to a point corresponding to the end of the second section of Book Three, Chapter II of the published book" (Millgate 184), and an examination of the manuscript facsimile confirms that the final words of the existing manuscript correspond very closely with the last words of the published version of 3.2.2 (all references to parts of novels will be indicated as book.chapter.section): "Are they going to feed them niggers before they do a white man? he thought, smelling the coffee and the ham"(Blotner et al., vol. 15, part 1: 474). (For an extended discussion of the manuscript, see Blotner et al., vol. 15, part 1: *vii—xxii*.) Blotner and Polk agree, reporting that "[b]y the time these novels [*Go Down, Moses*, *Intruder in the Dust*, *Requiem for a Nun*, and *A Fable*] were written, Faulkner composed almost exclusively at the typewriter rather than in longhand, which had been his practice up through the third book of *The Hamlet* (1940)" (*William Faulkner: Novels 1936–1940* 1104; see also Polk 9–10).

There seems, then, to be a general consensus that Faulkner normally composed his fiction directly on the typewriter after 1940, in spite of the following claim Faulkner made in a 1957 appearance at the University of Virginia:

> I write it out in longhand because I never have learned to think good onto the typewriter. [audience laughter] That I've got to—got to feel the pencil and see the words at the end of the pencil. Then if it's the wrong word, it's simple enough to scratch it out and try it again. I—I reckon I was—started writing too soon to have taken the typewriter as an extension of the hands, as—as the young man nowadays can do. I have to put—put it down on paper first. After that I do the rewriting on the typewriter, but something has got to be on paper first for me to look at and get the feel.
>
> *(Faulkner, "Local and UVA Communities")*

As for many authors, Faulkner's claims about his writing process cannot be taken at face value, especially because he nearly always added a great deal to any manuscript he typed, a process that obviously requires "thinking onto the typewriter." To take a single example, note that the typescript of *The Hamlet* contains thirteen pages (near the end of the third book) that are not present in the manuscript. The two quotations from interviewers at the beginning of this section also provide first-hand accounts of Faulkner composing at the typewriter in 1940 and 1953. Furthermore, in other University of Virginia events during 1957, he talks about trying to avoid revision because he is lazy, a claim that does not mesh well with the tremendous amount of revision he did on most of his novels (see Faulkner,

"Local and UVA Communities").[2] For example, there are many examples in the facsimiles of Faulkner's manuscripts of a text typed on the reverse of a discarded page from another manuscript that also has handwritten interlinear additions or replacements. At the very least, the fact that holograph manuscripts exist for the novels immediately preceding *The Hamlet* and for part of that novel, but not for those immediately following it, suggests a significant change in mode of composition that can be investigated. Naturally, *The Hamlet* will be one main focus of this investigation.

Compared with Tarkington's adoption of dictation in the face of blindness, Faulkner's abandonment of writing his first draft by hand in favor of composing directly at the typewriter seems intuitively less likely as a cause of stylistic change. The change in Faulkner's mode of composition seems more a matter of convenience than a change forced upon him. Faulkner was, after all, used to typing his initial handwritten draft very shortly after writing it, so that typing and correcting must have been quite familiar by this time in his career. At the same event at which he claimed never to compose on the typewriter, he commented of his handwriting that "somebody said my handwriting looks like a caterpillar that crawled through an ink well and out on to a piece of paper. If I leave it until tomorrow, I can't read it myself, [audience laughter] so it's got to be put down quick and then typed quick" (Faulkner, "Local and UVA Communities"). One further problem is that, as he often did, Faulkner adapted material written much earlier for inclusion in *The Hamlet*. Fortunately, the included earlier passages do not span the part of the novel where the change in mode occurred, and the location and extent of the earlier material, which was presumably handwritten, are fairly well documented.

As with other authors, it seems prudent to check for any chronological drift in Faulkner's style before addressing any possible effect of the change in mode of composition. The four novels that precede *The Hamlet*, for all of which complete holograph manuscripts exist, present no particular difficulty: *As I Lay Dying* (1930), *Light in August* (1932), *Absalom, Absalom!* (1936), and *If I Forget Thee, Jerusalem* (1939; originally published as *The Wild Palms*). (The tour-de-force nature of parts of the 1929 *The Sound and the Fury* makes it inappropriate for inclusion in this analysis.) Among the four novels that followed, *Intruder in the Dust* (1948) also presents no significant problems. For *Go Down, Moses* (1942), however, only a typescript manuscript exists. Yet this novel, like *The Hamlet*, incorporates some earlier material that was presumably handwritten, requiring careful selection of what parts can be safely analyzed. *Requiem for a Nun* (1951) and *A Fable* (1954), the other two novels immediately following *Go Down, Moses*, are much more problematic. There are "holograph drafts of extensive portions of *Requiem for a Nun* and of *A Fable*" (Blotner and Polk, *William Faulkner: Novels 1942–1954* 1104), and *Requiem* is part drama and part novel. The problems of genre and composition process seem so severe for these two novels that they cannot be safely included, and the next novel published, *The Town* (1957), is so distant in time from the change in mode of composition as to be unsuitable.[3] We are left, then, with seven novels for analysis—*As I Lay Dying* (1930), *Light in August* (1932), *Absalom, Absalom!* (1936), *If I Forget Thee, Jerusalem* (1939), *The Hamlet* (1940), *Go Down, Moses* (1942), and *Intruder in the Dust* (1948)—though the relatively long gap between the last two of these will need careful consideration.

A series of forty bootstrap consensus analyses based on cluster analyses of the five hundred to twelve hundred most frequent words, word two-grams, and character three-grams, four-grams, and five-grams, in increments of one hundred words or n-grams, and based on a range of culling percentages and eight different distance measures, shows that the three earliest of these novels group together very consistently but that the rest of the groupings are not very consistent. In about half (twenty-one) of the analyses, the two latest (typed) novels group separately from the rest, while the remaining four novels form two groups, one of which includes *The Hamlet*. This may sound promising, but, as a representative analysis shows (Figure 4.3), these analyses do not suggest a distinction between handwritten and typed novels. Rather, this looks more like three pairs of adjacent novels with *Absalom, Absalom!* isolated.

The four handwritten novels form a single group in only two of the forty analyses, and *The Hamlet* groups with the two typed novels in those analyses. Thus only two of the forty analyses could be said to argue for a stylistic effect of the change in mode. Also relevant to the question of a mode effect is the fact that partly typewritten *The Hamlet* consistently groups either with the immediately preceding handwritten *If I Forget Thee, Jerusalem* or with the immediately following typewritten *Go Down, Moses*. This suggests, as did the analyses in which the two typed novels form a pair, that a chronological effect may be operating even over this relatively short time span, especially because the gap between *The Hamlet* and *Go Down, Moses* is a year longer than that between *The Hamlet* and *If I Forget Thee, Jerusalem*, with which *The Hamlet* often groups. The fact that parts of *The Hamlet* were handwritten and parts were typed, however, suggests that a more careful analysis is required.

The composition and origin of the earlier materials incorporated into *The Hamlet* and *Go Down, Moses* also need to be clarified to allow this more careful analysis. First, *The Hamlet*. Faulkner's story "Barn Burning" (*Harper's*, 1939) originally seems to have begun the novel, and elements of that story are still to be found in 1.1, "Flem," but there is almost no textual correspondence between the story and the novel.[4] However, 1.2.2, closely corresponds to Faulkner's "Fool About a Horse (*Scribner's*, 1936). "Lizards in Jamshyd's Courtyard" (*The Saturday Evening Post*, 1932) is the basis of 1.3, but there is only a very minor textual correspondence between the chapter and the story. The second book, "Eula," does not seem to be based on any earlier material. In the third book, "The Long Summer," 3.1.2, is based on "The Afternoon of a Cow," which was written in 1937 but not published separately until after *The Hamlet* was published. This story, however, has "nothing textual in common" with the novel (Millgate 327). There is some

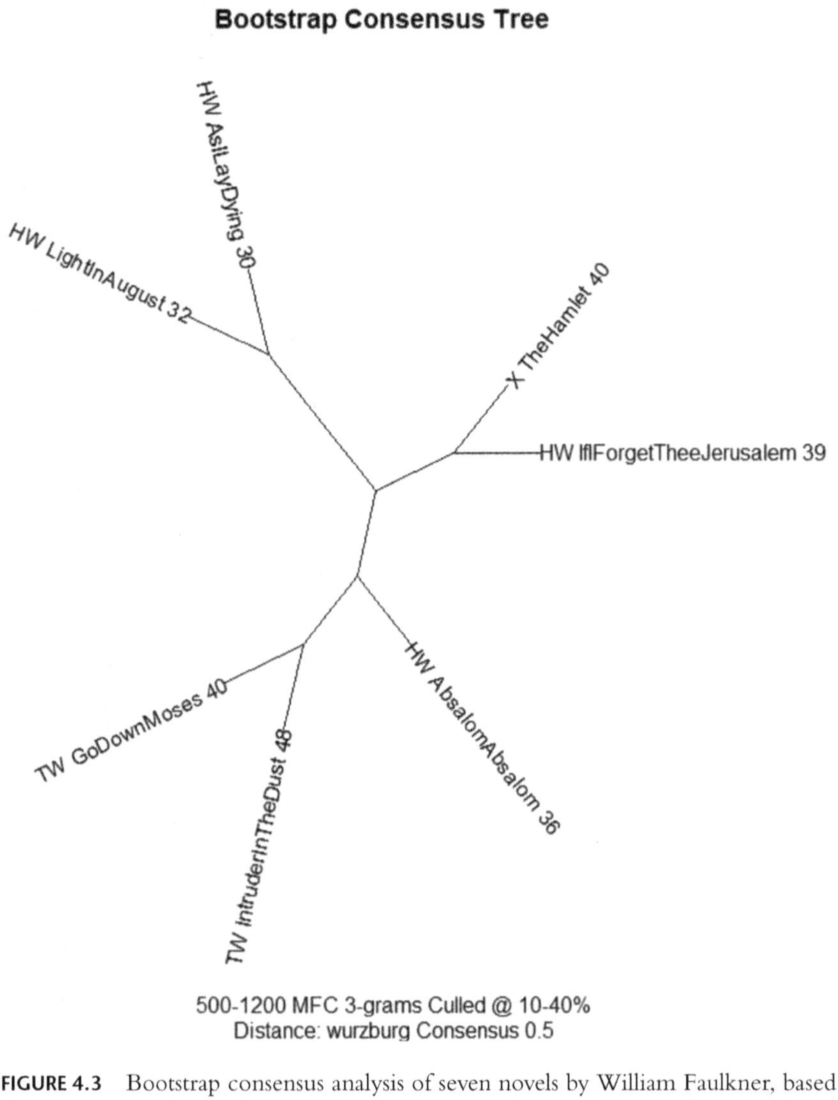

FIGURE 4.3 Bootstrap consensus analysis of seven novels by William Faulkner, based on the five hundred to twelve hundred most frequent character three-grams, culled at ten to forty percent, with Wurzburg Delta distance and a consensus of fifty percent

textual correspondence between "The Hound" (*Harper's*, 1931), a story of about fifty-four hundred words, and 3.2.2, but there are no more than a few hundred words of close parallel out of almost seventeen thousand. The manuscript ends at this point (Millgate 184), and there is no textual similarity between "The Hound" and the first typewritten section (the last section) of the third book (3.2.3). In the fourth book, much of 4.1.1 corresponds closely to "Spotted Horses" (*Scribner's*,

1931). As with 1.3, "Lizards in Jamshyd's Courtyard" (*The Saturday Evening Post*, 1932) is clearly the basis of 4.2, but close correspondence between the story and 4.2.1 amounts to only about one hundred words (out of more than ten thousand). Close correspondence between 4.2.2 and the story amounts to about 350 words (out of about 2,050). To prevent their earlier composition from artificially linking them with the earlier handwritten novels, I will either remove 1.2.2, 3.2.2, 4.1.1, and 4.2.2 from the analyses or analyze them separately.

For *Go Down, Moses*, the situation is simpler. The novel is divided into seven sections, as can be seen in Table 4.1. Most of the stories Faulkner combined into this novel had been written after he began typing his first drafts. The exceptions are the fourth section of the novel, "The Old People" (*Harper's*, 1940, but written in 1939), and "Lion" (*Harper's*, 1935), which was used as a basis for parts of "The Bear." Specifically, there is a close correspondence between the first section of "The Bear" (about six thousand words) and "Lion," consisting of perhaps a couple of hundred words. There is only a very small amount of correspondence, mainly consisting of isolated words or word pairs, between the second section (about fifty-five hundred words) and "Lion." The third section (about nine thousand words) shows a very substantial amount of textual correspondence with "Lion." Except for a few sporadic, isolated words, there is no correspondence between "Lion" and the fourth section (about eighteen thousand words), which Early describes as a "fresh creation of 1941" (40). Finally, there is some sporadic correspondence between the fifth section (about fifty-two hundred words) and "Lion," consisting of a couple of hundred words. The safest and most conservative course seems to be to eliminate "The Old People" and all but the fourth section of "The Bear" from the analysis (or analyze them separately), to avoid contaminating any possible effect of the change in mode of composition with a chronological effect.

Repeating the testing described earlier for the full seven novels, but with the early material that was included in *The Hamlet* and *Go Down, Moses* removed,

TABLE 4.1 Dates and origins of the seven sections of William Faulkner's *Go Down, Moses*

Sect. #	*Title*	*Date and Origin*
1	"Was"	An early version, "Almost," completed by 1 July 1940
2	"The Fire and the Hearth"	Three combined stories, completed by 3 February 1940
3	"Pantaloon in Black"	Sent to his agent March 1940
4	"The Old People"	Related to earlier hunting stories; sent to his agent in October 1939
5	"The Bear"	Completed in the last half of 1940? "Lion" (the earliest version) dates from 1935
6	"Delta Autumn"	Sent to his agent December 1940
7	"Go Down, Moses"	Sent to his agent July 1940

Source: Information about dates and origins from Blotner and Polk, *William Faulkner: Novels 1942–1954* 1106–7.

gives results in which the grouping of the three earliest novels is much less consistent. The later, typed, portion of *The Hamlet* quite consistently groups with the handwritten *If I Forget Thee, Jerusalem*. The later, typed portion of *Go Down, Moses* now groups quite consistently with the final, typed novel in this group, *Intruder in the Dust*. As before, there is no tendency for any consistent split between the handwritten and typed novels. A representative analysis is shown in Figure 4.4. Running the analysis again, but this time including only the early, handwritten

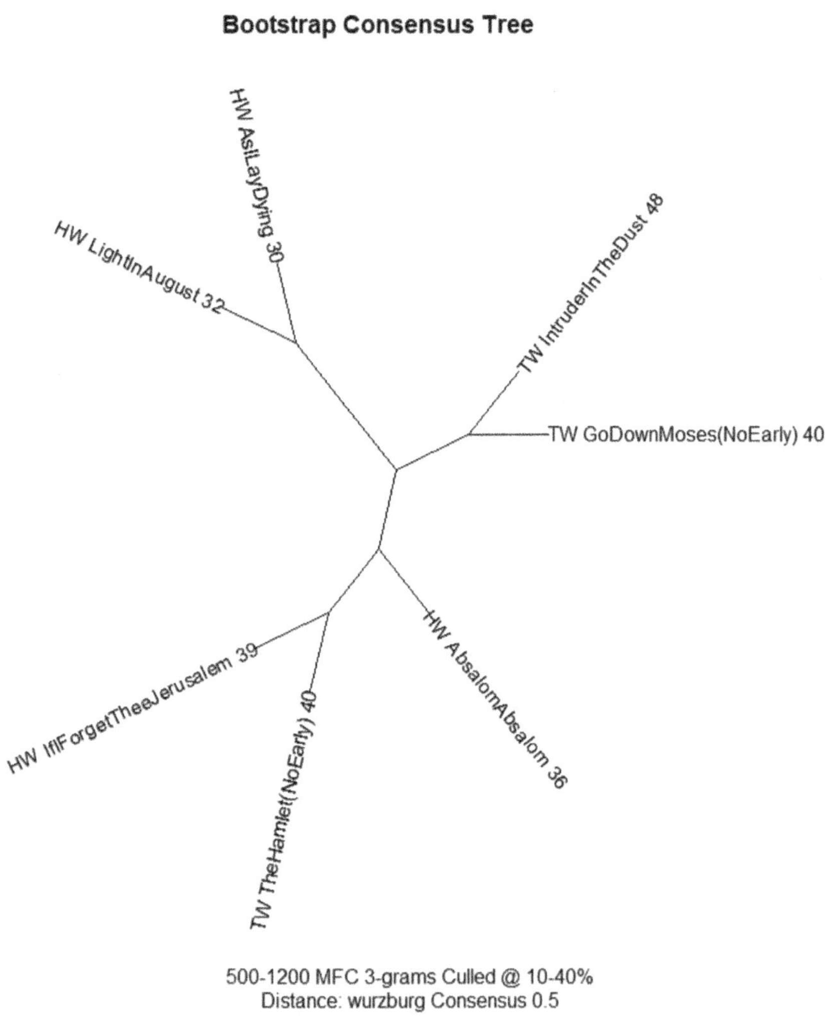

FIGURE 4.4 Bootstrap consensus analysis of seven novels by William Faulkner, with early material removed, based on the five hundred to twelve hundred most frequent character three-grams, culled at ten to forty percent, with Wurzburg Delta distance and a consensus of fifty percent

parts of *The Hamlet* and *Go Down, Moses*, gives much less consistent groupings overall but, curiously, shows a more consistent tendency for the three latest novels to group together. One of the most consistent groupings in these analyses is the handwritten parts of *The Hamlet* and the typed 1948 *Intruder in the Dust*. What remains constant throughout is that there is no hint of a separation by mode of composition.

Including both the handwritten and typed parts of *The Hamlet* and *Go Down, Moses* gives fairly chaotic results. The three earliest novels often group together, and the later, typed part of *Go Down, Moses* usually groups with the typed *Intruder in the Dust*. The typed part of *The Hamlet*, however, fairly consistently groups with the earlier, handwritten *If I Forget Thee, Jerusalem*. The fact that the handwritten and typed parts of *The Hamlet* and *Go Down, Moses* only rarely group together suggests that the early handwritten material incorporated into them is rather different from the later, typed material. The failure of any analysis to group the texts by mode of composition, however, suggests that any such differences are very unlikely to have been caused by Faulkner's composition directly at the typewriter.

The extensive analyses just described give no support to the idea that switching from handwriting to typing while writing *The Hamlet* caused any significant change in Faulkner's style. A series of cluster analyses of just this novel (in twenty-four sections of about four thousand words), with the parts based on or corresponding significantly to material written earlier removed, confirms this. Although the three sections composed directly on the typewriter consistently form a subgroup, that subgroup never shows any tendency to separate from the handwritten remainder of the novel. Instead, it groups loosely with a diverse cluster that includes sections from the beginning, middle, and end of the novel. Given that the typewritten sections are consecutive, it seems clear that they group together because of their place in the narrative, as do other contiguous sections, such as 15–17, 9–10, and 11–12. In a series of bootstrap consensus analyses, these three sections also typically form a subgroup, but again without any indication that they are distinct from all other sections, as would be expected if the change in mode of composition caused a distinct change in style.

Conclusion

The evidence strongly suggests that neither Booth Tarkington's change in mode of composition from handwriting to dictation nor William Faulkner's change from handwriting to typing materially affected their styles. Or, more precisely, multiple tests that have been shown to be sensitive to relatively subtle changes in style do not detect significant changes in the styles of these authors when they changed their modes of composition. Tarkington and Faulkner, for whom the change in mode was essentially permanent, thus join Hardy, Scott, and Conrad, who changed back and forth between handwriting and dictation in failing to provide significant evidence of an effect of change in mode of composition. The fact that these authors changed their mode of composition for reasons that vary from pain caused by illness, wrist pain, failing eyesight, time pressure, and convenience provides further evidence for the durability of authorial style.

Notes

1. I am grateful to Brianna Cregle, Special Collections Assistant, Public Services Division, Department of Rare Books and Special Collections, Princeton University Library, for checking the identity of the handwriting of some of the manuscripts.
2. The idea that the 1948 novel, *Intruder in the Dust*, was composed directly on the typewriter is supported by Samway, who gives an especially clear discussion of the fourth chapter of that novel (150–61). See also Blotner on Faulkner's typewritten first drafts (411).
3. For *Requiem for a Nun*, see Blotner et al. (vol. 19). For *A Fable*, see the introduction to Blotner et al. (vol. 20, part 1), which confirms the extreme complexity of the hundreds of pages of manuscript, typescript, and typescript with interlinear manuscript that make up the materials underlying the novel. Faulkner's almost unreadable handwriting greatly complicates any attempt to understand how the novel was composed.
4. Unless otherwise indicated, the information about the previously written parts of *The Hamlet* comes from Fargnoli et al. 117. The amount of textual overlap has been checked with *Juxta*.

References

Barron, Mark. "Tarkington Still Writes for Stage in Maine Retreat: Hoosier Author, Nearing 70, Busy Rewriting an Earlier Play." *The Washington Post*, 10 July 1938, p. TT2.

Biber, Douglas. *Variation Across Speech and Writing*. Cambridge UP, 1988, doi:10.1017/CBO9780511621024.

"Blindness Menaces Booth Tarkington: Is Writing Furiously to Finish Several Works, Author Refuses to Rest on Order of Eye Specialist." *Boston Daily Globe*, 27 Oct. 1927, p. 1.

Blotner, Joseph. *Faulkner: A Biography*. UP of Mississippi, 2005. muse.jhu.edu.

Blotner, Joseph, and Noel Polk, editors. *William Faulkner: Novels 1936–1940*. Library of America, 1990.

———. *William Faulkner: Novels 1942–1954*. Library of America, 1994.

Blotner, Joseph et al., editors. *William Faulkner Manuscripts*. 25 vols., Garland, 1986–87.

"Booth Tarkington Better: Author to Leave Johns Hopkins Hospital on Monday." *New York Times*, 6 Apr. 1930, p. 6.

"Booth Tarkington Cheered by First Eye Operation: Recovering from Operation." *New York Herald Tribune*, 29 Jan. 1929, p. 6.

Booth Tarkington Papers, 1812–1956. Manuscripts Division, Department of Rare Books and Special Collections, Princeton University Library.

"Booth Tarkington Still Writes at 71 Although Half Blind: Famous Indiana Author Painfully at Work on His Autobiography, Producing 1000 to 2000 Words Daily." *Los Angeles Times*, 16 Feb. 1941, p. 9.

Crane, Joan St. C. "Manuscript of *Mosquitoes* at Virginia." *Faulkner Newsletter and Yoknapatawpha Review*, vol. 8, no. 1, 1988, pp. 1, 3. egrove.olemiss.edu/cgi/viewcontent.cgi?article=1114&context=faulkner_nl.

Early, James. *The Making of Go Down, Moses*. Southern Methodist UP, 1972. archive.org/details/makingofgodownmo0000earl.

Eder, Maciej et al. "Stylometry With *R:* A Package for Computational Text Analysis." *R Journal*, vol. 8, no. 1, 2016, pp. 107–21. journal.r-project.org/archive/2016/RJ-2016-007/RJ-2016-007.pdf.

Fargnoli, A. Nicholas et al. *Critical Companion to William Faulkner*. Facts on File, 2008. books.google.com/books?id=dQca8cin24gC&q.

Faulkner, William. Local and UVA Communities, Tape 1, 30 May 1957. *Faulkner at Virginia*, created by Stephen Railton and Michael Plunkett. Rector and Visitors of the University of Virginia, 2010. faulkner.lib.virginia.edu/display/wfaudio18_1.html#wfaudio18_1.1.

Ford, Ford Madox. *It Was the Nightingale*. J. B. Lippincott Company, 1933. archive.org/details/itwasnightingale0000ford_p1m1.

Gottlieb, Robert. "The Rise and Fall of Booth Tarkington: How a Candidate for the Great American Novelist Dwindled into America's Most Distinguished Hack." *The Newyorker*. 4 Nov. 2019. www.newyorker.com/magazine/2019/11/11/the-rise-and-fall-of-booth-tarkington.

Hallet, Richard. "Booth Tarkington: At Sea at Home." *The Christian Science Monitor*, 20 Dec. 1941, p. WM7.

Hoover, David L. "Frequent Word Sequences and Statistical Stylistics." *Literary and Linguistic Computing*, vol. 17, no. 2, 2002, pp. 157–80, doi:10.1093/llc/17.2.157.

Juxta. Applied Research in Patacriticism, U of Virginia. www.juxtasoftware.org.

Karl, Frederick R. *William Faulkner, American Writer: A Biography*. Weidenfeld and Nicolson, 1989. archive.org/details/williamfaulknera0000karl.

Kibler, James E. Review of "The Making of *Sartoris:* A Description and Discussion of the Manuscript and Composite Typescript of William Faulkner's Third Novel" by Stephen Neal Dennis. *The Mississippi Quarterly*, vol. 24, no. 3, 1971, pp. 315–19.

———. "A Study of the Text of William Faulkner's *The Hamlet*." PhD dissertation, U of South Carolina, 1970.

Kunitz, Stanley. "Booth Tarkington." *Living Authors*. 1931. Edited by Dilly Tante, pseud. [Stanley Kunitz], H. W. Wilson, 1935, pp. 398–400. archive.org/details/in.ernet.dli.2015.260813.

MacDonald, A. B. "Tarkington, Nearly Blind. Hunts Whale: Doesn't Catch Creatures. Just Watches Them—Forbidden to Write, He Dictates Work." *The Hartford Courant*, 17 Sept. 1934, p. 15.

MacDougall, Sarah. "Authors Struggle to Get Down to Work: Homer Croy Takes off His Shoes, Will Irwin Starts at 5 A. M., Booth Tarkington Dons Bathrobe, Anne Parrish Seeks Garage." *The Hartford Courant*, 6 Feb. 1927, p. 5.

Mayberry, Susanah. *My Amiable Uncle: Recollections About Booth Tarkington*. Purdue UP, 1983. archive.org/details/myamiableunclere00mayb.

Mcdowell, Edwin. "Faulkner Manuscript Is Bought." *New York Times*, 10 Oct. 1987.

Meriwether, James B. *The Literary Career of William Faulkner: A Bibliographical Study*. Princeton University Library, 1961. archive.org/details/literarycar00meri.

Meriwether, James B., and Michael Millgate, editors. *Lion in the Garden: Interviews with William Faulkner 1926–1962*. U of Nebraska P, 1968. archive.org/details/lioningardeninte00meri.

Millgate, Michael. *The Achievement of William Faulkner*. U of Nebraska P, 1963. archive.org/details/achievementofwil0000mill_m1x2.

Minitab Release 19, Minitab, Inc., State College, PA, 2019.
Morehouse, Ward. "Tarkington Ill at Home: Noted Author Delayed From Leaving on Summer Trip to Maine Coast." *Los Angeles Times*, 30 May 1936, p. 10.
"Mrs. Tarkington Denies: Novelist's Wife Says He Is Not to Undergo Eye Operation Soon." *New York Times*, 13 Dec. 1928, p. 26.
Polk, Noel. *Children of the Dark House: Text and Context in Faulkner.* UP of Mississippi, 1998. archive.org/details/childrenofdarkho0000polk.
Russo, Dorothy Ritter, and Thelma L. Sullivan. *A Bibliography of Booth Tarkington: 1869–1946.* Indiana Historical Society, 1949. archive.org/details/biblibo00russ/.
Samway, Patrick H. S. J. *Faulkner's Intruder in the Dust: A Critical Study of the Typescripts.* Whitston Publishing Company, 1980. archive.org/details/faulknersintrude0000samw.
Tarkington, Booth. *Penrod Jashber.* Grosset and Dunlap, 1929. archive.org/details/penrodjashber00tark.
"Tarkington Blind; May Regain Sight: Writer, Who Will Be Operated On, Gets 'Thrill' Not Having to See Everything. Helps Him Concentrate He Did More Work in Year Than Ever Before, He Says—His Chief Interest Is Modern Woman." *New York Times*, 28 Mar. 1929, p. 29.
"Tarkington Is Gaining: Author Recovering After Third Eye Operation at Baltimore." *New York Times*, 21 Oct. 1930, p. 4.
William Faulkner: "Man Working," 1919–1962: A Catalogue of the William Faulkner Collections at the University of Virginia. Compiled by Linton R. Massey, and an introduction by John Cook Wyllie, UP of Virginia, 1968.
Woodress, James. *Booth Tarkington: Gentleman From Indiana.* J. B. Lippincott Company, 1954. archive.org/details/boothtarkingtong001459mbp.
———. "The Tarkington Papers." *The Princeton University Library Chronicle*, vol. 16, no. 2, 1955, pp. 45–53. www.jstor.org/stable/26402872.

5

CHANGING OVER FROM HANDWRITING OR TYPING TO WORD PROCESSING: ARTHUR CLARKE, OCTAVIA BUTLER, STANLEY ELKIN, AND IAN McEWAN

Introduction

Like Tarkington and Faulkner, the authors addressed in this chapter, Arthur C. Clarke (1917–2008), Octavia E. Butler (1947–2006), Stanley Elkin (1930–95), and Ian McEwan (1948–), changed their modes of composition more or less permanently. These writers, however, replaced their earlier modes with word processing rather than typing or dictation. For Clarke the change was from an electric typewriter, for Butler from a manual typewriter, and for Elkin and McEwan from handwriting. Clarke, Butler, and Elkin all switched to a word processor in the middle of a novel, but McEwan switched between novels. Testing for a change in Elkin and McEwan will, like the analyses of Tarkington and Faulkner, focus on a group of texts spanning the point of change. For Butler and Clarke, however, because of the nature of their careers and their works, the single novel in which they changed their modes of composition must be the focus of analysis, and it is with Clarke and Butler that I begin.

Arthur Clarke: Changing Over From an Electric Typewriter to a Word Processor

> The marvellous thing about Archie (Archives III, 5 megabytes Winchester disk, Wordstar program) is that he has totally eliminated the drudgery (mechanical, not mental!) from writing. I could no more imagine going back to a typewriter—I've not touched one since last year—than to a slide rule after using a pocket calculator (That's a pretty exact analogy.)
>
> *(McAleer 295)*

Arthur C. Clarke (1917–2008) is widely regarded as one of the most important science fiction authors of his time (along with Isaac Asimov and Robert Heinlein). In 1981, at the age of sixty-four, he began *2010: Odyssey Two* (1982), his sequel to the wildly successful *2001: A Space Odyssey* (1968). He had not planned to write a sequel, but his agent, Scott Meredith, persuaded him that his readers deserved to know what happens after the mysterious ending of *2001* (McAleer 292–4). He began writing the novel on his electric typewriter, which had been his normal mode of composition since at least the late 1960s, when he was working on *2001*. He had been typing his work on a manual typewriter since at least the late 1930s (McAleer 34, 194). By late 1981, he had about one hundred pages of "messy manuscript" completed, when he bought his first computer, an Archives III. He was an immediate convert:

> "As soon as I realized what word processing could do," Clarke says, "all writing came to an abrupt halt. I was in exactly the same position as an Egyptian scribe who had spent his life carving inscriptions on granite—and suddenly discovered ink and papyrus."
>
> *(McAleer 295)*

After paying to have his existing manuscript entered into the computer, he finished the last three-fourths of the novel at the computer (McAleer 295; Kirschenbaum 67). Clarke's delight in the way the computer eliminated the mechanical drudgery of writing, shown in the quotation at the beginning of this section, is remarkably similar to Tarkington's account of how dictation eliminated the "purely mechanical task of writing by hand" (MacDonald 15; see ch. 4), even though Clarke's change in mode of composition seems far less dramatic.

Although it would be preferable to test Clarke's writings over a several-year period that spans his change in mode, such an approach is not really legitimate. *2010: Odyssey Two* is a 1982 sequel to *2001*, which was published fourteen years earlier, and the next two parts of the series appeared in 1988 and 1997. The long time span and irregular spacing of the four parts make the series an unattractive focus for investigation. His sparse publishing record in the five years preceding and following 1982 and the fact that most of his books following *2010* were collaborations suggest that restricting the analysis to *2010* itself is the only valid option.

The possibility of a change in style caused by Clarke's change from electric typewriter to word processor can be tested first by dividing the novel into chapters, combined in pairs because they are quite short, ranging from about four hundred to thirty-four hundred words, with an average length of less than fourteen hundred words (in two cases, three very short chapters are combined). Initial cluster analyses of these chapter-blocks are quite chaotic; they show no evidence of a grouping of chapters from the first-fourth of the novel that was typed on the electric typewriter against the chapters from the last three-fourths that was typed on the word processor. (All cluster analyses in this chapter were performed in Minitab, with standardized variables, Ward linkage, and squared Euclidean distance.)

These blocks are not very consistent in length, however, ranging from about eighteen hundred to about five thousand words, so that a more evenly divided analysis seems appropriate. Dividing the novel into four equal parts of about nineteen thousand words each, and then dividing each fourth into three equal parts of about sixty-three hundred words, allows for a set of analyses that provide a fairer test for a word-processing effect. If Clarke's style was altered by his change in mode of composition, the first three sections, which were typed on an electric typewriter, should tend to form a separate group from the other nine word-processed sections. In addition, this division into twelve sections will allow for the possibility that the change in mode was either earlier or later than claimed. In dozens of analyses using Stylo's bootstrap consensus function (Eder et al. 113–15), however, there is no tendency of such a grouping by mode. These tests were based on various numbers of the most frequent words, word n-grams, and character n-grams, and using three different culling levels and eight different distance measures. (For an early argument for the effectiveness of the analysis of n-grams, there called "sequences," see Hoover, "Frequent Sequences"; all bootstrap consensus analyses in this chapter were performed in Stylo.)

Although there is some fairly consistent grouping of the first and second sections of the third quarter of the novel ("Three 1" and "Three 2") and the second and third sections of the fourth quarter, the three sections of the first quarter never form a group in any analysis. Indeed, it is very rare for even two sections of the first quarter to form a pair, as "One 2" and "One 3" do in Figure 5.1, and no analysis shows any tendency at all for the first quarter to group separately from the other three. The failure of these analyses to give any hint of a difference between the typed and word-processed parts of *2010* shows that, surprisingly or not, Clarke's change in mode of composition created no measurable difference in his style.

Octavia Butler: Changing Over From a Manual Typewriter to a Word Processor

> When she finally bought a computer after her mother's death in 1996, she created yet another hybrid journal/novel writing/note-taking system in place in addition to the notebooks she carried in her purse. (Her struggles learning to use WordPerfect and then with Microsoft Word are a topic for another day.)
>
> *(Ha)*

Octavia E. Butler (1947–2006) stands alone as the only prominent African American woman writing in the genres of science fiction and fantasy. Her often

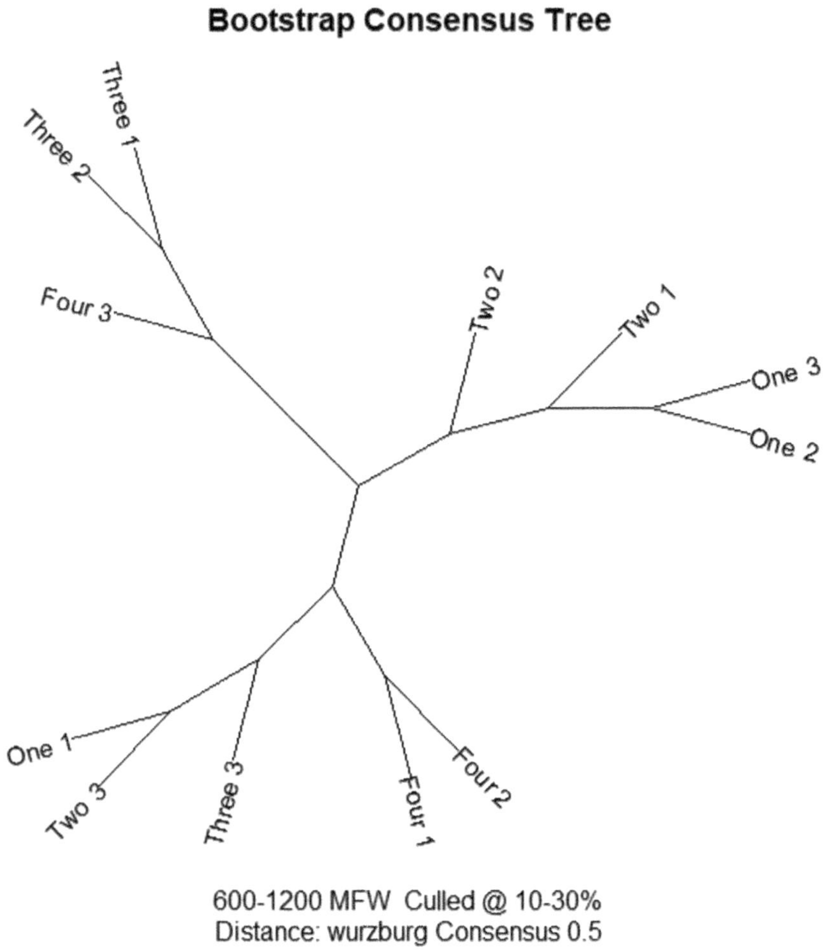

FIGURE 5.1 Bootstrap consensus analysis of three typewritten and nine word-processed sections of Arthur Clarke's *2010: Odyssey Two* in sections of sixty-three hundred words, based on the six hundred to twelve hundred most frequent words, culled at ten to thirty percent, with Wurzburg Delta distance and a consensus of fifty percent

disturbing and challenging novels and stories notably address questions of race, gender, feminism, class, and even human-alien sexual relationships. The first science fiction author to receive the prestigious MacArthur genius grant, she died relatively young, having published only twelve novels and two volumes of shorter works (one of them posthumous). Among other honors, she won two Nebula and two Hugo awards (Russell; Smith 389). During the writing of one of those

Nebula winners, *The Parable of the Talents* (1998), Butler changed her mode of composition from typing to word processing, and this section will explore the possibility that this change of mode affected her style.

As with Clarke, the shape of Butler's career makes a broad study inappropriate. Five of her twelve novels appear in her Patternmaster series, published in 1976, 1977, 1978, 1980, and 1984. Three more appear in her Xenogenesis series, published in 1987, 1988, and 1989, and *The Parable of the Talents* (1998) is the sequel to *The Parable of the Sower* (1993). Butler published only two standalone novels: *Kindred* (1979) and her last novel, *Fledgling* (2005). The absence of any group of novels surrounding the point at which she changed her mode of composition combined with the fact that all but two of the novels are parts of sequentially published series leave *The Parable of the Talents* as the only reasonable focus (see Calvin for an extensive bibliography of Butler's work and works about her).

Butler's main mode of composition from an early age was to type her work on a manual typewriter. As she recalls, "I pecked my stories out two-fingered on the Remington portable typewriter my mother had bought me. I had begged for it when I was 10, and she had bought it" (Butler 79). In 1997, an interview done during the writing of *The Parable of the Talents* reports that Butler has purchased a computer but that she is finishing the novel on a manual typewriter (Fry 58). However, as Kirschenbaum points out, the manuscript evidence suggests that the novel was actually completed on the computer (113–14, and 289–90n100). Fortunately, this claim can be examined more thoroughly by using the "Finding Aid" for the Octavia E. Butler Papers at the Huntington Library.

Butler left an enormous amount of written material to the Huntington Library: the material that is relevant here, labeled "manuscripts," alone fills more than two hundred boxes and dates from 1957 to 2006. Throughout this period there are autograph manuscripts and typescript manuscripts and, beginning in 1997, computer printouts. An exhaustive count of the materials of various kinds and in various modes is beyond the scope of this study, but a series of searches of years and types of material (notes, draft, fragment) through the more than five-hundred-page online "Finding Aid" of the Huntington collection (Russell) allows some secure generalizations about her writing process. Although the presence of large numbers of autograph materials shows that Butler clearly did not compose exclusively at the typewriter or computer, there is a strong tendency, throughout the collection, for the autograph materials to be "notes," "journal," or "fragments and notes," and for "drafts" to be typewritten manuscripts (1960 to 1996) or computer printouts (1997 to 2005).

The approximate place in the novel at which Butler changed her mode of composition can be determined by examining the nature of the very large amount of preliminary material for *The Parable of the Talents* in the collection. There are dozens of relatively short items labeled as "notes," "fragments and notes," or "fragment," dating mainly from 1996. Some of these are autograph manuscripts, but most of the items longer than a few pages are typewritten, and this is especially so for those labeled "fragment." The first items labeled as a "printout" also date from "ca. 1996," and the items labeled "fragments—drafts," also from ca. 1996, are all printouts. Among those labeled "partial draft," typically significantly longer than the ones previously mentioned and dating from late 1996, are typewritten drafts as long as 171 pages. Beginning early in 1997, "partial draft" printouts of more than 150 pages also appear, and all of the full drafts (nearly five hundred pages), all of which are from 1997, are printouts, as is the final draft sent to her publisher on 15 July 1998. About two hundred items of preliminary material exist for the unfinished "Parable of the Trickster," dating from 1998 and following. These are labeled "notes," "fragments," and "partial draft." Only about twenty-five of the two hundred are autograph, and only about five are typewritten; the rest are printouts. This presents a clear picture of an almost complete change in Butler's mode of composition in 1997, after writing about one-third of *The Parable of the Talents.*[1]

An initial set of cluster analyses of the novel in chapters, which range from about thirty-eight hundred to ninety-two hundred words long, shows some evidence of early chapters in one of the clusters, but no evidence of any sequence of early chapters alone grouping separately from the rest of the novel. Bootstrap consensus analysis confirms these findings. Dividing the novel into twenty-one sections of about sixty-three hundred words and doing dozens of analyses based on multiple numbers of the most frequent words, word n-grams, and character n-grams, multiple culling percentages, and eight different distance measures also shows no evidence of a stylistic shift caused by the change in mode. There is a good deal of grouping of early, middle, and late sections, but very little suggestion of a word processing effect. The most coherent clustering of sections based on narrative sequence is shown in Figure 5.2.

The ending groups nicely on the lower left of Figure 5.2, as does most of the middle on the center right. The grouping on the upper left suggestively contains the first five sections of the novel, yet it also contains the eighth and ninth sections but not the sixth and seventh, which group with the tenth section. The evidence of the manuscripts suggests that it is unlikely that Butler was still typing the eighth and ninth sections, and it must be emphasized that the pattern seen in Figure 5.2 is not a very common one. The great majority of analyses show much more chaotic groupings, though there is a fairly strong tendency for the final sections of the novel to group together. If Butler had switched to word processing after typing two-thirds of the novel rather than one-third, Figure 5.2 would provide evidence of a stylistic change caused by word processing. As it is, however, the only reasonable conclusion is that, as with Clarke, changing to word processing had no significant effect on Butler's style.

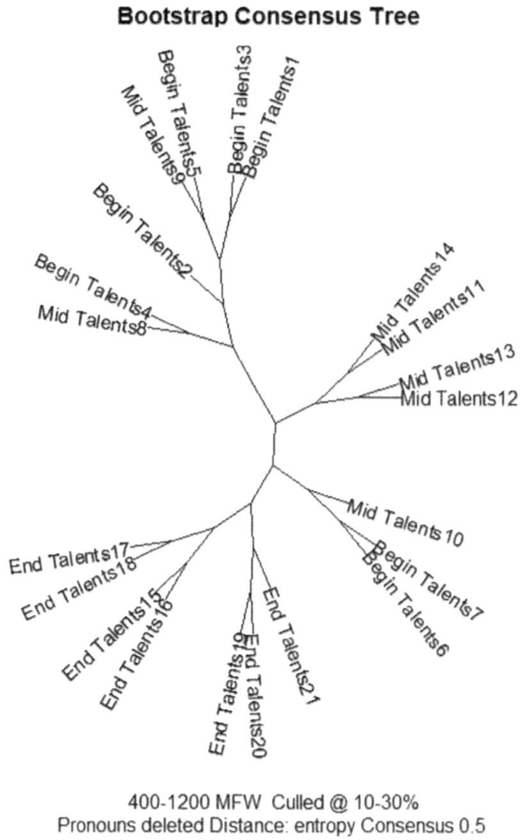

FIGURE 5.2 Bootstrap consensus analysis of sections of Octavia E. Butler's *The Parable of the Talents* in sections of sixty-three hundred words, based on the four hundred to twelve hundred most frequent words, with pronouns deleted, culled at ten to thirty percent, entropy distance, and a consensus of fifty percent

Stanley Elkin

> The word processor enables one to concentrate exponentially; you have absolute command of the entire novel all at once. You can go back and reference and change and fix and . . . so in a way, all novels written on the bubble machine ought to be perfect novels.
>
> *(Bailey 19)*

Stanley Elkin (1930–95) was highly regarded as a stylist and humorist and was a successful academic with a Ph.D. dissertation on William Faulkner and a long career of teaching at Washington University in St. Louis (Dougherty 4). Although his oeuvre is even smaller than Butler's (just ten novels and several collections of stories and essays), he won two National Book Critics Circle Awards for *George Mills* (1982) and for the posthumous *Mrs. Ted Bliss* (1995). He received nominations for the National Book Award in fiction for three other novels, *The Dick Gibson Show* (1971), *Searches and Seizures* (1973), and *The MacGuffin* (1991) (Tristman 36). (A series of articles in the summer 1995 issue of *Review of Contemporary Fiction* provides a good introduction to Elkin.) Much to his own disappointment, his recognized influence and importance among intellectuals and other writers never translated into a large readership, and he remains little-known and little-read today (Dougherty 1–3).

Elkin's importance for this study is the widely recognized fact that his *George Mills* "was one of the first novels by a 'serious' or 'literary' writer to have been composed in large measure on a word processor—an early CPU designed solely for word processing, in this case a Lexitron" (Dougherty 192). Elkin had been diagnosed with multiple sclerosis in 1972, and by 1979 his handwriting had deteriorated to an almost unreadable mass of "strong verticals and horizontals and acute angles" (Kirschenbaum 164). The key pressure required for typewriting was too agonizing. Fortunately, his dean found funds for a word processor, and he finished *George Mills* using it (Dougherty 192).

> When asked what was the most important event of his writing life, he replied "June 6, 1979, when my word processor was delivered. Not just any word processor, but a dedicated word processor. Not even just a dedicated word processor, finally, but a devoted one."
>
> *(Dougherty 192)*

As the quotation at the beginning of this section reveals, Elkin thought that using a word processor was especially important for plot rather than style, but his own perception that the word processor changed his writing suggests that his change in mode of composition may also have affected his style. This is especially true if, as Salztman suggests,

> [m]ost of Elkin's fiction is loosely episodic, as if to give the freest reign to the author's ingenuity on the levels of both occurrence and utterance. By Elkin's reckoning, form is rather intuitive: patterns are repeated from one episode to the next. . .; a sort of "rhyming" between episodes substitutes for conventional linear plot development. Sentence making is prior to structure.

Wilde's contention that Elkin displays "a bravura handling of language" (62), and that his "words so deliberately and relentlessly call attention to themselves" (63) also suggest that a stylistic analysis is appropriate.

Fortunately, the situation surrounding Elkin's change in mode of composition is fairly clear. He seems typically to have written the first drafts of his works by hand in university exam books from as early as 1964 until 1979, during the composition of *George Mills* (Dougherty 78, 143, 172, 192; Kirschenbaum 164). "The first several chapters [of that novel] were written in the famous university exam books and typed by someone else. But the final sections were composed and revised on the word processor; eleven 5¼ inch diskettes contain pages 260–466 of the printout" (Dougherty 192). Elkin continued to compose at the word processor for the rest of his career (Elkin). Analysis can thus proceed by examining the change in mode of composition that took place a little more than half way through *George Mills* (1982) and the two handwritten novels and a novella that preceded and the three word-processed novels that followed it: *The Dick Gibson Show* (1971), *The Franchiser* (1976), *The Living End* (1979), *The Magic Kingdom* (1985), *The Rabbi of Lud* (1987), and *The MacGuffin* (1991).

Preliminary cluster analyses of *George Mills* in eleven sections of about eighteen thousand words show no tendency of the novel to divide into halves. Sections 1, 3, and 8 consistently group together, sometimes also with 9 or with 9 and 10, but there is no hint of a word-processing effect somewhere near the middle of the novel. Analyzing the seven novels in sections of about twenty-five thousand words results in quite consistent clustering by novel, except for *The Dick Gibson Show* and *George Mills*. The sections of both of these novels typically form two separate groups. Ironically, however, it is *The Dick Gibson Show* that shows a consistent separation between sections 1–2 and sections 3–5. *George Mills* also shows a fairly clear separation, but with sections 1, 2, 3, 6, and 7 in one group and sections 4, 5, and 8 in the other (joined by section 3 in some analyses). Removing the earliest and latest novel and repeating this analysis gives very similar results. The crucial point here is that none of the analyses suggest a stylistic difference between sections composed in the two different modes. If Elkin's change in mode of composition altered his style, the handwritten novella and novels and the handwritten part of *George Mills* should be in one group and the word-processed half of *George Mills* and the later word-processed novels in the other. But this never happens.

George Mills is a notoriously digressive and various novel that tells part of the history of many generations of men named George Mills (for an interesting discussion of its structure and meaning, see Christensen 82–91). It begins in 1097 during the first crusade and recounts events from a George Mills in 1826, but about sixty percent of the novel deals with a George Mills of 1982, although there is a long flashback to a decade or so earlier (Dougherty 185–6). The five parts and twenty-three chapters of the novel vary widely in length. Even combining some chapters (always from the same part) into sections and extracting a very long letter from a very long chapter leaves sections varying from about 12,500 to 28,500 words. However, cluster analyses of these sections give results that generally agree with the analysis by sections of eighteen thousand words: no analysis shows a division of early versus late sections.

Dividing these sections into more nearly equal smaller sections of about sixty-two hundred to eighty-five hundred words and running dozens of Stylo bootstrap consensus analyses based on multiple numbers of the most frequent words, word n-grams, and character n-grams, multiple culling percentages, and eight different distance measures also show no evidence of a stylistic shift caused by the change in mode. The most consistent grouping found is shown in Figure 5.3. Although there is a group of seven early sections on the upper left, the other six early sections group with late sections (upper right), middle and late sections (lower

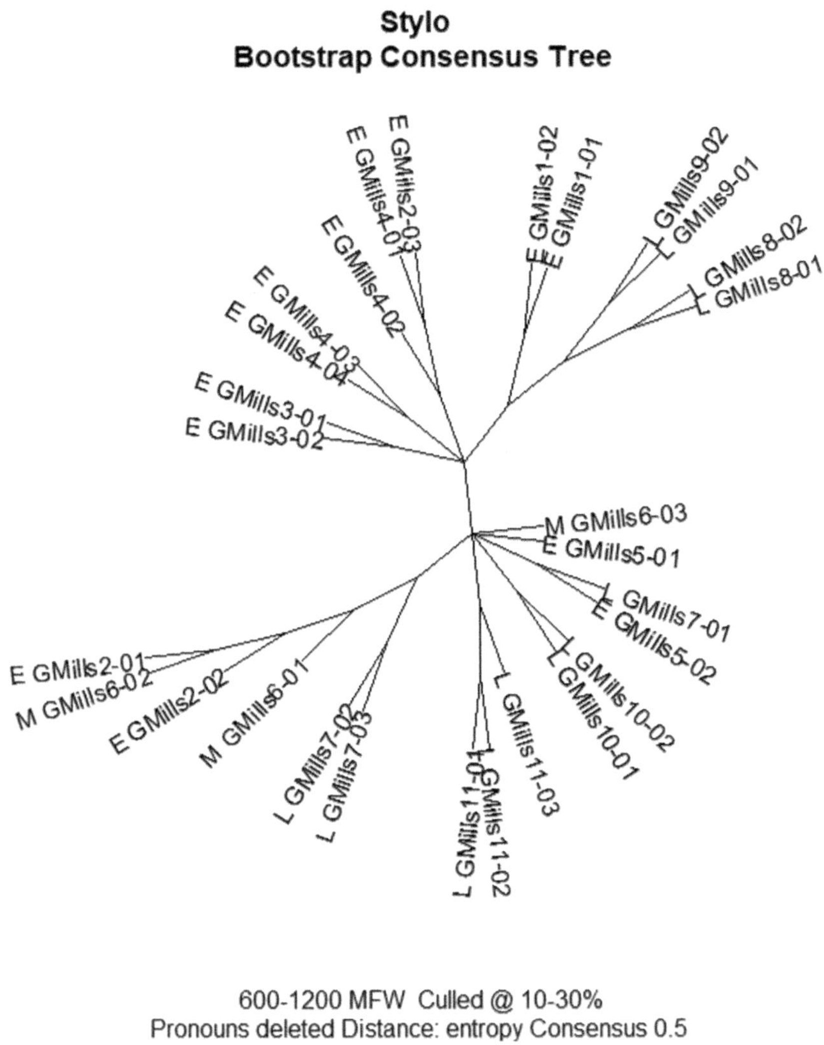

FIGURE 5.3 Bootstrap consensus analysis of Stanley Elkin's *George Mills* in sections of sixty-two to eighty-five hundred words, based on the six hundred to twelve hundred most frequent words, with pronouns deleted, culled at ten to thirty percent, entropy distance, and a consensus of fifty percent

left), or not at all, and it must be emphasized that this grouping is extremely rare among the dozens of analyses. Indeed, most analyses show very chaotic patterns in which early, middle, and late sections mix thoroughly.

Finally, testing *George Mills* in sections of about twenty thousand words with Stylo's classify function (Eder et al. 115–17) seems at first to suggest a word-processing effect. In these tests, the first six sections are assumed to be handwritten and the final four to be word processed, and these ten sections are tested against the preceding handwritten novel and novella and the following two word-processed novels: *The Franchiser* (1976), *The Living End* (1979), *The Magic Kingdom* (1985), and *The Rabbi of Lud* (1987). In most of these analyses the early and late sections of *George Mills* are classified as handwritten and word processed about forty to sixty-six percent of the time. A few analyses reach an accuracy of seventy to eighty percent, however. Although this might seem suggestive of a word-processing effect, further reflection suggests that even these relatively weak classification successes are far more likely to be a result of chronology than mode of composition. Although *George Mills* was published in 1982, Elkin had apparently been working on it since about 1975 (Dougherty 182–3, 189) and had finished about sixty percent of it by handwriting by 1979, when he got his word processor. Thus the beginning of *George Mills* may be similar to the two previous works, the novel *The Franchiser* (1976) and the novella *The Living End* (1979), especially the former, because of the date of composition. The same is true for the similarity of the end of *George Mills* and *The Magic Kingdom* (1985) and *The Rabbi of Lud* (1987). This becomes even more likely when *George Mills* is tested against just the preceding and following novels, when the accuracy of classification is almost never as high as fifty percent.

Although the complex structure and digressive nature of *George Mills* may be masking a word-processing effect, the fact that it might be masked also suggests that it cannot be very significant, and Stanley Elkin can join our other examples of writers whose change in mode of composition cannot be shown to have had any significant effect on their styles.

Ian McEwan

> Well, everything's changed a great deal with word processing. *The Child in Time* was the first novel I ever wrote on a word processor. Before that I was never quite settled on a way of doing drafts. *The Comfort of Strangers* was written in long-hand and sent out to be typed. I found that to be very unsatisfactory. *The Cement Garden* I wrote in longhand and typed up myself—slightly less unsatisfactory, but typewriters I found were a real problem: a machine seemed very much to interpose in the immediacy of writing by hand.
>
> *(Reynolds and Noakes 14)*

Unlike Stanley Elkin, Ian McEwan (1948–) has been very successful commercially. Several of his novels have been best sellers, and more than ten of his books (novels and a short story collection) have been made into movies. While commenting on the "problems" this popularity has caused him, John Sutherland opines:

> He's too popular, obviously; and too rich, too succinct, too soft. We should celebrate "Atonement", yet we do not. What, for the love of Keira, has Ian McEwan done to deserve us? If literature had its gold medals, Ian McEwan would be on the podium at Parnassus, festooned with them—he's the Mark Spitz of novelists. His latest novel, *On Chesil Beach*, has been in the best-seller list since publication: jostling shoulders with Danielle Steel.
>
> *(Sutherland)*

McEwan has also won the 1998 Man Booker prize (for *Atonement*) and has been named as one of the fifty greatest British writers since 1945 (Hosking and Wighton), although some critics find his fiction disappointing and suggest that his novels are more like stretched short stories (Schmidt 1040–1).

Also unlike Elkin, McEwan has a substantial body of work, with fifteen novels and three collections of short stories to his credit, though the investigation into a possible change in style caused by his change from handwriting to word processing will not address all of these. McEwan wrote his works by hand before composing *The Child in Time* (1987) and his following work on a computer. In this, he and Elkin are alike. In addition to his comments on the significance of word processing quoted at the beginning of this section, McEwan has also said in his Art of Fiction interview that

> Word processing is more intimate, more like thinking itself. In retrospect, the typewriter seems a gross mechanical obstruction. I like the provisional nature of unprinted material held in the computer's memory—like an unspoken thought. I like the way sentences or passages can be endlessly reworked, and the way this faithful machine remembers all your little jottings and messages to yourself. Until, of course, it sulks and crashes.
>
> *("Ian Mc Ewan")*

The Harry Ransom Center at the University of Texas is home to the Ian McEwan Papers, a very large collection of drafts of his work, notebooks, correspondence, and family papers. Although the finding aid does not distinguish between typewritten manuscript and printouts from word-processed files, it does support the idea of a relatively permanent transition from handwritten to word-processed first drafts beginning with *The Child in Time*.

The fact that McEwan's first novel, *The Cement Garden*, was published in 1978, just nine years before his change in mode of composition, suggests that any analysis should be limited to novels from 1978 to the 1997 *Enduring Love*. It has been suggested, however, that after the very dark and macabre tone of his early short stories and his first two novels,

> He varied his palette from all black and grey, adding other shades. In *The Child in Time* (1987) and *The Innocent* [1990] the moral world is the same but there is more resistance. *Black Dogs* (1992) marks the end of the initial phase in his work. When, five years later, he is back in action with *Enduring Love* (1997), he has become more conventional in plot and theme, an adjustment the critics welcomed.
>
> *(Schmidt 1041)*

These considerations suggest that the analysis should be limited to McEwan's first five novels: *The Cement Garden* (1978), *The Comfort of Strangers* (1981), *The Child in Time* (1987), *The Innocent* (1990), and *Black Dogs* (1992). This selection includes the two novels preceding the change in mode, the first word-processed novel, and the two novels following the change in mode.

Preliminary cluster analysis of these five novels in sections of about eleven thousand words is compatible with a change in style caused by the change from handwriting to word processing: in analyses based on the two hundred to the one thousand most frequent words, the sections of the two earliest handwritten novels invariably form a separate cluster from the later word-processed novels. Curiously, the sections of these two earliest novels also invariably cluster by novel, while all analyses show some intermingling of sections of the three later word-processed novels. Increasing the length of the sections to about twenty thousand words improves the clustering by novel and confirms the distinction between the two handwritten and the three word-processed novels. Given the range in the sizes of these novels, an analysis based on about thirty-six thousand words of each (taken at random) in sections of about nine thousand words seems appropriate. (See Hoover, "Microanalysis" for a discussion of the use of equal amounts of text taken at random from the texts to be analyzed.) This analysis gives completely consistent results based on the one hundred to one thousand most frequent words. In all analyses all sections of each novel cluster together and the two handwritten novels always appear in one cluster and the word-processed novels in the other.

As I have noted, these results are compatible with a stylistic change caused by a change in mode of composition, but they are also compatible with the kind of simple chronological change that is often seen in the career of writers whose mode of composition never changed. Note the six-year gap between the last handwritten novel, *The Comfort of Strangers*, and the first word-processed novel, *The Child in Time*. Note also that the two handwritten novels were written within a three-year time span and that the three word-processed novels were written within a five-year time span. Both spans are shorter than the gap between the last handwritten and the first word-processed novel. Another curious fact is that, among the word-processed novels, the first and last, *The Child in Time* and *Black Dogs*, most often group together before being joined by the middle one, *The Innocent*. This is especially puzzling because *The Innocent* and *Black Dogs* are both set in Berlin. If the change in mode of composition were responsible for the distinction between first two and the next three novels, one would expect either a substantial initial change followed by a reduction in effect or an increasing effect over time, rather than an oscillation.

Given these inconclusive findings, a look at the characteristic vocabulary of the earlier handwritten and the later word-processed novels may provide further insights. The characteristic vocabulary of the two sets of novels can be identified by using wide spectrum analysis (Hoover, "Text Analysis"). Initial testing shows that a large number of the words heavily used by one set and avoided by the other are proper nouns. However, even after deleting these words, wide spectrum analysis shows that the two sets of novels are as distinct some pairs of authors. When I collected the one hundred most distinctively distributed words for both groups, I noticed that past tense verbs and concrete nouns seemed prevalent in the handwritten novels and relatively rarer in the word-processed novels. The two lists below record the results of a more careful examination of the words that are characteristic of the two sets. In the lists, the past tense verbs are in bold type, the concrete nouns are in italics, and the abstract nouns are underlined.[2]

The one hundred most distinctive words of McEwan's two handwritten novels:

> **laughed**, till, *shoulder*, **lay**, round, **watched**, **ran**, suddenly, *legs*, **stared**, **nodded**, upstairs, *cellar*, *bedroom*, large, several, **turned**, **leaned**, *bed*, **smiled**, *hair*, outside, **rested**, *mother*, small, **picked**, **covered**, *mirror*, pale, *sisters*, very, *balcony*, **cried**, carefully, herself, *stairs*, us, **sat**, great, **folded**, **closed**, *table*, **appeared**, **pulled**, *sister*, *garden*, **moved**, oh, *clothes*, **played,** *finger*, *lips*, **whispered**, bright, **spoke**, *arms*, **called**, loudly, *voice*, asleep, **looked**, hold, *wrist*, **noticed**, **caught**, *arm*, *tower*, we, sitting, bottom, *door*, **tried**, *mum*, **finished**, **repeated**, briefly, loud, my, long, **locked**, **held**, slowly, blue, between, *father*, *brother*, **died**, *neck*, staring, **remained**, quickly, *cement*, **arranged**, **placed**, *smile*, **became**, <u>sound</u>, *mother's*, *plastic*, *school*, few

The one hundred most distinctive words of McEwan's three word-processed novels:

> <u>life</u>, <u>work</u>, <u>place</u>, young, new, himself, until, <u>years</u>, these, <u>thing</u>, *station*, *beer*, *tunnel*, can, <u>love</u>, **found**, *woman*, <u>thoughts</u>, thinking, *phone*, <u>government</u>, beginning, right, set, should, form, *man*, enough, might, <u>case</u>, twenty, happy, its, *road*, their, <u>war</u>, *army*, **knew**, taken, **arrived**, being, *field*, high, *building*, do, public, <u>matter</u>, *tree*, think, three, shaking, cold, among, within, <u>year</u>, any, *village*, *warehouse*, ten, has, <u>sense</u>, *world*, else, hundred, *seat*, <u>party</u>,

> *man's*, security, *coffee*, sector, give, **worked**, *apartment*, working, *train*, growing, whose, **needed**, good, however, bring, *traffic*, days, *equipment*, drunk, military, evidence, chance, physical, *office*, truth, true, **prepared**, far, *police*, speak, never, *home*, surely, spirit, six

The one hundred words most characteristic of handwritten novels include thirty-six past tense verbs, thirty-two concrete nouns, and just one abstract noun, while the one hundred words most characteristic of the word-processed novels include only three past tense verbs, but twenty-one abstract nouns and twenty-four concrete nouns. The concrete/abstract distinction is confirmed by the fact that the average concreteness score is 3.67 for the five hundred most distinctive words of the handwritten novels and only 3.12 for the five hundred most distinctive words of the word-processed novels. The presence of "till" as a characteristic handwritten word and "until" as a characteristic word-processed word in these lists is noteworthy as well, as this contrast is found frequently as a strong marker of authorship. It is odd, then, to see these words as characteristic of two periods in a single author's work.

There is thus no doubt that McEwan's style shifted rather dramatically between 1981 and 1987, but the kinds of differences just noted do not seem intuitively likely to be related to a change in mode of composition. Why would word processing cause an increase in abstract nouns, a decrease in concrete nouns and past tense verbs, and an overall decrease in concreteness? McEwan's comments on his own style add an intriguing dimension to this question:

> This [*The Cement Garden*] and my next novel, *The Comfort of Strangers*, brought to an end a ten-year stretch of writing—formally simple and linear short fiction, claustrophobic, desocialized, sexually strange, dark. After that I felt I had written myself into too tight a corner. I turned away from fiction for a while. I wrote a television film set against the code-breaking operation at *Bletchley Park* during the war. Then *The Ploughman's Lunch*, and an oratorio for *Michael Berkley*. By the time I set out on a new novel in 1983, *The Child in Time* [published in 1987], I was thinking in terms of precise physical locations, and times—even time itself—and of social texture and a degree of formal ambition.
>
> *(McEwan)*

Authors' comments about their own writing are not notably accurate, and McEwan's claim to have turned to "precise physical locations, and times" and "social texture" does not square particularly well with the decrease in concreteness seen in his later novels. His claim that his work changed direction after *The Comfort of Strangers* in 1981, however, does square with Schmidt's comment (quoted earlier) that his palette changed after 1981. The "Biographical Sketch" in the finding aid for the Ian McEwan papers at the Harry Ransom Center concurs about the place of change and notes that the first word-processed novel, *The Child in Time*, "marked a shift in the content of his novels, focusing less on individual morality and more on societal morality and social responsibility" (3).

The likelihood that the handwritten and word-processed novels may differ because of a change in subject matter, themes, and tone suggests one more kind of analysis: topic modeling. As noted in Chapter 2, topic modeling is a method of analysis that focuses on words that occur near each other more frequently than they would be expected to by chance. One of the outputs of a topic model is a set of lists of words in order of decreasing significance in each of a series of topics (the most frequent words, nearly all function words, are omitted as nontopical). These "topics" are not necessarily similar to what a reader might describe as the topics of the text, but many of them are readily interpretable by humans, and typically many of them seem intuitively appropriate for the text.

For my McEwan topic model, I broke the five novels to be analyzed into sections of about three thousand words (topic models seem to work best on sections of texts) and used Mallet to create thirty topics. It was immediately apparent that, as usually happens, character names are skewing the topics. After all, the character names in a novel tend to appear closer to many words than they would by chance. When I added the character names to the list of stop words for Mallet to ignore, the resulting model was quite interesting. About half of the topics were almost completely limited to a single novel. This is another indication of the textual coherence that typically makes sections of individual texts group together in analyses of multiple sections of multiple texts. The three topics with the most weight in these five novels are as follows (topics are numbered from 0 to 29; the weights of the topics, though not readily interpretable, are also given to show their relative strengths):

Topic 21: A generic topic, with a weight of 2.7, fairly strong in all texts, but decreasing in strength chronologically:

The thirty words with the greatest weight in topic 21 (note the heavy emphasis on body parts and physical objects and actions):

> *back, hand, head, door, hands, face, looked, room, eyes, stood, table, round, sat, put, turned, time, long, voice, light, floor, arm, side, spoke, bed, held, sound, arms, made, shoulder, open, nodded, small, air, chair, moved, standing, closed, watched, deep, hair, pushed, pulled, close, began, glass, kitchen, window, shook, ran, legs*

Topic 27: A generic topic, with a weight of 2.67, fairly strong in all texts, but increasing in strength chronologically:

The thirty words with the greatest weight in topic 27 (time seems an important aspect of this topic, along with speech and mental acts):

> *time, thought, wanted, it's, back, day, made, knew, make, i'm, felt, end, man, home, good, people, told, place, found, talk, work, thing, mind, years, hour, that's,*

find, talking, room, left, remember, began, kind, i've, feel, started, you're, point, things, speak, evening, days, free, coming, question, past, times, silence, gave, house

Topic 29: A generic topic, with a weight of 1.82, moderately strong in all texts, though significantly weaker than 21 and 27:

The thirty words with the greatest weight in topic 29 (here, walking seems central):

> *set, feet, front, man, wall, black, stopped, walked, passed, street, men, left, morning, side, water, high, clear, stood, raised, walk, line, brought, returned, road, red, appeared, space, empty, hand, stepped, full, top, walking, arrived, young, dark, turning, moment, ten, place, paper, thick, direction, flat, night, crossed, afternoon, windows, read, making*

These three topics are thus characteristic of all five novels, with the first two showing reverse chronological trends and the third showing a fairly steady use throughout all five. As can be seen in Figure 5.4, topic 21 seems especially characteristic of the two handwritten novels, and topic 27 especially uncharacteristic of them, except for a single spike near the end of *The Comfort of Strangers*.

The two next heaviest topics are these:

Topic 4: *The Child in Time*, *Black Dogs*, *The Innocent*, with a weight of 0.59, (descending strength):

The thirty words with the greatest weight in topic 4 (children and the family seem especially important):

> *long, life, made, parents, years, child, love, children, young, set, girl, friends, early, days, year, sense, months, word, summer, return, wife, feelings, growing, country, existence, presence, world, lost, speech, lives, account, personal, surely, spirit, terms, daughter, familiar, marriage, news, purpose, members, steady, press, language, subject, effect, evenings, social, official, intimacy*

Topic 20: *The Child in Time*, *Black Dogs*, *The Innocent*, with a weight of 0.23 (descending strength):

The thirty words with the greatest weight in topic 20 (this seems primarily a country topic):

> *trees, ground, tree, wood, path, platform, track, ahead, station, weeks, field, foot, miles, town, giant, brilliant, clearing, handle, grass, orange, climb, rock, climbed, inches, mile, swung, wild, deeper, dared, dried, countryside, nail, humour, tunnel, hundred, decided, build, thought, forgive, smiling, gate, rising, hearing, trunk, branch, underfoot, confident, posted, shrunk, branches*

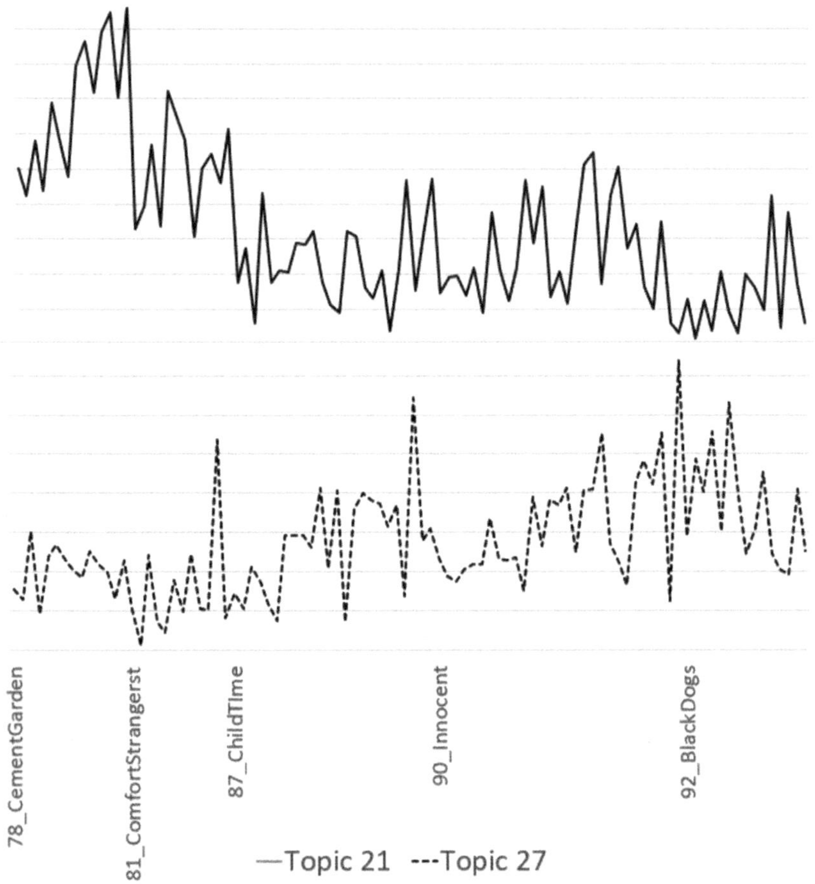

FIGURE 5.4 The weights of topics twenty-one and twenty-seven from a thirty-topic model in successive sections of five novels by Ian McEwan

Note that these two topics have substantial weight only in word-processed texts, and this is also true of seven of the remaining ten topics. Curiously, none of the topics have substantial weight only in the two handwritten novels, though, as shown in Figure 5.4, there is a fairly sharp decrease in the weight of topic 21 and a fairly sharp increase in the weight of topic 27 following the two handwritten novels. The two handwritten novels also score very low on topics 4 and 20.

The remaining topics with a weight of at least 0.07 that are not limited to a single text are shown in Table 5.1. These results seem to weaken further the case for a change in style caused by a change in mode of composition. The topic model shows a strong distinction between the handwritten and word-processed novels, but the distinction is more semantic than stylistic. Given all these considerations, it seems possible, but quite unlikely, that the differences between

TABLE 5.1 Topics not limited to one text (minimum weight: 0.07) in five novels by Ian McEwan

Topic #	*Texts in Which the Topic Is Heaviest (Descending Weight Order)*	*Weight*
2	*The Comfort of Strangers, The Child in Time, Black Dogs, The Innocent*	0.12
3	*The Innocent, Black Dogs* (minor in the latter)	0.14
6	*The Innocent, The Child in Time* (minor in the latter)	0.19
7	*The Child in Time, Black Dogs*	0.08
11	*Black Dogs, The Innocent, The Child in Time*	0.07
12	*Black Dogs, The Innocent, The Child in Time, The Comfort of Strangers*	0.18
18	*The Innocent, The Child in Time, The Comfort of Strangers, The Cement Garden, Black Dogs* (the last two minor)	0.15
22	*The Child in Time, The Innocent, Black Dogs*	0.10
25	*The Child in Time, The Innocent* (minor in the latter)	0.10
26	*The Innocent, The Child in Time, Black Dogs*	0.11

McEwan's handwritten and word-processed novels were caused by a change in mode of composition.

Conclusion

The four authors addressed in this chapter all made essentially complete changes in mode of composition, and all changed to word processing. Arthur Clarke and Octavia Butler abandoned typewriters (electric and manual, respectively) for word processors, while Stanley Elkin and Ian McEwan made the transition to word processing from handwriting. Although Clarke began composing on a word processor about one-fourth of the way through *2010: Odyssey Two*, multiple analyses give no hint of a difference between the typed and word-processed parts: Clarke's change in mode of composition created no measurable difference in his style. Similarly, Butler switched to a word processor after typing about a third of *The Parable of the Talents*, but it is the final third of the novel, rather than the first, that shows a significant difference in style from the rest of the novel. The only reasonable conclusion is that, as with Clarke, changing to a word processor did not significantly affect her style. For Elkin, the complex structure and digressive nature of *George Mills*, the novel in which he began using a word processor, make it possible that other kinds of style variation may be masking a minor word-processing effect, but the fact that it might be masked also suggests that it cannot be very significant. At the least, his change in mode of composition cannot be shown to have had any important effect on his style. Finally, although a marked difference exists between McEwan's handwritten and word-processed novels, that difference seems more semantic than stylistic. This fact, along with the presence of a long chronological gap between the novels in the two modes and some puzzling oddities in the similarities and differences among the novels, leaves McEwan as, at best, an equivocal case of a change in style caused by a change in mode of composition.

Notes

1. Canavan makes much of the false starts seen in the materials for the unfinished *The Parable of the Trickster*, but the preliminary material that exits for *The Parable of the Talents* is also voluminous and chaotic. The use of the computer is confirmed for late in Butler's career in an interview from 2004, in which her use of the computer for her writing is described as "almost-mandatory" (Govan and Butler 16).
2. Some of the word forms could represent more than one part of speech, so that the analysis cannot be considered definitive. The abstract/concrete indications are based on a set of about forty thousand words tested for human perceptions of concreteness (Brysbaert et al.). Based on my own sense of the boundary between concrete and abstract, I have labeled those words with scores of four or above as concrete, and those with scores below four as abstract. Both lists are scored in the same way, so that my somewhat arbitrary decision will affect the two lists in the same way.

References

Bailey, Peter J. "'A Hat Where There Never Was a Hat': Stanley Elkin's Fifteenth Interview." *Review of Contemporary Fiction*, vol. 15, no. 2, 1995, pp. 15–26.

Brysbaert, Marc et al. "Concreteness Ratings for 40 Thousand Generally Known English Word Lemmas." *Behavior Research Methods*, vol. 46, no. 3, 2014, pp. 904–11, doi:10.3758/s13428-013-0403-5.

Butler, Octavia E. "Birth of a Writer." *Essence*, vol. 20, no. 1, 1989, p. 74+.

Calvin, Ritch. "An Octavia E. Butler Bibliography (1976–2008)." *Utopian Studies*, vol. 19, no. 3, Octavia Butler Special Issue, 2008, pp. 485–516. www.jstor.org/stable/20719922.

Canavan, Gerry. "'There's Nothing New/Under The Sun,/But There Are New Suns': Recovering Octavia E. Butler's Lost Parables." *Los Angeles Review of Books*, 9 June 2014. lareviewofbooks.org/article/theres-nothing-new-sun-new-suns-recovering-octavia-e-butlers-lost-parables.

Christensen, Peter G. "The Escape From the Curse of History in Stanley Elkin's *George Mills*." *Review of Contemporary Fiction*, vol. 15, no. 2, 1995, pp. 79–91.

Dougherty, David C. *Shouting Down the Silence: A Biography of Stanley Elkin*. U of Illinois P, 2010. muse.jhu.edu/book/18460.

Eder, Maciej et al. "Stylometry with *R*: A Package for Computational Text Analysis." *R Journal*, vol. 8, no. 1, 2016, pp. 107–21. journal.r-project.org/archive/2016/RJ-2016-007/RJ-2016–007.pdf.

Elkin, Stanley. *Stanley Elkin Papers (MSS039), 1943–2013*. Washington University Libraries, Department of Special Collections, 2013. archon.wulib.wustl.edu/index.php?p=collections/findingaid&id=654&q=elkin&rootcontentid=1139248.

Fry, Joan. "'Congratulations! You've Just Won $295,000': An Interview With Octavia E. Butler." *Poets and Writers*, vol. 25, no. 2, 1 Mar. 1997, pp. 58–69. www.joanfry.com/congratulations-youve-just-won-295000.

Govan, Sandra Y., and Octavia E. Butler. "Going to See the Woman: A Visit With Octavia E. Butler." *Obsidian III*, vol. 6, no. 2; vol. 7, no. 1, 2005–06, pp. 14–39. www.jstor.org/stable/44511659.

Ha, Vi. LAPL BLOG: On Persistence: Octavia E. Butler and Central, Octavia Lab, Tuesday, 11 June 2019. www.lapl.org/collections-resources/blogs/lapl/persistence-octavia-e-butler-central-library.

Hoover, David L. "Frequent Word Sequences and Statistical Stylistics." *Literary and Linguistic Computing*, vol. 17, no. 2, 2002, pp. 157–80, doi:10.1093/llc/17.2.157.

———. "The Microanalysis of Style Variation." *Digital Scholarship in the Humanities*, vol. 32, suppl. 2, 2017, pp. ii17–ii30, doi:10.1093/llc/fqx022.

———. "Text Analysis." *Literary Studies in the Digital Age: An Evolving Anthology*, edited by Ken Price and Ray Siemens, MLA, 2013. dlsanthology.mla.hcommons.org/textual-analysis.

Hosking, Patrick, and David Wighton. "The 50 Greatest British Writers Since 1945." *The Times* [London], 5 Jan. 2008. www.thetimes.co.uk/article/the-50-greatest-british-writers-since-1945-ws3g69xrf90.

Ian McEwan Papers. Harry Ransom Center, the University of Texas at Austin, 2014.

"Ian McEwan, The Art of Fiction No. 173." Interviewed by Adam Begley. *The Paris Review*, Issue 162, Summer 2002. www.theparisreview.org/interviews/393/ian-mcewan-the-art-of-fiction-no-173-ian-mcewan.

Kirschenbaum, Matthew G. *Track Changes: A Literary History of Word Processing*. Belknap Press, 2016.

MacDonald, A. B. "Tarkington, Nearly Blind. Hunts Whale: Doesn't Catch Creatures. Just Watches Them—Forbidden to Write, He Dictates Work." *The Hartford Courant*, 17 Sept. 1934, p. 15.

McAleer, Neil. *Arthur C. Clarke: The Authorized Biography*. Contemporary Books, 1992.

McEwan, Ian. "The Art of Fiction No. 173." Interviewed by Adam Begley. *The Paris Review*, Issue 162, Summer 2002. www.theparisreview.org/interviews/393/ian-mcewan-the-art-of-fiction-no-173-ian-mcewan.

Minitab Release 19, Minitab, Inc., State College, PA, 2019.

Octavia E. Butler Papers. The Huntington Library, San Marino, CA.

Reynolds, Margaret, and Jonathan Noakes. *Ian McEwan: The Essential Guide*. Vintage, 2002. books.google.com/books/about/Ian_McEwan.html?id=cXkh1vk3TzwC.

Russell, Natalie M. "Finding Aid." *Octavia E. Butler Papers*, the Huntington Library, San Marino, CA, 2013. oac.cdlib.org/findaid/ark:/13030/c8hm5br8/entire_text.

Salztman, Arthur M. "Stanley Elkin: An Introduction." *Review of Contemporary Fiction*, vol. 15, no. 2, 1995, pp. 7–14.

Schmidt, Michael. *The Novel: A Biography*. Harvard UP, 2014.

Smith, Stephanie A. "Octavia Butler: A Retrospective." *Feminist Studies*, vol. 33, no. 2, 2007, pp. 385–93, doi:10.2307/20459148.

Sutherland, John. "The McEwan Problem." *Independent on Sunday*, 2 Sept. 2007. www.independent.co.uk/voices/commentators/john-sutherland-the-mcewan-problem-401145.html.

Tristman, Richard. "Tragic Soliloquy, Stand-up Spiel." *New England Review*, vol. 27, no. 4, 2006, pp. 36–40. www.jstor.org/stable/40244882.

Wilde, Alan. "Final Things: More Letters to Mzimmer Humanitas at Hub.Ucsb.Edu." *Review of Contemporary Fiction*, vol. 15, no. 2, 1995, pp. 61–9.

6

THE DURABILITY OF CHANGE: HANDWRITING, DICTATION, AND STYLE EVOLUTION IN HENRY JAMES

> And dictating, please, has moreover nothing to do with it. The value of that process for me is in its help to do over and over, for which it is extremely adapted, and which is the only way I can do at all. It soon enough, accordingly, becomes, intellectually, absolutely identical with the act of writing—or has become so, after five years now, with me; so that the difference is only material and illusory—only the difference, that is, that I walk up and down: which is so much to the good.
>
> *(James,* Letters *411)*

> That brought back to Maisie—it was a roundabout way—the beauty and antiquity of her connexion with the flower of the Overmores as well as that lady's own grace and charm, her peculiar prettiness and cleverness and even her peculiar tribulations. A hundred things hummed at the back of her head, but two of these were simple enough. Mrs. Beale was by the way, after all, just her stepmother and her relative. She was just—and partly for that very reason—Sir Claude's greatest intimate ("lady-intimate" was Maisie's term) so that what together they were on Mrs. Wix's prescription to give up and break short off with was for one of them his particular favourite and for the other her father's wife.
>
> *(James,* What Maisie Knew *[1897])*

Introduction

It may seem paradoxical to include in this discussion of the durability of style a writer whose style is so well known to have changed dramatically over his long career. No author's style is likely to remain constant over a forty-year time span like that between James's first novel in 1871 and his last complete novel in 1911, but the change in James's style is so extreme that many readers and critics consider the later novels too obscure and enjoy only the early novels. Others champion the later novels and consider the early novels immature. One critic notes that James's late "distortions" often "obliterate the normal elements of connection and cohesion. When he has undone the usual ties, his meanings float untethered, grammatically speaking, like particles in colloidal suspension" (Short 73–4). James W. Tuttleton, the editor of the Norton Critical Edition of James's *The American* (James, *The American* [Norton]), rejected the heavily revised text that James prepared for his New York Edition (James, *The American* [Scribner]) in favor of the first edition. In a reminiscence of James, E. F. Bensen puts it this way:

> "All my earlier work was subaqueous, subaqueous," he [James] said, "Now I have got my head, such as it is, above the water, such as it was." I did not know him personally in the pellucid "subaqueous" days of his early work, before he got his head above that crystal clearness and (to my mind) emerged into a fog. Enormously admiring, as I do, the beautiful direct simplicity of such a book as "Roderick Hudson," it is only natural that I should find his later methods dim and nebulous.
>
> *(279)*

Most of the critical attention to James's style has been focused on syntax, and much has been made of the length and self-interrupting complexity of the sentences in the late style, a fine example of which can be seen in the final sentence from the quotation from *What Maisie Knew* at the beginning of this chapter. Curiously, although there is a slight trend toward longer sentences in the twenty novels published before James's death, the 1886 novels *The Bostonians* and *The Princess Casamassima* have by far the greatest average sentence lengths (the two unfinished posthumous novels have somewhat longer sentences). Yet changes in James's vocabulary are equally dramatic, and, as I have shown, the frequencies of the most frequent words alone very effectively identify when each novel was written ("Corpus Stylistics" 178–80, 193–6). The question for this chapter, whether or not James's change in mode of composition is responsible for the genesis of his later style, seems both important from a literary perspective and especially amenable to computational investigation.

In 1897, while writing *What Maisie Knew*, James began dictating because of persistent pain in his wrist. At first, his hired stenographer, William McAlpine, took down his dictation in shorthand and typed a clean copy for revision the following day. The delay bothered James enough, however, that he soon purchased a typewriter so that McAlpine could type directly from James's dictation (Novick 265). James's most famous typist, Theodora Bosanquet, who worked with him as he prepared his New York Edition, beginning in 1907, discusses

James's disappointment with his earlier work and her view of the significance of dictation as follows:

> One catches echoes of a plea that these elderly youngsters [the early novels] may not be too closely compared, to their inevitable disadvantage, with the richly endowed, the carefully bred, the highly civilised and sensitised children of his second marriage, contracted with that wealthy bride, Experience. Attentive readers of the novels may perhaps find the distinction between these two groups less remarkable than it seemed to their writer. They may even wonder whether the second marriage was not rather a silver wedding, with the old romantic mistress cleverly disguised as a woman of the world. The different note was possibly due more to the substitution of dictation for pen and ink than to any profound change of heart.
>
> *(39–40)*

Many critics have also accepted this view, as does Leon Edel in his biography of James (though these comments suggest that he thinks of the late style as appearing "several years" after *What Maisie Knew*). He claims that

> some of his friends claimed they could put their finger on the exact chapter in *Maisie* where manual effort ceased and dictation began. Henry James writing, and Henry James dictating, were two different artists. His sentences were to become, in time, elaborate—one might indeed say baroque—filled with qualifications and parentheses; he seemed often in a letter to begin a sentence without knowing what its end would be, and he allowed it to meander river-like into surprising turns and loops. Out of several years of consistent dictating the "later manner" of Henry James emerged.
>
> *(176)*

Recent interest in media and technology, especially at the turn of the twentieth century, has sparked new interest in the claim that dictation changed James's style (Cappello 205; Thurschwell 103–4, 110–13; Seltzer 25–7; Kittler *Gramophone* 216). In a discussion that owes a good deal to Kittler's *Discourse Networks 1800/1900*, Matthew Schilleman argues that "[r]eplacing his own conscious intentions with the rhythms of his writing machine, James refashioned himself into precisely the kind of authorial subject that would produce the representations of mind for which he was famous" (15).

The claim that dictation changed James's style is also mentioned by Marshall McLuhan (McLuhan and Zingrone 193; McLuhan 182). It appears in *Barron's BookNotes* (a study guide for students), the online guide to the *Dragon Naturally Speaking* dictation-to-text program (Newman 153), in an article on voice recognition in composition (Honeycutt 85–6), in *Wikipedia* ("Henry James"), in *The Ivanhoe Game* (Bethany), and in Cynthia Ozick's novel, *Dictation: A Quartet*. It is discussed more extensively in *The Iron Whim* (Wershler-Henry 98–104) and in *Thinking in Henry James* (Cameron 32–3). These multiple appearances testify to its widespread appeal and to its relevance to media studies and computational stylistics (see also Curley-Egan; Layne; Vericat).

The fact that James's later style is generally dated to the late 1890s, just when he begins dictating, has undoubtedly helped to foster the idea that the adoption of dictation in 1897 helped to bring that late style into being. A simple cluster analysis of the seven earliest and the seven latest James novels shows that there is a very clear distinction between the novels up to 1881 and those of 1901 and later—a distinction that helps to explain the attractiveness of the idea that the switch to dictation changed James's style. (All cluster analyses in this chapter were performed in Minitab, with standardized variables, Ward linkage, and squared Euclidean distance.) In spite of the widespread currency of this idea, however, Campbell points out that neither traditional scholarship nor media theory has made much progress (164–5). After a discussion of the oral/written dichotomy in James, she asks why, if James's late fiction bears traces of his talking voice, "do readers (both contemporary with James, and still today) have such trouble following it? Why isn't reading James easy in the way listening to someone talk is easy?" (166–7). She suggests that James's talk was not, in fact, easy, noting a comment by Bosanquet that James spoke to the local fishmonger or railway clerk in the language "coined in the same mint as his addresses to the Academic Committee of the Royal Society of Literature" (Bosanquet 47). Campbell then concludes:

> The typist's remarks reaffirm that the movement between the oral and the written for James was not unidirectional: it wasn't simply that dictation changed the sentences of his novels—it may have altered his speech as well. That his characters' voices were often indistinguishable, that their voices sounded like his, that his writing voice was his speaking voice and vice versa—his use of language blurs the line between literary and non-literary uses of language as they have conventionally been associated with the written and oral, respectively.
>
> *(170–1)*

On the question of speech and writing, E. F. Bensen suggests some qualification of Campbell's claims:

> Nothing would be further from the truth than to say that he talked like a book, but most emphatically he talked like a book of his own in the making, just as he used to dictate it, with endless erasures of speech, till he got the exact and final form of his sentences. Just so in his talk he tried word after word to express the precise shade he required; he avoided, just as he avoided in his writing, any definite and final statement, if what he meant to say could be conveyed in a picturesque and allusive periphrasis. The most

> trivial incident thus became something rich and sumptuous with the hints of this cumulative treatment. I remember, as the simplest instance, how he described a call he paid at dusk on some neighbours at Rye, how he rang the bell and nothing happened, how he rang again and again waited, how at the end there came steps in the passage and the door was slowly opened, and there appeared in advance on the threshold, "something black, something canine."
>
> *(324–5)*

Comments on James's complex and involved speech by his friend Edith Wharton seem relevant as well:

> His slow way of speech, sometimes mistaken for affectation—or, more quaintly, for an artless form of Anglomania!—was really the partial victory over a stammer which in his boyhood had been thought incurable. The elaborate politeness and the involved phraseology that made off-hand intercourse with him so difficult to casual acquaintances probably sprang from the same defect.
>
> *(177–8)*

Some critics, however, have been skeptical of the view that the change to dictation in 1897 was largely responsible for the radical change in James's style from his early novels and those written after 1900, in spite of its wide currency. For example, Wood remarks that

> A lot has been said about the connection between James's dictation to MacAlpine [sic] at the typewriter and his famous late sentences—those beautiful, maddening, loaded convoys. . . . But *The Spoils of Poynton*, written before MacAlpine's arrival, has its share of fairly appalling sentences ("I may not perhaps too much diminish the merit of that generosity if I mention that it could take the flight we are considering just because really, with the telescope of her long thought, Fleda saw what might bring her out of the wood"), and the speedy and compact *What Maisie Knew* in fact has very few.
>
> *(106)*

(It seems fair to point out, however, that the final sentence of the quotation from *What Maisie Knew* at the beginning of this chapter seems to qualify as a "maddening, loaded convoy.")

I share Michael Schmidt's intuitive view (which also echoes Campbell's question about speech normally being easy to understand):

> One might have expected that writing for the stage or dictation might have shortened James's sentences. If we remember blind Milton unfolding

> the huge periods of *Paradise Lost* to his daughters, we will know that the writer aloud need not become laconic, though Milton had the mnemonic of meter and for James the units of energy are not the foot and line but the phrase, sentence, and paragraph, and some of the sentences run on for half a page or more. James Thurber regarded this as the chief problem with the late style: he got bored. "James is like—well, I had a bulldog once who used to drag rails around, enormous ones. . . . He loved to get them in the middle and you'd hear him growling out there, trying to bring the thing home." The problem was the garden gate: "Crash, he'd come up against the gateposts." James sometimes tries to get the rail through a gate not wide enough.
>
> *(503)*

Although he does not discuss dictation, Le Roy Phillips, one of James's early bibliographers, argues for a gradual development in James's style rather than an abrupt revolution and writes, in his introduction to his edition of James's *Views and Reviews* in 1908:

> Those whose palates are accustomed to the subtle flavours of the wines of the Rhine and Moselle can smack their lips and name the vintage at the first taste. Likewise any one fairly familiar with the work of Mr. James during his forty years of literary activity can, after the reading of a single page taken at random, judge with a remarkable accuracy the date of its composition. Yet the transition has not been abrupt and the styles of writing which the author has adopted, early, middle and late, have blended in such a way that he has been bringing many of his earlier readers, though some have fallen by the wayside, along with him to a genuine appreciation of his present work.
>
> (v)

Finally, R. P. Blackmur, in his introduction to James's *The Art of the Novel*, suggests that the later style was an organic development, born of a desire for the expression of increasingly subtle and complex human interactions:

> He enjoyed an excess of intelligence and he suffered, both in life and art, from an excessive effort to communicate it, to represent it in all its fullness. His style grew elaborate in the degree that he rendered shades and refinements of meaning and feeling not usually rendered at all.
>
> *(James, "Art"* xiii*)*

One might quote James's first preface from the New York Edition in (a rather vague) support of this idea: "These notes represent, over a considerable course, the continuity of an artist's endeavour, the growth of his whole operative consciousness and, best of all, perhaps, their own tendency to multiply, with the implication, thereby, of a memory much enriched" (James, "Art" 4).

In spite of these demurrers, however, the idea that dictation was a major cause of the changes in James's style is an initially plausible one that accords well with critical opinion about when those changes took place and remains very widely held. What has been lacking thus far has been any solid objective evidence for or against the view. The analyses in this chapter, however, will show that James's style exhibits a gradual and unidirectional development over his entire career with no significant evidence for an effect of his mode of composition. James's style undeniably changes significantly over time, but this chronological development is itself durable: it begins before the change in mode and continues after it, with no evidence of a rupture around 1897.

The Early and Late Styles of James's Fiction

A cluster analysis of all of James's major novels, including his two late, unfinished, and posthumously published ones, based on the one thousand most frequent words, shown in Figure 6.1, does a remarkable job of arranging the novels in order of publication, with the exception of the late, topical novel, *The Outcry*. Note that, even within the large, dated clusters, there is a finer-grained chronology. Within the 1871–81 cluster, the 1880–81 novels cluster separately, as do the 1875–77 novels, with James's first novel somewhat of an outlier, as first novels often are. Within the 1901–17 cluster, the two posthumous novels group separately from the 1901–04 novels. As precise as these groupings are, they do not support a transformation after *What Maisie Knew*, which groups most closely with the handwritten *The Spoils of Poynton* within a group of handwritten and dictated novels that are clearly chronologically linked, except for *The Outcry*. The exceptional behavior of *The Outcry*, which is a novelization of a 1909 play, raises interesting questions. According to Bosanquet, James's typist, the play version of the novel was handwritten in order to keep its length under control (35). It might be possible to argue that this could account for its placement among the novels of 1896–99, but two of those novels were handwritten and two were dictated. Furthermore, the genre difference between drama and fiction is a much more likely cause for the odd placement of *The Outcry* than is the mode of composition. Finally, note that the plays also divide into similar periods of early, middle, and late, in spite of the fact that, according to Bosanquet, they seem likely to have been handwritten throughout James's career (35–6).

The pattern shown in Figure 6.1 is stable when different numbers of the most frequent words are analyzed. Perhaps one could use the fact that the novels after 1900 tend to cluster separately from those before to argue that the changes caused by dictation took time to develop, as Edel suggested (176), but this would not explain the consistent clustering of all the novels from 1896 and after in the late group, whether they were handwritten or dictated, nor the sharp difference

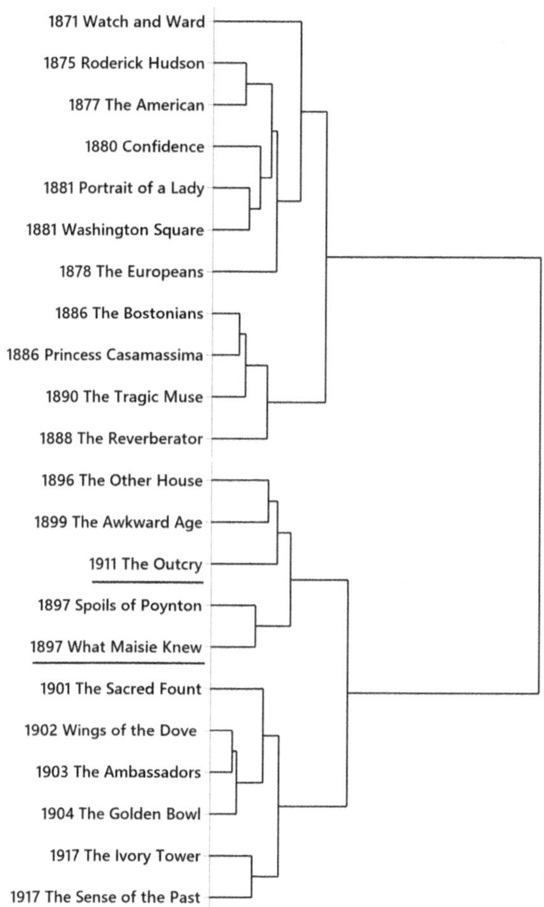

FIGURE 6.1 Cluster analysis of twenty-two novels by Henry James, based on the one thousand most frequent words, with pronouns deleted, culled at eighty percent

between the novels from 1871 to 1881 and those from 1886 to 1896, all of which were handwritten.

Consider also the extraordinary pattern of adoption of characteristically late words and abandonment of characteristically early words over time shown in Figure 6.2. To produce this figure, I created a combined word frequency list for eighteen of James's novels, novellas, and long stories, nine published between 1868 and 1881 and nine published after 1901, in order to create a twenty-year gap (there are about 680,000 words in each group). I then selected all words that are at least three times as frequent in the early texts as in the late texts or at least three times as frequent in the late texts as in the early texts: 3,368 early James words and 2,058 late James words. Finally, I added all the frequencies of the early words (an "early" score) and all the frequencies of the late words (a "late" score) that appear

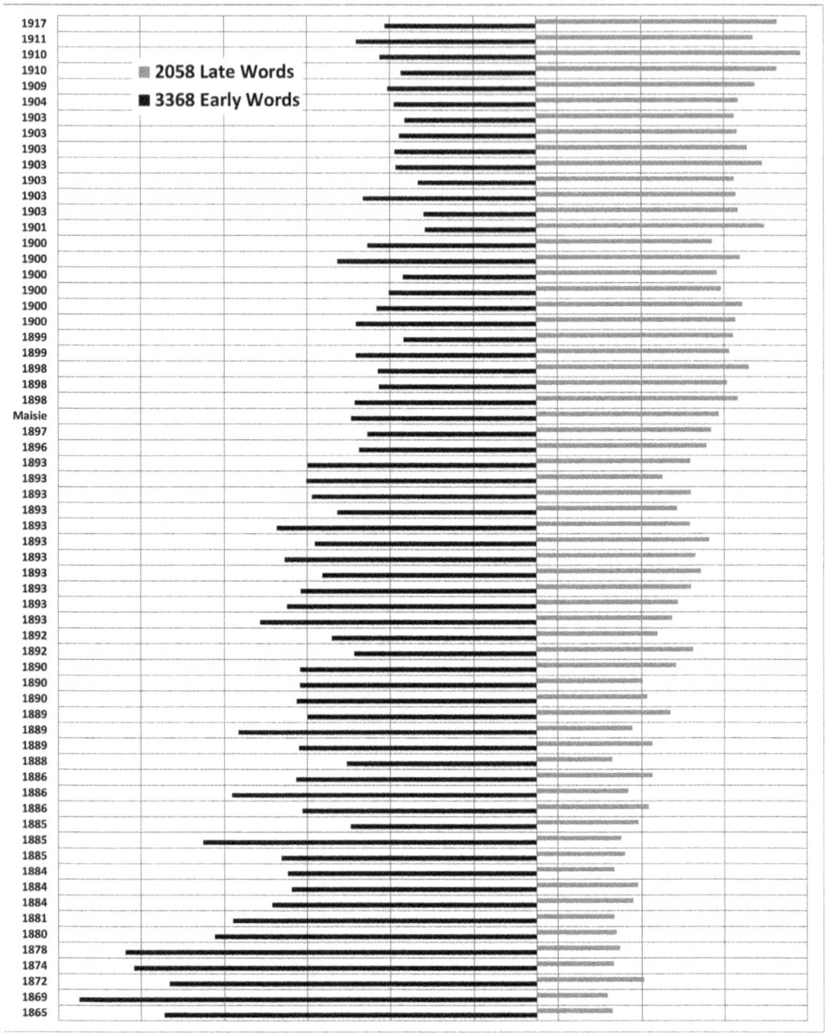

FIGURE 6.2 Distinctively early and late vocabulary in Henry James's fiction, 1865–1917

in each of sixty-four *additional* James novels, novellas, and long stories published between 1865 and 1917 and graphed the early and late scores for each text. I multiplied each early score by −1 so that it appears on the left; only the year is given for each text except *What Maisie Knew*, to make the graph more readable.[1]

Note how regularly the frequency of early words declines and the frequency of late words increases over time, even through the middle period, in spite of the fact that no texts from the middle period and none of the texts shown in Figure 6.2

were used in creating the word lists. The later style has often been associated more with syntax than with vocabulary, but the regularity of the vocabulary changes shown here certainly offers no support for an abrupt shift between the handwritten novels that precede and the dictated novels that follow *What Maisie Knew*. It is also important to note that, according to his final typist, Theodora Bosanquet, "there were to the end certain kinds of work which he was obliged to do with a pen" (35). This included much of his short fiction, which was initially handwritten, with James later dictating from his handwritten draft, and invariably adding substantially to the lengths of most of the stories (35). Thus much of the late short fiction in Figure 6.2 may have been at least initially handwritten, though the almost total absence of manuscripts of James's work prevents any firm conclusions. Remember also that a wide spectrum analysis of multiple genres of James's work in Chapter 1 showed that fiction, criticism, drama, and letters can all be identified as early or late, whether they were handwritten or dictated (see also Hoover, "Text Analysis").

This simple method of analysis can be confirmed by the precise method of bootstrap consensus analysis, performed in Stylo (Eder et al. 113–15) and concentrating on texts written just before and after James's adoption of dictation. (All bootstrap consensus analyses in this chapter were performed in Stylo.) A series of dozens of such analyses of eleven novels, novellas, and long stories published between 1895 and 1899 never results in a consensus tree in which all the texts published before the partly dictated *What Maisie Knew* in 1897 group separately from those published after it. These analyses were based on multiple numbers of the most frequent words, word n-grams, and character n-grams, multiple levels of culling, and multiple different distance measures. (For an early argument for the effectiveness of the analysis of n-grams, there called "sequences," see Hoover, "Frequent Sequences.") In fact, in almost all analyses, *What Maisie Knew* groups most closely with *The Spoils of Poynton*, the last handwritten novel, and the handwritten *The Other House* (1896) almost as consistently groups with the later, dictated novel, *The Awkward Age* (1899). None of these results suggests any significant dictation effect.

The Evidence From Handwritten and Dictated Letters

James's letters provide an opportunity for a subtler test for evidence of stylistic change caused by dictation. When James took up dictation, he initially intended to dictate only his voluminous correspondence, hoping that reducing the stress on his wrist would make the handwriting of his fiction less painful (Edel 175–6). Although he soon began dictating his novels, he also continued to dictate many of his letters for the rest of his life. An initial set of bootstrap consensus analyses of handwritten and dictated letters from 1897, when James first began to dictate, to 1912 shows, as expected, that the letters strongly tend to group chronologically, rather than by mode of composition. These analyses were based on multiple numbers of the most frequent words, word n-grams, and character n-grams, multiple levels of culling, and multiple different distance measures. Selecting groups of long handwritten and dictated letters from a relatively brief period, however, minimizes the effects of the strong chronological drift in James's style to allow for more accurate testing for an effect of mode of composition. For this testing, I selected letters from 1897 to 1903 because of the large numbers of both handwritten and dictated letters James produced during those years.

Another variable that seems potentially problematic is the identity and nature of the addressee. One might expect James's choice of handwriting or dictation for his letters to be affected by his addressee. For example, a plausible hypothesis is that family members or more intimate friends would be more likely to receive the more personal handwritten form, a hypothesis that receives some initial support from James's many apologetic comments about his dictated letters. For example, he writes to his old friend Grace Norton:

> I don't write to you for a hideous age, and then, when at last I do, I take the romantic occasion of this particular day to write in this unsympathetic ink. But that is exactly what, as I say, the horrid time has made of me. The use of my hand, always difficult, has become impossible to me; and since I am reduced to dictation, this form of dictation is the best. May its distinctness make up for its indirectness.
>
> (Letters, *275–6)*

However, multiple addressees, including Edmund Goss, Mrs. Humphry Ward, Edith Wharton, William James (his brother), Mrs. William James (his sister-in-law), Percy Lubbock, Lady Wolseley, and William Dean Howells, received letters in both modes during this period. Thus, there does not seem to be any strong correlation between the mode of composition of a letter and the addressee. It seems certain, however, that the content of letters will often vary systematically with the addressee, and initial testing showed some tendency for letters to group by addressee. Consequently, I also avoided including letters to the same addressee in both the handwritten and dictated groups of letters (see Hoover et al. 82–4 for a discussion of distinguishing fictional addressees when analyzing epistolary novels).

A series of dozens of analyses using bootstrap consensus (based on multiple numbers of the most frequent words, word n-grams, and character n-grams, multiple levels of culling, and multiple different distance measures), PCA, and multidimensional scaling show only a very weak tendency for the letters to group by mode of composition. Only occasionally do more than half of the letters group by mode, and such groupings by mode that do exist are not consistent or regular. Instead, they seem chaotic. Furthermore, many analyses show a greater (though still weak) tendency for the letters to group by date than by mode, even within this short chronological span.

The Composition of *What Maisie Knew*

Although analyses of James's fiction before and after *What Maisie Knew* and of his handwritten and dictated letters have not provided any support for the idea that dictation changed his style, it seems worthwhile to examine *What Maisie Knew* itself for evidence of any significant local shift in style that might have been caused by the switch to dictation, even if that shift did not survive in later novels. The external evidence concerning the composition of *What Maisie Knew* is helpful, but inconclusive. It is known that James suffered wrist pain in the autumn of 1896, that it was so severe that he was unable to write for two weeks in December of that year (Novick 264), and that he first hired a typewriter (at this period, the term refers to both the machine and its operator) in February of 1897 (Edel 175). Because *What Maisie Knew* had already begun its serial publication on 15 January in the United States (Worden, "Cut Version" 495), a substantial portion of the novel must have been written by hand. An entry in James's *Notebooks* for 26 October 1896 adds information to this, discussing eight chapters as complete and describing his planning for chapters 9 to 12 (James, "Complete Notebooks" 163–7). The final notebook entry for *What Maisie Knew*, dated 21 December 1896, reports that he has ten thousand more words "of this interminable little *Maisie*" to write, though without reporting how many words have been written since October. Further information is lacking because James made no notebook entries from January of 1897 to May of 1898, perhaps because of his wrist pain (James, "Complete Notebooks" 167).

This apparently simple scenario is complicated by the fact that the first eight chapters of the completed novel comprise only about seventeen thousand and the first twelve only about twenty-nine thousand of the total ninety-six thousand words of the finished novel and by a December 1896 advertisement in *Bookman* for *What Maisie Knew* as a "novelette" of about twenty-five thousand words to be published serially beginning in January of 1897 (Worden, "Cut Version" 495). James was notorious for allowing short stories to expand into novels, so that one likely scenario is that his original plans for a long story of about twenty-five thousand words changed during the late fall. In any case, the story eventually nearly quadrupled in size. It is unclear how much of the novel James could have written between late October and late December, especially with severe wrist pain and two weeks off in December. If his planned story of twenty-five thousand words had already expanded to twenty-nine thousand (through chapter 12) by December, however, he might possibly have referred to such a story as "interminable" with the addition of another ten thousand words.

Consider also the fact that chapters 18 to 31 of *What Maisie Knew* were rather severely cut in its almost simultaneous British serial publication in the *New Review*, beginning in February 1897 (Worden, "Cut Version" 493), perhaps so that it would finish about the time of the book publication (496–7). Furthermore, the existence of about forty thousand words of *What Maisie Knew* in January is confirmed by a letter that James Henley, the editor of the *New Review*, wrote to a friend on 19 January 1897, in which he reported, "My Directors have landed me for about 100 pages of Henrietta James. So I fear the N.R. will scarce survive the year" (qtd. in Worden, "Cut Version" 496). Edel reports that James spent the winter working on *What Maisie Knew* by dictation and that he was finishing it as late as July (178–80). This seems reasonable, given that the serial ran through September 1897 (Worden, "Cut Version" 494) and that the British edition of the novel was published late the same month (495). If James was dictating the novel from March or April to July, it seems likely that at least the last ten chapters, 22 to 31, were dictated.

We are left, then, with the fairly certain knowledge that at least the first twelve chapters of the novel were handwritten and that probably at least the last third of the novel was dictated. It also seems likely that the change in mode of composition was after chapter 17 (chapters 1 through 17 comprise about forty-four thousand words) and before chapter 22 (the last ten chapters comprise about thirty-five thousand words).[2] Probably the most reasonable scenario is that James had finished about twenty-nine thousand words by 21 December. If he kept to his normal habits, the "ten thousand" more words of the interminable *What Maisie Knew* that he mentions could easily have stretched to the fifteen thousand more that brought the novel through chapter 17 before he turned to dictation. Add to this the fact that James at first used dictation for letters only (Edel 175–6), so that his dictation of *What Maisie Knew* seems unlikely to have begun before March or April. This seems to provide sufficient time for the completion of the first seventeen chapters. The page proofs for "more than one third of the planned book" are known to have existed by 10 June 1897, already revised by James (Worden, "Cut Version" 495). It seems very likely that the length of a book to be published in September would be "planned" by June, and one-third of the completed novel, about thirty-two thousand words, would comprise chapters 1 to 14. The existence of revised page proofs for fourteen chapters surely means that more than fourteen chapters existed by 10 June.

But there is a final complication: there are significant plot twists in chapter 14 and after chapter 19, and, while the events of chapters 1 to 19 span a few years, those of the final twelve chapters, 20 to 31, occur within only about one week. Chapters 20 to 21 move the action from London to Folkstone, and chapters 22 to 31 are set in France (Worden, "Henry James's" 374–5). Thus there are other possible reasons for stylistic shifts in the novel after chapters 14, 19, and 21 than a change to dictation, and these potential shifts annoyingly fall within the span where the change from handwriting to dictation also seems most likely to have taken place. Finally, it is also important to note that "James habitually revised his works as they passed from manuscript to typescript (if he dictated them as he did *The Ambassadors*) to print," so that he had an opportunity to remove any *unwanted* changes he noticed in his dictated works (James, *Ambassadors* 361).

Dictation and Style in *What Maisie Knew:* Internal Evidence From the Novel

I turn, then, from this fascinating but inconclusive external evidence to internal evidence, with special attention to the middle of the novel. For the sake of simplicity, I begin with a series of chapter-by-chapter cluster analyses based on the most frequent words. Although most of the analyses discussed thus far have involved culled word lists with the pronouns removed, I have neither culled the word list nor removed pronouns for analyses of *What Maisie Knew* alone. This seems appropriate because, within a single novel, pronouns and words with high local frequencies may be indicators of local changes associated with a change in mode of composition, plot, characters, or setting. (See Hoover, "Multivariate Analysis" 350–1 for a more thorough discussion of this issue.) In these initial cluster analyses, most of the early chapters appear in one cluster, and most of the middle and later ones in another. This result might seem encouraging, but there is no realistic possibility that James started dictating in chapter 8 (the earliest chapter in the "late" cluster), and the presence of chapters 11 and 17 in the "early" cluster would be problematic in any case, as would the clustering of chapters 15 and 16 with chapters 29 to 31. Furthermore, the pattern just described is found only in the analyses based on the seven hundred, eight hundred, and nine hundred most frequent words. Those based on the one thousand most frequent words and on smaller numbers of words consistently mix earlier and later chapters even more fully, adding chapters in the twenties to the "early" cluster. (Among the scores of novels I have analyzed, *What Maisie Knew* is unusual in how weakly its narrative structure is reflected in the relationships among the chapters.)

Because no chapter after 17 appears in the "early" cluster, this analysis is problematically compatible with a change to dictation after chapter 17 (the latest chapter in the first group). Except for chapter 17, chapters 12 through 31 are all in the "late" cluster, which is problematically compatible with a change to dictation after chapter 11. The first of these divisions fits the external evidence fairly well but has errors for chapters 7, 8, 10, and 12 through 16. The second is unlikely on the basis of external evidence and has errors for chapters 7, 8, 10, and 17. It would be foolhardy to place any confidence in either of these suggested divisions into handwritten and dictated parts. Analyzing the chapters using n-grams of two and three words gives similar but less consistent results.

The great discrepancy of the lengths of the chapters (one thousand to six thousand words) suggests that it would be more appropriate to test the novel divided into sections of equal size, as large differences in size are known to cause problems with the frequencies of less frequent words. An analysis of the novel in twenty-two sections of about forty-three hundred words each (based on the one thousand most frequent words, with pronouns, not culled) produces two main clusters. One includes sections 1 to 6 and section 10, but sections 1 to 6 cover chapters 1 to 11, and this is not a likely place for the switch to dictation. This pattern is very similar to those in analyses based on the nine hundred and eight hundred most frequent words, and dividing the novel into sections of about thirty-four hundred words produces a similar pattern in analyses based on the nine hundred and eight hundred most frequent words, but with the break after chapter 12. When the novel is divided into sections of twenty-two hundred words, this pattern disappears. There is still a tendency for sections from the beginning of the novel to cluster together, but the clustering is much more chaotic. If there were a significant stylistic shift in the novel, all of these analyses would agree with each other.

A set of bootstrap consensus analyses based on multiple numbers of the most frequent words, word n-grams, and character n-grams, multiple levels of culling, and multiple different distance measures tells a similar story, with fairly chaotic and inconsistent results. One of the most coherent analyses can be seen in Figure 6.3.

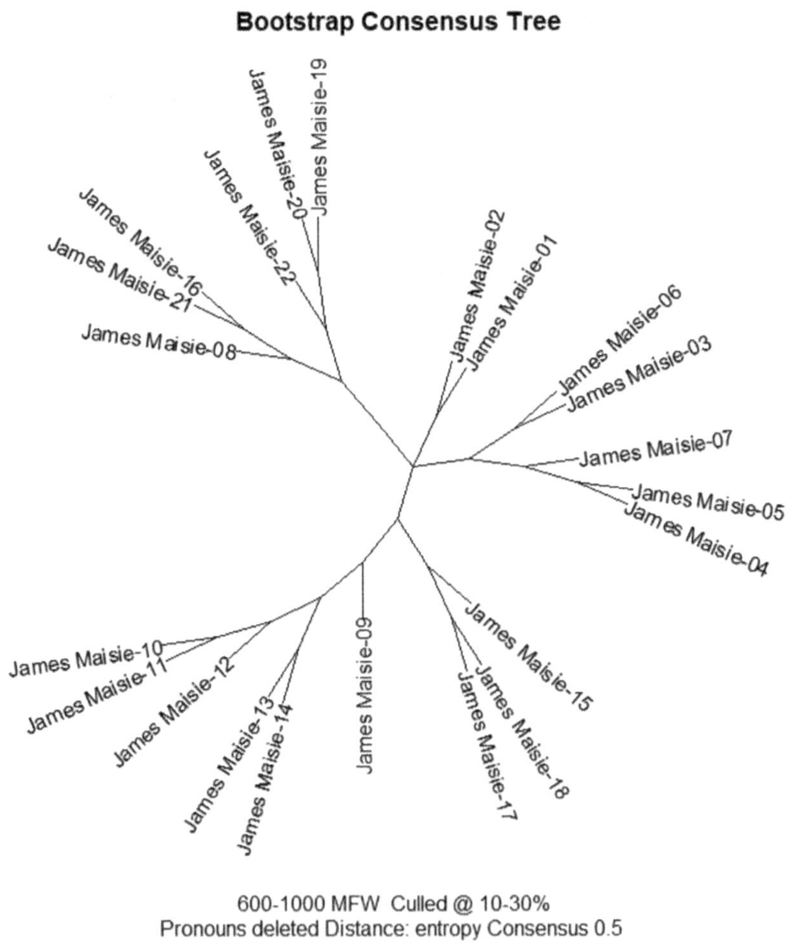

FIGURE 6.3 Bootstrap consensus analysis of *What Maisie Knew* in sections of about forty-three hundred words, based on the six hundred to one thousand most frequent words, with pronouns deleted, culled at ten to thirty percent, entropy distance, and a consensus of fifty percent

As in some of the cluster analyses, the first sections of the novel form a group, and it is possible that the change in mode could have taken place after section 7 (roughly chapter 12). The bottom group consists of sections 9 through 18 (except for 16). The top-left group tempts interpretation, but the inclusion of sections 8 and 16 is problematic, and section 19 is much later than seems possible for the change to dictation. In any case, this kind of coherence is rare among the dozens of analyses and, with three clear groups, is not compatible with a significant change in style when James changed to dictation.

Dictation and Style in *What Maisie Knew:* Evidence From Dialogue and Narration

Because of the well-known genre differences between dialogue and narration, an additional test on pure narrative seems appropriate. It seems reasonable that dictation might have had different effects on narration and dialogue, especially given the obvious similarity of the latter to speech. For this test, I removed all the dialogue and cut the narrative into seventeen sections of about four thousand words each.[3] In a cluster analysis of these sections of narrative (based on the eight hundred most frequent words, with pronouns, not culled), the narrative alone forms two chronological clusters. Section 8 begins in chapter 16 and ends in chapter 17, suggesting a stylistic change beginning with chapter 17 that could mark the beginning of dictation, but this pattern is found only in this one analysis. Analyses based on the one thousand and the nine hundred most frequent words cluster sections 1 through 5 and section 8, but not sections 6 or 7, and those based on the seven hundred and six hundred most frequent words cluster sections 1 through 6 and section 8. Section 5 covers chapters 9 and 10, and section 6 covers chapters 11 through 13. (Analyses based on word two-grams and three-grams again give similar but less consistent results.) Dividing the narration into sections of about three thousand words gives a set of consistent analyses in which sections 1 through 7 and section 11 form a cluster. Section 7 is approximately the narration of chapter 11, which would suggest a change to dictation in chapter 12. Sections of two thousand words again give a more confused picture without supporting either of the suggested divisions based on longer sections. It is also important to remember that it is quite normal for the beginning or ending sections of a novel (or both) to cluster separately, so that the division at section 7 need have no relationship to dictation.

Dividing the dialogue into sections in the same way as the narrative suggests a major break after chapter 25, but this is likely caused by the much larger proportion of dialogue by Mrs. Wix and Maisie in the final chapters, is not supported by any other analyses, and is ruled out on external grounds as the point at which James began dictating. The failure of the analyses of dialogue and narration to suggest a consistent and plausible place in the novel where a change of mode of composition may have taken place is sufficient to cast even further doubt on the idea that dictation changed James's style in any significant way.

Tests on variables that are generally less effective in authorship attribution confirm these results. It seems intuitively possible that sentence length (measured in words) and vocabulary richness (the number of different words in a given amount of text) could be altered by a shift to dictation, but the lengths of the sentences in the narrative sections of *What Maisie Knew* fail to suggest any change caused by dictation. The length of the sentences generally declines over sections 1 through 7 of the narrative, then increases in sections 8 through 10, only to decline rapidly in sections 11 through 17. This is especially difficult to reconcile with the claim that dictation caused James's sentences to become long and diffuse. There is also no directional change in vocabulary richness in the middle of the novel. Bosanquet reports that, in dictating, James never left out punctuation, except sometimes the period (34). However, the frequencies of various marks of punctuation, which might also be affected by the mode of composition, also fail to provide any consistent evidence of a directional change. Perhaps one could argue that the increase in the frequencies of periods, semicolons, colons, and possibly question marks in the late sections of narration might support the suggestion of a change

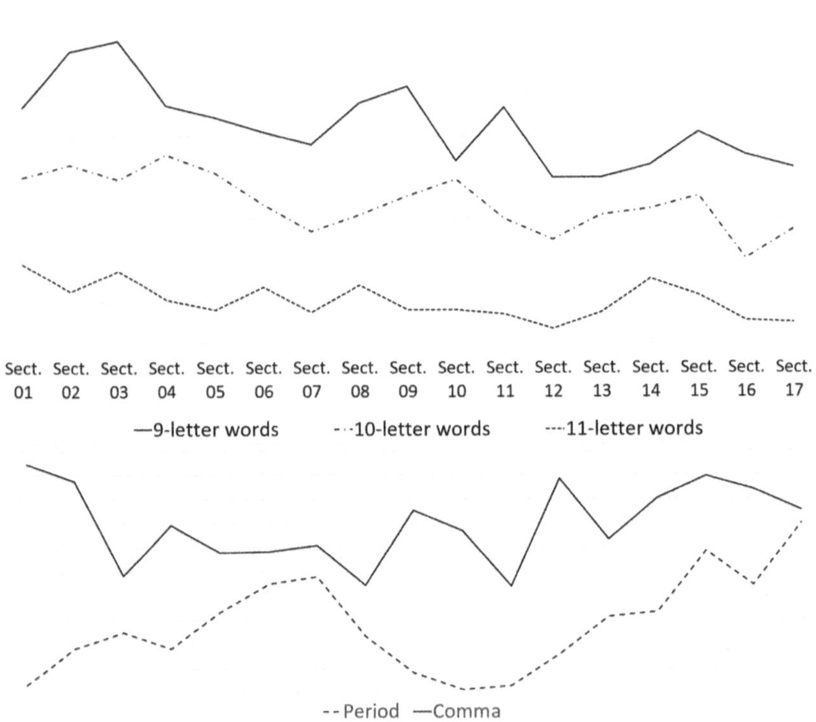

FIGURE 6.4 The frequencies of commas, periods, and words of nine, ten, and eleven syllables in the narration of Henry James's *What Maisie Knew* in sections of four thousand words

to dictation, but these increases do not occur at the same places and are all later than any of the potential points of change suggested in the earlier analyses and later than points of change that are likely on external grounds. The frequencies of words of different lengths in these sections of narration also show some trends, with long words decreasing somewhat in frequency and short words increasing slightly in frequency after section 10 or 11 of the narrative. The frequencies of commas, periods, and words of nine, ten, and eleven syllables in the seventeen sections of narration, some of the variables that show the strongest trends, are graphed in Figure 6.4.

The frequencies of the comma and period, like many of the variables mentioned earlier, fluctuate rather chaotically, and the downward trend in the frequencies of the long words operates throughout the novel rather than showing a sharp change at any particular point. Surely, if dictation were responsible for the radical change from the pellucid early novels to the turgid and difficult late ones, there would be clear and consistent differences between texts written just before the change in mode and those written just after it, or between the handwritten and dictated parts of *What Maisie Knew*.

Conclusion

Analyses of James's fiction over his whole career, analyses of his handwritten and dictated letters, analyses of chapters or sections of *What Maisie Knew*, and separate analysis of dialogue and narration in those sections, all fail to offer any substantial support for the hypothesis that James's change in mode of composition had a major effect on his style. Rather, the change in mode simply falls roughly at the midpoint of his career, and his gradual, unidirectional style evolution both predates and continues after it, with no substantial deviation in 1897 and without any indication of a stylistic change within *What Maisie Knew*.

It seems possible that James's attempt at writing plays (in hope of recapturing his diminishing readership) may have had some influence on his style evolution. Although he had written a few plays in the late 1860s and early 1870s, he returned more seriously to drama in the 1890s and wrote six plays between 1890 and 1893. The catastrophic and embarrassing failure of the premier of *Guy Domville* in 1895, when James was booed off the stage, however, put an end to his dramatic efforts for more than a decade (Flatley 103). Leon Edel suggests, as others have, that this failure led him to employ a more scenic kind of writing in his fiction and that this is another source of the chronological change in his style (164). By the end of July 1897, he was at work on the final pages of *What Maisie Knew* (179–80), and the Notebook entry for 21 December 1896 insists that the scenic method is the only good way for the end of *What Maisie Knew* (167). It is unclear, however, how the adoption of a scenic approach could account for the convoluted later style.

As reasonable as the idea that dictation changed James's style has seemed, and as productive as it has been for speculation about the relationship between media, machines, and literary production, the new kinds of computational evidence presented here suggest that perhaps we should take seriously James's own claim that dictating and writing soon became intellectually identical, except for his walking up and down (quoted at the beginning of this chapter, from a 1902 letter). When questioned about the potential effects of dictation on his style by Morton Fullerton much earlier, in March of 1897, soon after he began dictating, James assured him, "I can be trusted, artless youth, not to be simplified by any shortcut or falsified by any facility" (Edel 176). Perhaps we should accept his assurance.

Notes

1. The idea of collecting words at least three times as frequent in the early or late texts is related to Ellegård's "distinctiveness ratio" (Kenny 69–70). To avoid division by zero errors, I replace zero frequencies by 0.5, which allows the calculation of the DR without overemphasizing words absent from early or late texts. This method is also used by Clement and Sharp (430).
2. Intriguingly, the Morgan Library has a typescript of chapters 17 and 18 of *What Maisie Knew* with James's autograph corrections. Infuriatingly, there are erased and largely unreadable notations that seem to have something to do with the typing of these chapters, along with an erased signature of James's on the top left of the first page of this typescript. It is impossible to know for certain whether this was a dictated draft or a typed version of an earlier handwritten or dictated draft, but the presence of the word "July" in red ink above the erased note, apparently also in James's hand, suggests that it is probably too late to be a dictated draft (the novel was probably finished in July).
3. The process of dividing narrative from dialogue manually is extremely tedious and error-prone. My method here is partly automated one using an Excel spreadsheet and macros. The spreadsheet and detailed instructions are available online ("Analyze Textual Divisions").

References

Barron's BookNotes: "The Turn of the Screw." Barron's Educational Series, Inc., 1986. www.pinkmonkey.com/booknotes/barrons/turnscr2.asp.

Bensen, E. F. *As We Were: A Victorian Peep Show.* Longmans, Green and Co., 1930. archive.org/details/aswewere030125mbp.

Bethany [Nowviskie]. "The Turn of the Screw." *The Ivanhoe Game*, 2002. speculativecomputing.org/greymatter/ivanhoe/roles/archives/00000019.htm.

Bosanquet, Theodora. *Henry James at Work. 1924.* Edited by Lyall H. Powers, U of Michigan P, 2006. muse.jhu.edu/book/7215.

Cameron, Sharon. *Thinking in Henry James.* U of Chicago P, 1989. archive.org/details/thinkinginhenryj0000came/.

Campbell, Sarah. "The Man Who Talked Like a Book, Wrote Like He Spoke." *Interval(le)s*, II.2–III.1, 2008–09, pp. 164–73. labos.ulg.ac.be/cipa/wp-content/uploads/sites/22/2015/07/18_campbell.pdf.

Cappello, Mary. *Awkward: A Detour.* Bellevue Literary Press, 2007. archive.org/details/awkward00mary.

Clement, Ross, and David Sharp. "Ngram and Bayesian Classification of Documents." *Literary and Linguistic Computing*, vol. 18, no. v4, 2003, pp. 423–47, doi:10.1093/llc/18.4.423.

Curley-Egan, James. "The Master's Voice: A Close Reading of James." *PMLA*, vol. 133, no. 5, 2018, pp. 1251–8, doi:10.1632/pmla.2018.133.5.1251.

Edel, Leon. *Henry James: The Treacherous Years, 1895–1901*. Lippincott, 1969. archive.org/details/henryjamestreach00edel.

Eder, Maciej et al. "Stylometry With *R*: A Package for Computational Text Analysis." *R Journal*, vol. 8, no. 1, 2016, pp. 107–21. journal.r-project.org/archive/2016/RJ-2016-007/RJ-2016-007.pdf.

Flatley, Jonathan. "Reading Into Henry James." *Criticism*, vol. 46, no. 1, Special Issue: Materia Media, 2004, pp. 103–23. www.jstor.org/stable/23127340.

"Henry James." *Wikipedia*. en.wikipedia.org/wiki/Henry_James.

Honeycutt, Lee. "Researching the Use of Voice Recognition Writing Software." *Computers and Composition*, vol. 20, no. 1, 2003, pp. 77–95, doi:10.1016/S8755-4615(02)00174-3.

Hoover, David L. *The Analyze Textual Divisions Spreadsheet*. 2017. wp.nyu.edu/exceltextanalysis/analyzetextualdivisions.

———. "Corpus Stylistics, Stylometry, and the Styles of Henry James." *Style*, vol. 41, no. 2, 2007, pp. 174–203. www-jstor-org.proxy.library.nyu.edu/stable/10.5325/style.41.2.174.

———. "Frequent Word Sequences and Statistical Stylistics." *Literary and Linguistic Computing*, vol. 17, no. 2, 2002, pp. 157–80, doi:10.1093/llc/17.2.157.

———. "Multivariate Analysis and the Study of Style Variation." *Literary and Linguistic Computing*, vol. 18, no. 4, 2003, pp. 341–60, doi:10.1093/llc/18.4.341.

———. "Text Analysis." *Literary Studies in the Digital Age: An Evolving Anthology*, edited by Ken Price and Ray Siemens, MLA, 2013. dlsanthology.mla.hcommons.org/textual-analysis.

Hoover, David L. et al. *Digital Literary Studies: Corpus Approaches to Poetry, Prose, and Drama*. Routledge, 2014. ebookcentral.proquest.com/lib/nyulibrary-ebooks/detail.action?docID=1619572.

James, Henry. *The Ambassadors*. Norton Critical Editions. 2nd ed., edited by S. P. Rosenbaum, Norton, 1994.

———. *The American*. Norton Critical Editions, edited by James W. Tuttleton, Norton, 1978. archive.org/details/americanauthorit0000jame.

———. *The American*. Scribner, 1907. archive.org/details/theamerican02jameuoft.

———. *The Art of the Novel*. Edited by R. P. Blackmur, Scribner, 1934. archive.org/details/artofnovel00jame.

———. *The Complete Notebooks of Henry James*. Edited by Leon Edel and Lyall H. Powers, Oxford UP, 1987. archive.org/details/completenotebook00henr.

———. *The Letters of Henry James*. Vol. 1, edited by Percy Lubbock, Palgrave Macmillan, 1920. archive.org/details/lettersofhenryja01jamerich.

———. *Views and Reviews*. Introduction by Le Roy Phillips, Hall, 1908. www.gutenberg.org/files/37424/37424-h/37424-h.htm.

———. *What Maisie Knew*. New York: Stone, 1897. ia331316.us.archive.org/0/items/whatmaisieknew00jamerich/whatmaisieknew00jamerich_djvu.txt.

Kenny, Anthony. *The Computation of Style*. Pergamon Press, 1982, doi:10.1016/C2009-0-10976-5.

Kittler, Friedrich A. *Discourse Networks 1800/1900*. Stanford UP, 1990.

Kittler, Friedrich A. *Gramophone, Film, Typewriter*. Stanford UP, 1999.

Layne, Bethany. "'Henry Would Never Know He Hadn't Written It Himself': The Implications of 'Dictation' for Jamesian Style." *The Henry James Review*, vol. 35, no. 3, 2014, pp. 248–56, doi:10.1353/hjr.2014.0039.

McLuhan, Eric, and Frank Zingrone. *Essential McLuhan*. House of Anansi, 1995. epdf.pub/essential-mcluhan.html.

McLuhan, Marshall. *Understanding Media: The Extensions of Man*, Gingko Press, 2013. ebookcentral.proquest.com/lib/nyulibrary-ebooks/detail.action?docID=1222206.

Minitab Release 19, Minitab, Inc., State College, PA, 2019.

The Morgan Library and Museum, New York, NY.

Newman, Dan. *The Dragon Naturally Speaking Guide*. 2nd ed. Waveside Publishing, 2000. lib.store.yahoo.net/lib/sayican/onlinebook.html.

Novick, Sheldon M. *Henry James: The Mature Master*. Random House, 2007. archive.org/details/henryjamesmature00novi.

Ozick, Cynthia. *Dictation: A Quartet*. Houghton Mifflin, 2008.

Schilleman, Matthew. "Typewriter Psyche: Henry James's Mechanical Mind." *Journal of Modern Literature*, vol. 36, no. 3, 2013, pp. 14–30, doi:10.2979/jmodelite.36.3.14.

Schmidt, Michael. *The Novel: A Biography*. Harvard UP, 2014. ebookcentral.proquest.com/lib/nyulibrary-ebooks/detail.action?docID=3301447.

Seltzer, Mark. "The Graphic Unconscious: A Response." *New Literary History*, vol. 26, no. 1, 1995, pp. 21–8. www.jstor.org/stable/20057262.

Short, R. W. "The Sentence Structure of Henry James." *American Literature*, vol. 18, no. 2, 1946, pp. 71–88.

Thurschwell, Pamela. *Literature, Technology and Magical Thinking, 1880–1920*. Cambridge UP, 2001. doi:10.1017/CBO9780511484537.

Vericat, Fabio L. "Her Master's Voice: Dictation, the Typewriter, and Henry James's Trouble With the Speech of American Women." *South Atlantic Review*, vol. 80, no. 1–2, 2015, pp. 1–23. www.jstor.org/stable/soutatlarevi.80.1-2.1.

Wershler-Henry, Darren. *The Iron Whim: A Fragmented History of Typewriting*. Cornell UP, 2007.

Wharton, Edith. *A Backward Glance*. Appleton-Century, 1934. archive.org/details/backwardglance030620mbp.

Wood, James. "Cult of the Master." *Atlantic Monthly*, vol. 291, no. 3, 2003, pp. 102–8.

Worden, Ward S. "A Cut Version of *What Maisie Knew*." *American Literature*, vol. 24, no. 4, 1953, pp. 493–504.

———. "Henry James's *What Maisie Knew*: A Comparison With the Plans in the Notebooks." *PMLA*, vol. 68, no. 3, 1953, pp. 371–83.

7

THE DURABILITY OF STEPHEN KING'S STYLE

> One night . . . I asked Amy [Tan] if there was any one question she was never asked during the Q-and-A that follows almost every writer's talk—that question you never get to answer when you're standing in front of a group of author-struck fans and pretending you don't put your pants on one leg at a time like everyone else. Amy paused, thinking it over very carefully, and then said: "No one ever asks about the language." . . . Amy was right: nobody ever asks about the language. They ask the DeLillos and the Updikes and the Styrons, but they don't ask popular novelists. Yet many of us proles also care about the language, in our humble way, and care passionately about the art and craft of telling stories on paper. What follows is an attempt to put down, briefly and simply, how I came to the craft, what I know about it now, and how it's done. It's about the day job; it's about the language.
>
> *(King,* On Writing *"First Foreword")*

Introduction

Stephen King (1947–) is, by any measure, an immensely popular writer, who, by 2016, "with more than fifty titles, has also sold an estimated 350 million books" (Heller). In some ways, even this is inadequate as a measure of his popularity. In 1987, King

> became the first author to have four hardcover books on the *New York Times* bestseller list in a single year, an achievement that led David Streitfeld to remark, even before the publication of *The Tommyknockers* that year, "King has passed beyond bestsellerdom into a special sort of nirvana reserved for him alone."
>
> *(Rolls ch. 11)*

As noted in Chapter 5, Ian McEwan, also very popular, has had ten movies based on his books, but King dwarfs all other living authors, with thirty-four feature films based on his novels and short stories, as well as many television movies and miniseries (Temple). Although overshadowed financially by James Patterson and by J. K. Rowling (the first billionaire author), King had earned some $450 million in his career up to 2019 (Fernandez). It is not his popularity that is relevant here, however, but rather the shape of his career, and, related to what King suggests in the quotation at the beginning of the chapter, it is about possible changes in the language of his texts.

King is especially appropriate as my final author to be investigated for a change in style caused by changes in his modes of composition and for the durability of his style for several reasons. King's earliest stories were written by hand, including his earliest known story, "Jhonathan [*sic*] and the Witches," written in 1956 or 1957, when he was nine (Wood, *Literary Companion* "Jhonathan and the Witches"). This story was published (with a reproduction of the first page in King's handwriting) in 1993 (Mandelbaum 117–20). King produced his first published novels on a manual typewriter in the early 1970s but switched to a word processor in 1981. He also wrote two later novels by hand. Like Conrad's, King's changes in mode of composition have also been for multiple reasons, including convenience, pain from an accident, and a desire to try a slower mode. But King's case is exceptionally complex in other ways.

Intersecting with and complicating the changes in mode of composition is a complex history of alcohol and drug abuse that King has often discussed openly. For example, he reports that he wrote or at least revised his first four published novels while drinking heavily. While writing the next eight novels, he was also using cocaine almost continuously, during both composition and revision. At this point, his wife staged an intervention, and he wrote his following novels sober, except for a period after a nearly fatal accident when he wrote one novel, *Dreamcatcher* (2001), under the influence of Oxycontin. To add complexity to complexity, both *Dreamcatcher* and *Bag of Bones* (1998) were written by hand long after he had taken up word processing and about ten years after he quit using alcohol and other drugs. These handwritten novels interrupted a long string of word-processed novels, with one word-processed novel between them.

King has also written several books under the pseudonym Richard Bachman and is well known to be an author who writes in multiple genres and in mixed genres. The strengths of these various possible influences on King's style are undoubtedly different (on the strengths of various stylistic variables, see Jockers ch. 6). Despite the challenges King presents, however, teasing apart the multiple variables that might affect his style also provides an opportunity for a thorough examination of any possible changes in his style caused by his changes in mode of composition.

Genre and Stephen King's Style

> As far as I'm concerned, genre was created by bookstores so that people who were casual readers could say, "Well, I want to read romances." "Well, right over there, that's where romances are." But if you go over there, you're going to find Harlequin this and Harlequin that, and maybe you're going to find *Fifty Shades of Grey* or whatever the newest series of whatever erotic romantic fiction is. But what you're not going to find is *Rebecca*, you're not going to find *The Time Traveler's Wife*, you're not going to find *One Hundred Years of Solitude*. All of those things have genre elements to them, and my fiction has genre elements.
>
> *(King, "The Blue-Collar King")*

Although King is best known for horror novels, some of his work has also been classified as psychological horror, science fiction, thriller, literary naturalism (Strengell), mystery, adventure, epic, magical realism, and even romance. In fact, according to one critic, "King is actually a genre novelist; that is, he writes in all of the major popular genres now marketed to the country's largest reading population: horror, fantasy, science fiction, the western, the mystery, and the romance" (Casebeer 42). In her book-length study of King, Strengell concurs:

> The premise of my argument has now been established: King is a horror writer with an uncommonly wide interest in other literary genres. The following chapters will view him as a Gothic writer, as a writer of myths and fairy tales, and as a literary naturalist. I have chosen to focus on the Gothic first, because it provides King's brand of horror with a historical background and perspective. Since the Gothic atmosphere permeates King's myths and fairy tales, the fantastic genres have been placed next to each other.
>
> *(26)*

This widespread consensus of King's genre variety and genre-bending is supported by the fact that Worldcat labels most of King's novels as belonging to more than one genre, giving some of the novels as many as four different genre labels. Finally, as Rothman puts it:

> If there were a Stephen King Plot Generator somewhere out there on the Web, it would work, most of the time, by mashing up ideas from all of what used to be called speculative fiction—including sci-fi, horror, fantasy, historical (and alternate-history) fiction, superhero comic books, post-apocalyptic tales, and so on—before dropping the results into small-town Maine. Often, too, some elements of the Western, or of Elmore Leonard-esque crime fiction, are mixed in.

Fortunately for the purposes of this study, King is such a prolific writer that some novels written in genres that might disrupt analyses of other variables or in genres that are infrequent among his works can simply be omitted from study, while leaving a substantial number for analysis. For example, the seven novels of The Dark Tower series, which is normally labeled "fantasy," sometimes along with "adventure" or even "epic," will be ignored. Not only are they problematic because of genre, they appeared sporadically over a period of twenty-two years, with individual novels published in 1981, 1986, 1990, 1991, 1996, 2002, and 2003. Other novels to be omitted from analysis are the fantasy novel *The Eyes of the Dragon* (1984), the mystery or detective novel *The Colorado Kid* (2005), and the bildungsroman *Hearts in Atlantis* (1999). Finally, I will omit *Dolores Claiborne* (1989–92) from analysis, even though this novel is labeled as both "horror" and "thriller" by Worldcat. The fact that it is a monologue without chapters or paragraph breaks might well disrupt any analysis. King's two collaborations with Peter Straub, *The Talisman* (1984) and *The Black House* (2001), will also naturally be omitted. A few novels with potentially problematic genres seem useful for the investigation of the possible stylistic effects of alcohol and drug abuse, chronology, and mode of composition and will have been included, in spite of the fact that their genres will need to be considered carefully.

Before turning to the question of any genre effect on King's style, however, it will be useful to indicate, in tabular form, the dates, genres, and modes and circumstances of composition for the twenty-eight novels that will comprise the corpus to be analyzed in this chapter (see Table 7.1). These novels were published between 1974, the year of his first published novel, *Carrie*, to 2008, eight years after his last handwritten novel (not including those mentioned earlier as having been omitted). This long time span is required to include all of King's changes in mode of composition and to cover his drinking and drug abuse and the period of sobriety that followed. The long time span will also allow the creation of two series of novels—one that spans several years before and after the first significant change in mode or circumstances of composition and another that spans several years before and after the last. These two series will facilitate the investigation of possible stylistic changes caused by genre, chronology, and mode and circumstances of composition. The dates of publication are indicated parenthetically after the titles, and the dates listed in the "Date" column are dates of composition. These come mainly from King's helpful habit of indicating a span of dates of composition at the ends of most of his novels. The dates have been supplemented from Rolls's biography and from King's *On Writing*, which are also the main sources for the modes and circumstances of composition, supplemented by some journal entries printed in King's *Song of Susannah* (2004).

Testing for any possible genre effects on King's style can begin with bootstrap consensus analysis in Stylo (Eder et al. 113–15) of the eight early novels typewritten under the influence of alcohol or alcohol and cocaine. These novels have been chosen because they were written over a relatively short time span

TABLE 7.1 Circumstances of composition, composition dates, and genres, for twenty-eight novels by Stephen King

Novel and Circumstances of Composition	*Date Written*	*Worldcat Genres*
Drinking/Typewritten		
Carrie (1974)	1972–73	horror
'Salem's Lot (1975)	1972–74	horror
The Shining (1977)	1974–75	horror/occult/paranormal
The Stand (1978)	1975–78	horror
The Dead Zone (1979)	1975–78	horror/sci-fi/paranormal
Drinking/Using Cocaine/Typewritten		
Firestarter (1980)	1977–80	horror/thriller/paranormal
Cujo (1981)	1977–81	horror
Pet Sematary (1983)	1978–82	horror
Drinking/Using Cocaine/Word processed		
Thinner (as Bachman) (1984)	1981?-82	allegories/horror
Christine (1983)	1979–83	horror
It (1986)	1981–85	horror
Misery (1987)	1984–86	horror/psychological fiction
The Tommyknockers (1987)	1982–87	horror
The Dark Half (1989)	1987–89	horror
Sober/Word processed		
Needful Things (1992)	1988–91	horror
Gerald's Game (1992)	1990?-91	horror/psychological fiction
Insomnia (1994)	1990–93	horror
Rose Madder (1995)	1993–94	love stories/psychological fiction/horror/romance
Desperation (1996)	1994–95	horror/psychological fiction
The Regulators (as Bachman) (1996)	1994–95?	horror
The Green Mile (1996)	1995–96	horror
Sober/Handwritten		
Bag of Bones (1998)	1997–98	ghost stories
Sober/Word processed		
The Girl Who Loved Tom Gordon (1999)	1998–99	psychological fiction/adventure/action adventure
Using Oxycontin/Handwritten		
Dreamcatcher (2001)	1999–2000	horror
Sober/Word processed		
From a Buick 8 (2002)	1999–2001	horror/thrillers
Lisey's Story (2006)	2003–05	horror/ghost stories/fantasy
Cell (2006)	2005	horror/psychological fiction
Duma Key (2008)	2006–07	paranormal fiction/horror

(ten years) and were all written while King was drinking or drinking and using cocaine. They show almost no tendency to group by genre in a series of bootstrap consensus analyses based on multiple numbers of the most frequent words, word n-grams, and character n-grams, multiple different culling percentages, and several different distance measures. (For an early argument for the effectiveness of the analysis of n-grams, there called "sequences," see Hoover, "Frequent Sequences"; all bootstrap consensus analyses in this chapter were performed in Stylo.) *Firestarter* and *The Dead Zone*, both of which have paranormal elements, often group together, but they are almost invariably joined by the horror novel *The Stand*. One other fairly consistent grouping is *Carrie* with *'Salem's Lot*, both of which are simple horror novels, but they are also the two earliest. Another is the grouping of *Cujo* and *Pet Sematary* with *The Shining*, a group that is doubly incoherent, with two genres and a long chronological spread.

The six sober word-processed novels beginning with *Needful Things* and ending with *The Green Mile* (with *The Regulators* omitted because it and *Desperation* share a number of characters) also fail to show any strong tendency to group by genre. The horror novels *Needful Things* and *Insomnia* form the only very consistent group, but they are almost never joined by *The Green Mile*, the other horror novel. Similarly, *Rose Madder* and *Gerald's Game*, both of which have strong psychological features, pair fairly consistently but without the other psychologically inflected novel, *Desperation*. The fact that *The Green Mile* tends to be an outlier suggests that perhaps the Worldcat "horror" label is suspect. In fact, Wikipedia labels this novel "magical realism" ("*The Green Mile* [novel]").

These inconclusive analyses suggest that any genre effects on King's style are not strong ones. King's known penchant for mixing genres or the inherent vagueness and inaccuracy of the labels themselves may be preventing any consistent grouping by genre. Unlike the genre distinctions that were analyzed in Chapter 2 (between Nesbit's adult and children's fiction, between Alcott's sensational and normal fiction, and between Doyle's Holmes and non-Holmes stories), the genres of King's fiction can probably be safely ignored for the purposes of this chapter. If they disrupt the analyses of chronology or mode or circumstances of composition, that will be readily apparent in any case.

Alcohol and Drug Abuse and Stephen King's Style

> By 1985 I had added drug addiction to my alcohol problem. . . . I was wiping my ass with poison ivy again, this time on a daily basis, but I couldn't ask for help. That's not the way you did things in my family. . . . Yet the part of me that writes the stories, the deep part that knew I was an alcoholic as early as 1975, when I wrote *The Shining*, wouldn't accept that. Silence isn't what that part is about. It began to scream for help in the only way it knew how, through my fiction and through my monsters. In late 1985 and early 1986 I wrote *Misery* (the title quite aptly described my state of mind), in which a writer is held prisoner and tortured by a

> psychotic nurse. In the spring and summer of 1986 I wrote *The Tommyknockers*, often working until midnight with my heart running at a hundred and thirty beats a minute and cotton swabs stuck up my nose to stem the coke-induced bleeding.
>
> (King, *On Writing* 37)

Stephen King has been remarkably candid about his abuse of alcohol and cocaine, and the basic pattern of his abuse is as indicated in Table 7.1. His comments are not always entirely consistent, however. In his 2014 *Rolling Stone* interview, King claims, "I didn't drink in the days. Sometimes if I had, like, two things going—which I did a lot, sometimes I still do—I would work at night. And if I was working at night, I was looped. But I never wrote original stuff at night, I just rewrote" (King, "Stephen King: The *Rolling Stone* Interview"). Yet, in his *On Writing*, published fourteen years earlier, he had reported: "At the end of my adventures I was drinking a case of sixteen-ounce tallboys a night, and there's one novel, *Cujo*, that I barely remember writing at all" (38). He also reports that for the six years beginning in 1981, he sat at his desk "either drunk or wrecked out of my mind," presumably writing (39).

Although King admits being addicted to cocaine by 1985 (King, *On Writing* 37), he began using cocaine in 1978 or 1979 and continued until his wife staged an intervention in 1987 (King, "Stephen King: The *Rolling Stone* Interview" and "Stephen King Interview"). When asked whether or not he quit immediately after the intervention, King replied, "So it took me about a year to get my shit together, get back on track. The worst of it was 87 to 88 when I was looking for a detente, a way I could live with booze and drugs without giving them up altogether" (King, "Stephen King Interview"). According to a journal entry printed in "Pages from a Writer's Journal" in the 2004 Dark Tower novel, *Song of Susannah*, King celebrated his one-year anniversary of sobriety on 19 June 1989. This confirms the intervention in 1987, and this is broadly supported by another journal entry from *Song of Susannah* that reports an incident on 19 June 1987, when he got drunk to celebrate receiving his first author copy of the Dark Tower novel, *The Drawing of the Three*.

King indicates that *The Tommyknockers*, published in 1987 and written from 1982 to 1987, "was the last one I wrote before I cleaned up my act" (King, "Stephen King: The *Rolling Stone* Interview"). In his *Paris Review* interview, he described *Needful Things*, published in 1991 and written from 1988 to 1991, as "the first thing that I'd written since I was sixteen without drinking or drugging" ("Stephen King"). Rolls confirms this, in part, reporting that King was drinking heavily as early as 1972 (Rolls ch. 3). These statements seem to conflict with the fact that *The Dark Half*, written from 1987 to 1989, was published in 1989, after *The Tommyknockers*, but before *Needful Things*. The conflict is resolved by the fact that *The Dark Half* "was built using material from a book King had almost completed in the early 1980s and had considered releasing as a Bachman novel" (Rolls ch. 12). These facts provide the basis for the boundary between alcohol and drug influence and sobriety in Table 7.1.

King's use of Oxycontin while writing *Dreamcatcher* in 1999–2000 is also well documented in his *Rolling Stone* interview (King, "Stephen King: The *Rolling Stone* Interview"), but, because this novel was also handwritten, the effects of Oxycontin cannot be analyzed here. This novel will rather be addressed later in this chapter in the discussion of King's modes of composition.

There are some minor inconsistencies in King's various interviews and written comments about his alcohol and drug abuse, and I have mentioned in other chapters the relative unreliability of writers' comments on their own lives and work. As a pertinent reminder, consider Rogak's revelation that King even inaccurately reports the date of his mother's death in *On Writing* (5–6). The circumstances of composition indicated in Table 7.1 should therefore not be taken as definitive, but they seem accurate enough in outline to allow for some testing for the possibility of any effects of alcohol and drugs on King's style.

Analyzing the novels from several years before and after the intervention should reveal any change-point that might be caused by sobering up. My first test is a cluster analysis of the ten novels from *Christine* (1979–83) to *Desperation* (1994–95), the five novels written before and the five written after he became sober (see Table 7.1). (All cluster analyses in this chapter were performed in Minitab, with standardized variables, Ward linkage, and squared Euclidean distance.) All were word processed (for simplicity, these will be designated as "pre-intervention" and "post-intervention," in the following discussion). An analysis based on the nine hundred most frequent words almost perfectly places all sections of each novel in a single group. The single exception is one section of *The Tommyknockers* (1982–87) clustering with the sections of *The Dark Half* (1987–89). Both are pre-intervention. The grouping by novel is undoubtedly largely a result of topic and theme, given that most of these nine hundred words are content words, so it is important to compare analyses based on smaller numbers of words, where the proportion of function words is higher.

An analysis based on the five hundred most frequent words shows more mixing of sections of different novels, but it does not consistently group sections of pre-intervention novels separately from post-intervention novels. Reducing the number of most frequent words to one hundred, most of which are function words, removes most of the thematic or other content-based similarities. This analysis shows some groups consisting entirely of pre-intervention or post-intervention novels and including sections from more than one novel; for example, one post-intervention cluster consists of all of *Desperation*, two sections of *Insomnia*, and four sections of *Needful Things*. This cluster has eight sections of the pre-intervention *It* as its nearest neighbor, however, and elsewhere other sections of *Needful Things* join inconsistent mixed clusters with the pre-intervention *Misery*, *The Tommyknockers*, and *Thinner*.

Reducing the number of words that are analyzed to twenty-five removes all content words but tells much the same story. There is thus no evidence that removing the content words is revealing an alcohol or drug influence on King's style. Rather, the reduction in the amount of information available in analyses based on fewer words results in a reduction of the accuracy of the groupings by novel. Clearly, the individual identity of each text produces a stylistic signal that is stronger than that associated with sobriety or alcohol and drug abuse. These results are consistent with the results of cluster analyses discussed in Chapter 2, where the use of the most frequent words was similar enough among sections of individual novels to allow them to group by novel.

A clear chronological effect can be seen throughout all of the cluster analyses just described. Chronology will be treated more fully in the next section of this chapter, but removing the first two and last two of the novels, and thereby reducing the time span greatly, lessens the effect of chronology on these novels. A large number of bootstrap consensus analyses based on various different numbers of the most frequent words, word n-grams, and character n-grams, and multiple culling percentages and distance measures fail to show any examples of consistent groupings of pre-intervention and post-intervention novels. This also means there are no consistent groupings of earlier or later novels.

Similar analyses of just the final two pre-intervention and the first two post-intervention novels give results that are compatible with the analyses of larger groups. The groupings are not consistent, except for the fact that all of them produce only pairs consisting of one pre-intervention and one post-intervention novel. The surprising lack of any detectable difference between the styles of Stephen King's novels written while he was drinking heavily and using cocaine and those written after he became sober is echoed by one of his biographers, who remarks, "One of the amazing aspects of Stephen King's life is that his copious drug and alcohol abuse didn't interfere with either the quantity or the quality of his prodigious output" (Rogak 2). Fortunately, this durability of King's style in the face of alcohol and drug use suggests that it should be possible to detect any effects of change in mode of composition that may exist, provided that such effects can be disentangled from those of chronology, the subject of the next section.

Chronological Drift and Stephen King's Style

> My children-protagonists are just about finished because I'm getting too old. . . . I don't want to retrace territory that I've already covered . . . because it is too easy to rehash all the things which have occurred there over the years—the rabid dog, the crazy cop, those kids who ended a summer in search of a dead body along some railroad tracks. If I have one real interest in the next 10 or 15 years of my life, it is not to lose my courage as a writer. I want to try new projects and big, challenging projects. . . . A stronger draw

> than the money is the knowledge that people are coming to my books for one specific thing—to get scared, to learn something about their childhoods or the world they live in, whatever—and when they pick up a new book maybe they will discover that this book isn't the same as any of the others, isn't what they expected. There is a great siren's song to keep giving them whatever it is they want. And I could probably do that, but it wouldn't necessarily be giving myself what I want or what I need in order to grow as a writer. I want to continue to grow, but I don't think anybody knows how to do that.
>
> *(Magistrale 17)*

This quotation is taken from a 1989 interview with Stephen King. If 1969, the year he sold his first story (Rolls ch. 2), is considered the beginning of King's career, this interview occurred only twenty years into what is now a career of more than fifty years, but it already suggests that King did not want to become stagnant. The question to be answered here is whether or not, intentionally or not, his style evolved or drifted, irrespective of any effects of changes in mode of composition, in the thirty-five years from 1972 to 2007, during which the texts in my King corpus were written.

In the analysis of possible effects of alcohol and drugs on King's style earlier in this chapter, it was apparent that chronology was relevant, but the significance of any chronological drift needs further testing. An exploratory cluster analysis of all twenty-eight of the novels written between 1972 and 2007 that are included in my King corpus, based on the one thousand most frequent words (no pronouns, culled at eighty percent), shows strong chronological groupings, as can be seen in Figure 7.1 (some titles have been shortened to make the graph easier to read). With three exceptions, the novels form three consistent chronological groups by date of composition, 1973–85, 1986–94, and 1995–2007 (using the dates of completion). The first exception is the 1981–82 novel, *Thinner*, written under the Bachman pseudonym, which appears in the 1986–1994 group. (The other Bachman novel in this set, the 1995 *The Regulators*, groups normally, pairing with the related *Desperation*.) The second exception is the 1982–87 novel, *The Tommyknockers*, which appears in the 1973–1985 group, but note that it was begun in 1982. The third exception is the 1998–99 novel, *The Girl Who Loved Tom Gordon*, which is an outlier that groups very loosely with both the 1986–1994 group and the 1995–2007 group.

Testing these novels in sections of sixty thousand words gives similar results and shows that, as would be expected, the sections of each novel strongly tend to group together. There is only minor mixing of sections of *Cujo*, *The Stand*, *It*, and *Rose Madder*. Indeed, the chronological grouping is even more consistent than that shown in Figure 7.1. One section of the 1981–85 *It* and all sections of the 1982–87 *The Tommyknockers* now group with the 1986–1994 novels. *The Girl Who Loved Tom Gordon* (1998–99) remains somewhat of an outlier, though here it groups with the 1990–91 novel, *Gerald's Game*. The strength of the chronological

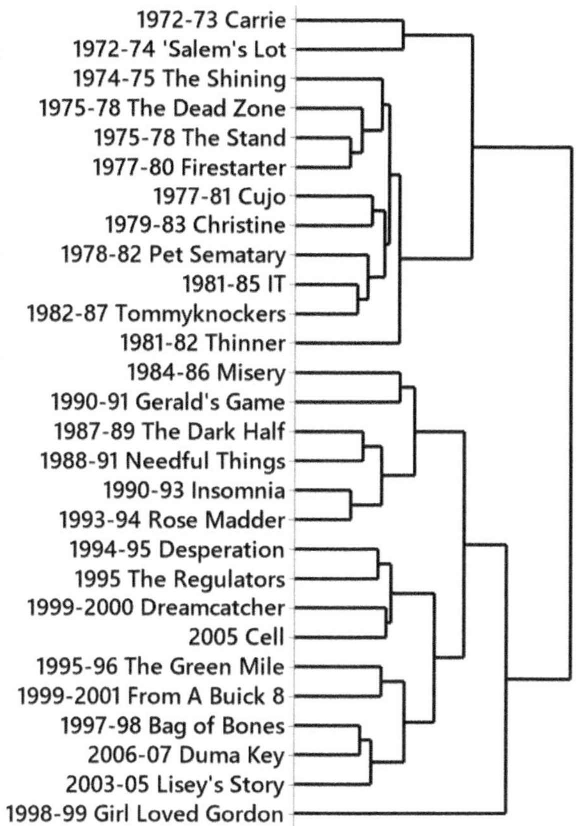

FIGURE 7.1 Cluster analysis of twenty-eight novels by Stephen King, based on the one thousand most frequent words, with pronouns deleted, culled at eighty percent

effect can be further evaluated by testing of the seven earliest and the seven latest novels in the corpus with a large number of bootstrap consensus analyses, based, as usual, on multiple numbers of most frequent words, word n-grams and character n-grams, multiple culling levels, and multiple distance measures. The results vary consistently and sharply distinguish the early and late novels.

Chronological drift can be tested more precisely by limiting the analysis to the eight pre-intervention typewritten novels, ignoring genre. Another set of bootstrap consensus analyses like the ones just described and based on the same variables and methods, while not entirely consistent, *are* consistent in separating the first two novels from the rest. Given the time spans in the years of composition for these novels, it is hardly surprising that the groupings by year of completion for the rest of the novels are not very accurate.

Finally, consider the results of testing just the post-intervention novels completed from 1991 to 2007, but omitting *The Girl Who Loved Tom Gordon*, which was an outlier in earlier analyses, and the handwritten 1998 *Bag of Bones* and 2000 *Dreamcatcher* (the latter written under the influence of Oxycontin). The omission of these three novels creates an artificial gap in composition from 1997 to 2000, which should make any chronological effect more visible and avoid complications. A final set of bootstrap consensus analyses of these eleven novels based on various different numbers of the most frequent words, word n-grams, and character n-grams, and multiple culling percentages and distance measures produces consensus trees in which there is a strong consensus for the novels completed from 1991 to 1994 to group separately from the rest and a weaker tendency for the last two novels to form a separate group.

King's style does not show the same kind of very strong chronological drift found in the works of Henry James in Chapter 6, but there is enough evidence of a significant effect of chronology on his style that testing for a possible stylistic effect of his changes in mode of composition will need to be designed so as to factor out chronology as much as possible.

Modes of Composition and Stephen King's Style

> "I need the sound of the keys, the keys of a manual typewriter," Don DeLillo once said in an interview. Now there are ways to recapture them. . . . There are contraptions that turn old manual typewriters into word-processing machines. The actor Tom Hanks is such a devotee of manual typewriters that he has created Hanx Writer, an app that simulates a manual typewriter on tablets and phones. If fetishism is in play, why stop there? Retro writing tastes find many justifications. *The Wall Street Journal* has reported that notes taken by hand are more effectively retained than those typed into a computer. Styluses are now being used on tablets that function like brushes or pens. And there is much to be said for the fountain pen. Who knows? Maybe such reversions to older writing tools will shape different thoughts or inspire an alternate prose style. Or maybe, I more soberly think, they will do nothing at all.
>
> *(Rothstein)*

Early Typing and Late Word Processing

Stephen King received a Royal typewriter for Christmas in 1958, when he was eleven, and composed the first story he remembers submitting for publication on it in 1960 (it was declined) (*On Writing* 13). He also seems to have used it to produce his first paid writing work, which he typed on a roll of yellow paper. This was a sports column he wrote, while still in high school, for a local newspaper, at the munificent rate of half a cent a word (*On Writing* 21). He later used an Underwood typewriter, and it was this typewriter he used to type the first draft of his first Dark

Tower novel, *The Gunslinger*, in 1970, at the age of twenty-three (King, "Politics"). He married Tabitha Spruce in 1971 (Rogak 61) and used her Olivetti to type his first two novels, *Carrie* and *'Salem's Lot*, from 1972 to 1974 (*On Writing* 4).

After his early success with *Carrie* in 1974, he bought an IBM Selectric, which he remembers using to type 450 pages of what he was then calling *The Cannibals*, the novel that was to become *Under the Dome* (2009):

> So, for your amusement, and as an appetizer to *Under the Dome*, here are the first sixty pages or so of *The Cannibals*, reproduced, warts and all, from the original manuscript which was dredged up by Ms. Mod from a locked cabinet in a back room of my office. I'm amused by the antique quality of the typescript; this may have been the last thing I did on my old IBM Selectric before moving on to a computer system.
>
> *(King, "The Cannibals"; see Kirschenbaum 83–4)*

King does not provide an explicit date for *The Cannibals*, but he reports typing it in Pittsburgh, during the filming of *Creepshow* (Romero), filming that took place in 1981 (Considine). He is presumably referring to the same typewriter in his 1983 *Playboy* interview, where, after mentioning his Wang word processor, he talks about typing *Pet Sematary* (1978–82) on his typewriter (King, "Stephen King: *Playboy* Interview"). The first draft of this novel was finished in early 1979 (Rolls ch. 6).

The evidence that King composed at the typewriter until 1981 accords well with the report that he bought his first computer, a Wang Model 5, in 1981, in preparation for collaborating with Peter Straub on *The Talisman* (1984) (Rolls ch. 6; Kirschenbaum 60, 83–4; Beahm *A to Z 224* "*The Talisman*"). Curiously, Rogak dates King's purchase of the Wang to 1976, though without documentation (81). This earlier date is just possible, as the first Wang word processors date from that year, but it seems unlikely, based on the other evidence discussed previously. In addition, King reports that he began his story "Word Processor of the Gods" (which features a modified Wang word processor with DELETE and INSERT keys that delete and insert things in the real world) the month after he got his word processor (*Skeleton Crew* "Introduction"). Given King's macabre imagination, it is hardly surprising that the main character uses the DELETE key on his wife and son so that he can INSERT better ones (see Kirschenbaum 79–81). The fact that "The Word Processor of the Gods" was published in the January 1983 *Playboy* (Rolls ch. 9) further supports 1981 as the year of the purchase of the Wang.

The situation is complicated somewhat by conflicting statements about how King initially used the word processor and by the manuscript evidence for some of his texts. For example, Rolls claims that "King, over the next few years, would continue using an electric typewriter for most of his writing, having his secretary transfer it to the Wang, on which he would do his editing (ch. 7)." He later argues that the main character's use of his computer in "The Word Processor of the Gods" to delete and insert was based on King's own use of the computer (ch. 9). This idea is (rather weakly) supported by a 1991 interview in which King was asked how he gets past points at which the writing does not come easily. He responded, "For me, a lot of times the real barrier to get to work—to get to the typewriter or the word processor—comes before I get there" (King, "Digging").

Kirschenbaum claims that, after King purchased his Wang in 1981, the computer "quickly became integral to the workflow of the office" (76). The integration that he specifically mentions, however, suggests the possibility that King continued to compose at the typewriter after 1981.

> Marsha DeFilippo, King's longtime personal assistant who came to work for him in 1986, recalls that some of her first assignments consisted of using the Wang to key in the then-typewritten manuscripts of *The Eyes of the Dragon* and the *Tommyknockers* so they could be mailed to Viking on disk.
>
> *(76)*

The suggestion that King was still composing on the typewriter significantly later than 1981 is problematic, however. According to King's notation at the end of *The Tommyknockers*, the novel was written from "August 19th, 1982" to "May 19th, 1987," and this date range seems to indicate only the final phase of writing. In 1985, when King was scheduled to publish *It* (1986), *The Eyes of the Dragon* (1987), *The Tommyknockers* (1987), and *Misery* (1987) in just over a year, he was asked whether this wasn't perhaps too much (the original, limited edition of the Dark Tower book, *The Drawing of the Three*, was actually also published in 1987).

> "Sure," he says. "But those books are there, and I'm tired of just seeing them sit in a drawer. They're not doing me any good, they're not doing anybody else any good. One of them has been there since 1981, 'The Tommyknockers.' So it was Tabby's (his wife's) idea. She said publish them all at once, and get done with them, and then don't publish any more for a couple of years."
>
> *(Weingarten 10)*

What this suggests is that DeFilippo was entering the 1981 or earlier preliminary typewritten draft of *The Tommyknockers* into the computer rather than that King was still composing that novel on the typewriter significantly later than 1981. Rolls suggests that *The Drawing of the Three* was another of the books that had been in the drawer for some time (ch. 10).

A stronger case can be made for King's typing of *The Eyes of the Dragon*. Rolls reports that he began the novel, which was originally titled, "The Napkins," in January of 1983, though "[h]e had been considering doing such a book for some months" (ch. 9). The fact that the book was privately published in 1984, in a deluxe limited edition, however, raises the question of what specific typescript DeFilippo was entering into the computer. "The mass market edition, first published in 1987, contains important differences in the text, including character changes and an entire chapter which was not included in the later edition" (Wood, *Literary Companion* "Eyes of the Dragon"), changes that were suggested, in part, by freelance editor Deborah Brodie (Rogak 151–2). It thus seems possible that DeFilippo was entering the text of the limited edition itself into the Wang. In any case, even if she was entering a typescript of the limited edition, that typescript could not have been typed later than early 1983.

One other peculiar question surrounding King's use of typewriters and word processors involves the restored, or "uncut," version of *The Stand*, published in 1990. In a 2009 podcast, King recalled his process of restoration, which included using his Selectric typewriter to re-type the entire existing novel, as well as the four hundred pages that had been cut from the original 1978 version:

> I had the manuscript on one side of an IBM Selectric typewriter, because this was pre-computers. So I had the manuscript on one side and I had the pages of a book that I had just simply torn out of the binding on the other side. And I went through the book and I started at the beginning and I updated the dates, because by then it was, I don't know, I think about seven or eight years out of date. So I changed the years to bring them a little bit into the eighties, and I added in all the pages, and I wrote new material besides, and that's how it came to be.
>
> *(King, "Stephen King on His Longest Novels"; my transcription)*

It is puzzling that the restored version was not published until 1990 and that its dates of composition are given by King, at the end of the book, as "February 1975" to "December 1988." Equally puzzling is the fact that the dates in the restored version do not extend "a little bit into the eighties" but rather into the 1990s. Most of the novel seems to have been drafted in 1975, though it was based on "Night Surf," a story first written in the late 1960s and published in 1974 (Rolls ch. 4; Wood, *Literary Companion* "Introduction"). Thus, in spite of the confused situation, King's "seven or eight" years out of date would put the revision in 1981 to 1983, broadly consistent with the other available information.

King's change in mode of composition from typewriting to word processing around 1981 is thus fairly firmly established, at least to a degree sufficient for testing whether or not the change in mode resulted in a change in style. Before that testing can begin, however, one further question about King's modes of composition has to be addressed: his occasional handwritten compositions.

Early and Late Handwriting

Although he clearly composed mainly at the typewriter from his teens until 1981, and then on the computer, it is also clear that King sometimes wrote longhand in notebooks. According to Beahm, "When traveling, King has written in notebooks, subsequently turned over to his secretaries for retyping into the computer at the office, which was linked to his home office, the site of the main CPU for his Wang word processor" (*A to Z* 247 "Writing Tools"). Wood confirms that "King keeps thoughts and stories in handwritten journals, some containing up to ten different pieces"; one of these journals, containing parts of four stories, seems to date from 1989–91 (*Literary Companion* "Movie Show"). King himself has sometimes commented on his occasional use of handwritten notebooks. For example, he recalls writing the first part of the first draft of *Misery* (1987) by hand at a desk in a London Hotel in the early 1980s, remarking, "I filled sixteen pages of a steno notebook. I like to work longhand, actually; the only problem is that, once I get jazzed, I can't keep up with the lines forming in my head and I get frazzled" (*On Writing* 6; see also Wood, *Literary Companion* "*Misery*"). In 1995, he also commented on the handwritten composition of part of *The Green Mile* (1996):

> So I got to work, but in a tentative, stop-and-start way. Most of the second chapter was written during a rain delay at Fenway Park! When Ralph called, I had filled a notebook with scribbled pages of *The Green Mile*, and realized I was building a novel when I should have been spending my time clearing my desk for revisions on a book already written.
>
> *(*The Two Dead Girls *"Foreword: A Letter";*
> *see also Beahm,* Companion *379)*

King's occasional donations of handwritten drafts for charitable purposes are also informative. For example, he donated ten handwritten pages of "The Raft" to benefit the American Repertory Theatre in 1996 (Beahm, *A to Z* 6 "Auctions and Benefits"). Although this text was published in 1982, it was written in 1968 and sold in 1969 (King, *Skeleton Crew* "Notes"), which means that it predates the period to be addressed in this study. Earlier, King had donated three items in 1985 that are described as follows:

> 48. KING, STEPHEN holographic notebook containting [*sic*] portions of three manuscripts. (1) *The Drawing of the Three* A portion of the unpublished 2nd Dark Tower novel. (2) "The End of the Whole Mess" A portion of the story, to be published in "Omni" (10/86 issue). (3) *The Doors* A portion of an unpublished novel.
>
> *(Wood,* Uncollected *95; see also Spignesi, "Keyholes")*

These seem to be genuine examples of partly handwritten texts. *The Drawing of the Three* was finished by 1986, according to the "Afterword." The publication details of "The End of the Whole Mess" are given in the description, and the presence of *The Doors* in the same notebook indicates that it was probably written about the same time. This suggests that King may have been writing longhand in the notebook as late as 1985, though there is no specific evidence of the date of the composition of these handwritten drafts, and Rolls's suggestion that *The Drawing of the Three* was one of the books King had in a drawer in 1985 (ch. 10) leaves open the possibility that the notebook could date from much earlier. In 1988, King also "donated a notebook containing holographic pages from an unpublished novel, *Keyholes*" (Beahm, *A to Z* 6 "Auctions and Benefits") that was apparently written about 1984 (Wood et al. 175). This is a fragment of only two-and-a-half pages and only about eight hundred words, so perhaps a story rather than a novel (Spignesi, "Keyholes"). The notebook also contained a handwritten revision of the script of the 1985 movie, *Silver Bullet*, based on *Cycle of the Werewolf* (1983) (Wood, *Literary Companion* "Keyholes").

Another indication of King's longhand work is a chapbook of "The New Lieutenant's Rap," entirely in his handwriting. This story was "provided to guests at a 1999 New York City party celebrating King's twenty-fifth anniversary in book publishing" (Wood, *Literary Companion* "The New Lieutenant's Rap"). The 1995 story "Luckey Quarter" was also written " 'longhand, on hotel stationery' in a Nevada hotel while on a Harley-Davidson motorcycle trip across America, promoting *Insomnia*" (Wood, *Literary Companion* "Luckey Quarter"). The evidence suggests, then, that King wrote longhand very early in his career and that he has occasionally worked longhand in notebooks when he was away from his typewriter or word processor. The fragmentary and relatively obscure nature of these handwritten works, however, suggests that handwriting has not normally been a major mode of composition for King. It also seems significant that there are no known holograph drafts of whole novels, except for *Bag of Bones* (1997–98) and *Dreamcatcher* (1999–2000).

Well after King's major change in mode of composition from typing to word processing in 1981, and about ten years after he stopped drinking and using drugs, he wrote *Bag of Bones* (1997–98) and *Dreamcatcher* (1999–2000) longhand. These two were interrupted by the word-processed *The Girl Who Loved Tom Gordon* (1998–99). From the point of view of computational analysis, the circumstances surrounding the handwritten composition of these two novels are both fortunate and unfortunate. Fortunately, the circumstances surrounding the handwritten novels are quite clear, and the time frame in which they were written is short enough that chronology should not be a significant factor. Unfortunately, King has given conflicting reasons for writing the novels by hand, and, for *Dreamcatcher* (and only this novel), the change in mode coincides with his use of Oxycontin for pain. Also, as noted in the section on chronological drift earlier in this chapter, the intervening short word-processed novel, *The Girl Who Loved Tom Gordon*, is quite different in genre and tends to be an outlier in chronological analyses.

In his "Author's Note" to *Dreamcatcher* (1999–2001), King comments on his use of handwriting, claiming, "To write the first draft of such a long book by hand put me in touch with the language as I haven't been for years. I even wrote one night (during a power outage) by candlelight." His *Paris Review* Interview (conducted in 2001 and 2006) gives a somewhat fuller comment on both of his handwritten novels:

> I've occasionally gone back to longhand—with *Dreamcatcher* and with *Bag of Bones*—because I wanted to see what would happen. It changed some things. Most of all, it made me slow down because it takes a long time. Every time I started to write something, some guy up here, some lazybones is saying, Aw, do we have to do that? I've still got a little bit of that scholar's bump on my finger from doing all that longhand. But it made the rewriting process a lot more felicitous. It seemed to me that my first draft was more polished, just because it wasn't possible to go so fast. You can only drive your hand along at a certain speed. It felt like the difference between, say, rolling along in a powered scooter and actually hiking the countryside.
>
> *("Stephen King")*

Years later, in his 2014 *Rolling Stone* interview, however, he gave a different reason for the mode of composition of *Dreamcatcher:*

> Well, I don't like *Dreamcatcher* very much. *Dreamcatcher* was written after the accident. . . . I was using a lot of Oxycontin for pain. And I couldn't work on a computer back then because it hurt too much to sit in that position. So I wrote the whole thing longhand. And I was pretty stoned when I wrote it, because of the Oxy, and that's another book [besides *The Tommyknockers*] that shows the drugs at work.
>
> *(King, "Stephen King: The* Rolling Stone *Interview")*

Handwriting, typing, word processing, and the durability of Stephen King's style

It seems appropriate to test King's more minor and problematic change in mode of composition first: his temporary change to handwriting for two novels, long after his transition from typing to word processing. As I have noted, King's use of Oxycontin during the composition of *Dreamcatcher*, coinciding as it does with his turn to handwriting, makes testing for a stylistic effect problematic. The odd behavior of the immediately following novel, *The Girl Who Loved Tom Gordon*, in chronological analyses, where it tends to be an outlier, is also problematic, possibly because of its genre (adventure, action, psychological fiction). Nevertheless, omitting *The Girl Who Loved Tom Gordon* and testing the *The Green Mile* (1995–96), *Bag of Bones* (1997–98), *Dreamcatcher* (2001), and *From a Buick 8* (1999–2001) seems an appropriate way of determining whether or not the two handwritten novels tend to group together and separate from the chronologically adjacent word-processed novels.

A set of initial cluster analyses of these four novels in sections of about thirty thousand words gives little suggestion of an effect of handwriting on King's style. In analyses based on the one hundred and two hundred most frequent words, there is some mixing of sections of novels, but no mixing of *Bag of Bones* with *Dreamcatcher*. The only mixing of these two handwritten novels occurs in analyses involving the one thousand most frequent words and the nine hundred most frequent words, in which just the final section of *Bag of Bones* clusters with *Dreamcatcher*. The novels are otherwise very distinct, a pattern hardly consistent with the operation of any significant effect of mode of composition.

A series of bootstrap consensus analyses of the same sections of these four novels based on various different numbers of the most frequent words, word n-grams, and character n-grams, and multiple culling percentages and distance measures shows some inconsistency, including analyses in which sections of handwritten and word-processed novels mix. The majority of the analyses (more consistently in those based on character n-grams) show the four novels appearing in three main groups: one containing the two word-processed novels, with their sections grouped separately; one containing the sections of *Dreamcatcher*; and one containing the sections of *Bag of Bones*.

Bootstrap consensus analyses of the four novels as whole texts (using the same variables and methods) shows multiple different pairings of the novels, including some in which the novels form two pairs, one handwritten and one word processed. The most common pattern, however, is two chronological pairs, one containing the two earliest and one containing the two latest novels, so that each pair contains a handwritten and a word-processed novel. Again, these patterns show, at the most, the possibility of a very weak effect of mode of composition. It also remains possible that the effect of Oxycontin on *Dreamcatcher* prevents it from grouping with the other handwritten novel, *Bag of Bones*, though the absence of discernable effects of alcohol and cocaine on King's style shown earlier in this chapter makes that unlikely.

I now turn to King's major change in mode of composition: typing versus word processing. As I have noted, King bought a Wang word processor in 1981 and used it and other computers and word-processing software from that time forward to write his novels, except for the two handwritten novels just discussed and the other minor exceptions noted earlier. The chronological drift shown in the section on chronology is weaker than the regular evolution of Henry James's style, but it is pronounced enough to require that its interference with any possible effect of mode of composition on King's style be taken into account.

Perhaps surprisingly, cluster analysis of the last six typewritten and first six word-processed novels does not group the typewritten novels separately from the handwritten ones, and thus also shows no chronological grouping into early and late novels. There are, however, some very consistent groupings, perhaps most clearly evident in an analysis based on the one thousand most frequent words, shown in Figure 7.2 (some titles have been shortened to make the graph easier to

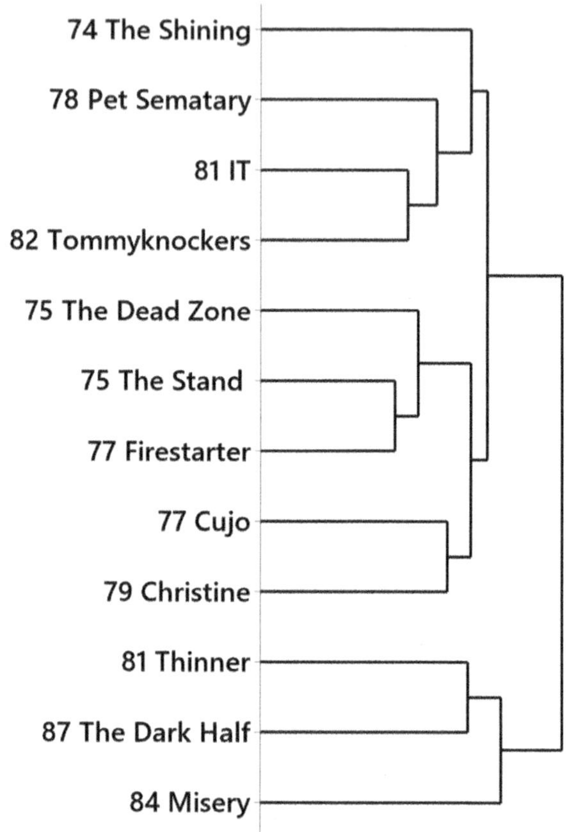

FIGURE 7.2 Cluster analysis of Stephen King's last six typewritten and first six word-processed novels, based on the one thousand most frequent words, with pronouns deleted, culled at eighty percent

read). When the whole range of analyses from the one hundred to one thousand most frequent words is examined, four relatively consistent clusters are evident, as shown in Table 7.2 (arranged in descending order of consistency).

Some of these groupings also occur sporadically in bootstrap consensus analyses of these texts, especially in analyses based on the most frequent words, but analyses based on word n-grams or character n-grams tend to give widely varying and rather chaotic results. The one consistency is that in none of the analyses do all the typewritten or all the word-processed novels form a single group. In fact, only very rarely do even four of the six novels written in a single mode form a group, and the typical pattern is several small groups of novels, most of which contain both typewritten and word-processed novels.

Dropping the three earliest and three latest of these novels and retesting the remaining six novels using the same range of bootstrap consensus analyses that was used for the twelve novels gives similarly chaotic results. Occasionally, an analysis

TABLE 7.2 Consistent groupings of six typewritten and six word-processed novels by Stephen King in ten cluster analyses based on the one hundred to one thousand most frequent words (arranged in descending order of consistency)

Group	*Members and Consistency of the Group*	*Worldcat Genres and Other Notes*
1	The three consecutive typewritten novels, *The Dead Zone* (1975–78), *The Stand* (1975–78), and *Firestarter* (1977–80), group together over the whole range of analyses based on the one hundred to one thousand most frequent words.	Worldcat includes the label "paranormal" for both *The Dead Zone* and *Firestarter.*
2	The 1978–82 typewritten *Pet Sematary* groups with the word-processed 1981–85 *It* and 1982–87 *The Tommyknockers* in all analyses based on the two hundred to one thousand most frequent words.	Worldcat labels all of these simply "horror," but *The Tommyknockers,* which features a buried alien spacecraft, has clear science fiction elements (Spignesi, "*The Tommyknockers*").
3	The three word-processed novels, *Thinner* (1981–82), *Misery* (1984–86), and *The Dark Half* (1987–89), group together in analyses based on the four hundred and the six hundred to one thousand most frequent words.	These seem disparate: Worldcat labels *Thinner* as "allegories" and "horror," *Misery* as "horror" and "psychological fiction," and *The Dark Half* simply as "horror." They were also written from 1981 to 1989, and *Thinner* is a Bachman novel.
4	The typewritten *Cujo* (1977–81) groups with the word-processed *Christine* (1979–83) in analyses based on the six hundred to one thousand most frequent words.	Rabid Dog *vs.* Malevolent Haunted Car.

produces one pair of typewritten and one pair of word-processed novels, but only three of thirty-two analyses place the three typewritten novels in one group and the three word-processed novels in the other.

Bootstrap consensus analyses of just the final two typewritten and the first two word-processed novels, again using the same variables and methods, give slightly more encouraging results. In seventeen of thirty-two analyses, the typewritten and word-processed novels form two separate pairs. Curiously, this occurs in only three of the sixteen analyses based on words or word two-grams, but in fourteen of the sixteen analyses based on character four-grams and five-grams. Even more curiously, when the four novels are analyzed with the same method in sections of about thirty thousand words, the sections of each novel almost always form a group in analyses based on the most frequent words and usually do so in analyses based on character four-grams and character five-grams but never in analyses based on word two-grams. More important, however, only two of thirty-two analyses (among those based on the most frequent words) place the sections of the two typewritten novels in one group and the two word-processed novels in another. A typical analysis is shown in Figure 7.3, in which the word-processed *Christine* and *Thinner* appear at the upper left and bottom right and the typewritten *Pet Sematary* and *Cujo* appear at the bottom left and upper right.

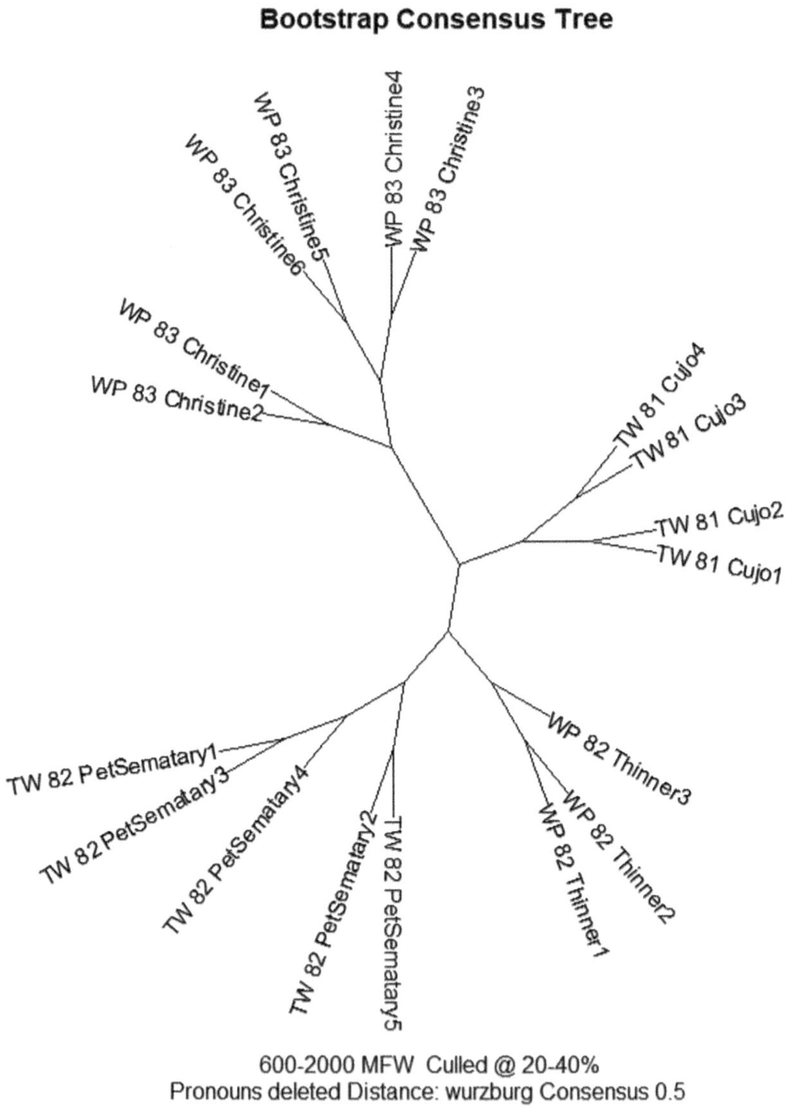

FIGURE 7.3 Bootstrap consensus analysis of Stephen King's last two typewritten and first two word-processed novels, based on the six hundred to two thousand most frequent words, with pronouns deleted, culled at twenty to forty percent, Wurzburg Delta distance, and a consensus of fifty percent

Conclusion

The analyses in Chapter 2 showed that even relatively subtle stylistic variation, such as that between the narrators or characters in novels or plays, can typically be detected computationally. In such cases, the results of multiple methods based on different numbers of the most frequent words are consistent with each other. The equivocal, varied, inconsistent, and often chaotic results of testing for a stylistic effect of Stephen King's changes in mode of composition from typing to word processing to handwriting suggest that, if such an effect exists, it is weaker than the subtle differences tested in Chapter 2. As Beahm puts it, "No matter what writing tool King uses, one thing is clear: It is the tale and the teller that count" (*A to Z*, 247 "Writing Tools"). As the results of this chapter have shown, Stephen's style was not only durable in the face of changes in mode of composition, it was also durable in the face of his abuse of alcohol and drugs and his recovery from that abuse.

References

Beahm, George. *The Stephen King Companion: Four Decades of Fear From the Master of Horror*. Palgrave Macmillan, 2015.

———. *Stephen King from A to Z: An Encyclopedia of His Life and Work*. Andrews McMeel Publishing, 1998. archive.org/details/stephenkingfromt00beah.

Casebeer, Edwin F. "Stephen King's Canon: The Art of Balance." *A Dark Night's Dreaming: Contemporary American Horror Fiction*, edited by Tony Magistrale and Michael A. Morrison, U of South Carolina P, 1996, pp. 42–54. archive.org/details/darknightsdreami0000magi.

Considine, Austin. "How a *Walking Dead* Guru Brought *Creepshow* Back to Life." *New York Times*, 26 Sept. 2019. www.nytimes.com/2019/09/26/arts/television/creepshow-reboot-greg-nicotero.html.

Eder, Maciej et al. "Stylometry With *R*: A Package for Computational Text Analysis." *R Journal*, vol. 8, no. 1, 2016, pp. 107–21. journal.r-project.org/archive/2016/RJ-2016-007/RJ-2016-007.pdf.

Fernandez, Henry. "Stephen King, One of the Richest Authors, Still Out to Scare You." *FOXBusiness*, 17 Aug. 2019. www.foxbusiness.com/media/stephen-king-richest-horror-authors.

"*The Green Mile* (novel)." *Wikipedia*. en.wikipedia.org/wiki/The_Green_Mile_(novel).

Heller, Karen. "Meet the Writers Who Still Sell Millions of Books. Actually, Hundreds of Millions." *The Washington Post*, 20 Dec. 2016. www.washingtonpost.com/lifestyle/style/meet-the-elite-group-of-authors-who-sell-100-million-books-or-350-million/2016/12/20/db3c6a66-bb0f-11e6-94ac-3d324840106c_story.html.

Hoover, David L. "Frequent Word Sequences and Statistical Stylistics." *Literary and Linguistic Computing*, vol. 17, no. 2, 2002, pp. 157–80, doi:10.1093/llc/17.2.157.

Jockers, Matt. *Macroanalysis: Digital Methods and Literary History*. U of Illinois P, 2013, doi:10.5406/illinois/9780252037528.001.0001.

King, Stephen. *Bag of Bones*. Scribner, 1998.

———. "The Blue-Collar King: An Interview With Stephen King." Interviewed by Angela S. Allan. *Los Angeles Review of Books*, 25 Oct. 2015. lareviewofbooks.org/article/the-blue-collar-king-an-interview-with-stephen-king.

———. "The Cannibals." Unpublished Works—A to Z, 2019. www.stephenking.com/library/unpublished/cannibals_the.html.
———. *Carrie*. Doubleday, 1974.
———. *Cell*. Scribner, 2006.
———. *Christine*. Scribner, 1983.
———. *The Colorado Kid*. Simon and Schuster, 2005.
———. *Cujo*. Scribner, 1981.
———. *Cycle of the Werewolf*. Land of Enchantment, 1983.
———. *The Dark Half*. Scribner, 1989.
———. *The Dark Tower II: The Drawing of the Three*. Donald M. Grant Publisher, Inc., 1987.
———. *The Dead Zone*. Scribner, 1979.
———. *Desperation*. Scribner, 1996.
———. "Digging Up Stories With Stephen King." Interviewed by Wallace Stroby, *Writer's Digest*, 16 Sept. 1991. wallacestroby.com/writersonwriting_king.html.
———. *The Drawing of the Three*. Signet, 2003.
———. *Dreamcatcher*. Scribner, 2001.
———. *Duma Key*. Scribner, 2008.
———. *The Eyes of the Dragon*. Philtrum Press, 1984.
———. *Firestarter*. Scribner, 1980.
———. *From a Buick 8*. Scribner, 2002.
———. *Gerald's Game*. Scribner, 1992.
———. *The Girl Who Loved Tom Gordon*. Scribner, 1999.
———. *The Green Mile*. 1996. Orion, 1998.
———. *The Gunslinger*. Donald M. Grant, 1982.
———. *Hearts in Atlantis*. Scribner, 1999.
———. *Insomnia*. Scribner, 1994.
———. *It*. Scribner, 1986.
———. *Lisey's Story*. Scribner, 2006.
———. *Misery*. Scribner, 1987.
———. *Needful Things*. Scribner, 1992.
———. *On Writing: A Memoir of the Craft*. Scribner, 2000. archive.org/details/onwritingmemoir000king.
———. *Pet Sematary*. Scribner, 1983.
———. "The Politics of Limited Editions." *The Truth Inside the Lie: A Blog About Stephen King . . . Mostly*, by Bryant Burnett. thetruthinsidethelie.blogspot.com/2017/10/a-guided-tour-of-kingdom-chronological_26.html.
———. *The Regulators*. Hodder and Staughton, 1996 (as Richard Bachman).
———. *Rose Madder*. Signet, 1995.
———. *'Salem's Lot*. Doubleday, 1975.
———. *The Shining*. Doubleday, 1977.
———. *Thinner*. Scribner, 1984 (as Richard Bachman).
———. *Skeleton Crew*. Signet, 1985.
———. *Song of Susannah*. Scribner, 2004.
———. *The Stand*. Doubleday, 1978.
———. *The Stand*. Doubleday, 1990.
———. "The Stephen King Interview." *The Guardian*, 14 Sept. 2000.
———. "Stephen King on His Longest Novels: *The Stand*." Podcast, interviewed by Gilbert Cruz, 6 Nov. 2009. pdl-stream.timeinc.net/time/audio/2009/thestand_dl.mp3.

———. "Stephen King: *Playboy* Interview (1983)." Interviewed by Eric Norden, *Playboy*, vol. 30, no. 6, June 1983. scrapsfromtheloft.com/2018/03/08/stephen-king-playboy-interview-1983.

———. "Stephen King: The *Rolling Stone* Interview." *Rolling Stone*, 31 October, 2014. www.rollingstone.com/culture/culture-features/stephen-king-the-rolling-stone-interview-191529.

———. *The Tommyknockers*. Scribner, 1987.

———. *The Two Dead Girls*. Scribner, 1995.

King, Stephen, and Peter Straub. *The Black House*. Random House, 2001.

———. *The Talisman*. Ballantine, 1984.

Kirschenbaum, Matthew G. *Track Changes: A Literary History of Word Processing*. Belknap Press, 2016.

Magistrale, Tony. *Stephen King, the Second Decade, Danse Macabre to the Dark Half*. Twayne Publishers, 1992. archive.org/details/stephenking00tony.

Mandelbaum, Paul, editor. *First Words: Earliest Writing From Favorite Contemporary Authors*. Algonquin Books of Chapel Hill, 1993.

Minitab Release 19, Minitab, Inc., State College, PA, 2019.

Rogak, Lisa. *Haunted Heart: The Life and Times of Stephen King*. St. Martins, 2008. archive.org/details/isbn_9780312377328.

Rolls, Albert. *Stephen King: A Biography*. Greenwood Press, 2008.

Romero, George A. *Creepshow*. Creepshow Films Inc., 12 Nov. 1982.

Rothman, Joshua. "What Stephen King Isn't." *The New Yorker*, 11 Oct. 2013. www.newyorker.com/books/page-turner/what-stephen-king-isnt.

Rothstein, Edward. "Undo Influence: Stephen King Began Using a Word Processor in 1981. Toni Morrison Writes Longhand. Does It Matter?" *The Wall Street Journal*, 10 June 2016.

Spignesi, Stephen. *Stephen King, American Master: A Creepy Corpus of Facts About Stephen King and His Work*. Permuted Press, 2018.

"Stephen King, The Art of Fiction No. 189." Interviewed by Nathaniel Rich and Christopher Lehmann-Haupt, *Paris Review*, vol. 48, no. 178, 2006. www.theparisreview.org/interviews/5653/stephen-king-the-art-of-fiction-no-189-stephen-king.

Strengell, Heidi. *Dissecting Stephen King: From the Gothic to Literary Naturalism*. U of Wisconsin P, 2005. archive.org/details/dissectingstephe0000stre.

Temple, Emily. "The Living Authors With the Most Film Adaptations: An Infographic to Confirm Your Suspicions. . . " Literary Hub, 15 Mar. 2017. lithub.com/the-living-authors-with-the-most-film-adaptations.

Weingarten, Paul. "Meeting the Tiger." *Chicago Tribune*, 27 Oct. 1985, p. C10.

Wood, Rocky. *Stephen King: A Literary Companion*. McFarland, 2017.

———. *Stephen King: Uncollected, Unpublished*. Revised and Expanded ed. Cemetery Dance Publications, 2010.

Wood, Rocky et al. *Stephen King: Uncollected, Unpublished*. Kanrock Publishing, 2006.

Worldcat. OCLC Online Computer Library Center, Inc. www.worldcat.org.

8

WHY A CHANGE IN MODE IS NOT ENOUGH: TRANSLATION AND THE RADICAL DURABILITY OF STYLE

> Not only do "translators receive minimal recognition for their work" (Venuti 1995: 8) in fame and fortune and law; not only is their work usually best praised when it is not mentioned at all—as I know from my own experience as a literary translator. Now this study seems to be adding an additional dimension to "the translator's shadowy existence": statistics—what is more, simple statistics of word usage—make them invisible too. . . . In other words, multivariate analysis of most-frequent word usage further—and in a novel way—condemns translators to stylometric invisibility. In the context of this study, they only emerge from it when they do something wrong, or at least controversial, like deleting fragments of a novel or adding their own two pence to the original writer's guinea.
>
> *(Rybicki, "The Great Mystery" 246)*

Introduction

A careful study of eleven authors has uncovered only one equivocal, though unlikely, case—in Ian McEwan (Chapter 5)—in which a change in mode of composition might have caused a significant change in style. This chapter examines the durability of style from a different perspective: that of translation. Translators normally replace almost all of the original author's vocabulary except proper nouns with their own vocabulary in another language. Yet the computational stylistics methods employed in this study are based on the frequencies of the most frequent words or n-grams, the latter themselves derived from the sequence of words. It seems reasonable, under these conditions, to expect these methods to attribute translations to their translators rather than their original authors. Surprisingly, that does not happen. Rather, as Rybicki's comment quoted earlier points out, despite the replacement of the original author's language by that of the translator, translations are normally attributable to their original authors, rendering the translators virtually invisible. The style of the original author somehow survives the process of translation, remaining a stronger signal than that of the translator, in spite of the fact that the text now consists of the translator's words rather than the author's. It is difficult to see how this is possible, but it is, nonetheless, demonstrably true.

The Puzzle of the Invisible Translator

Jan Rybicki, himself an accomplished translator, has presented some important discussions of the surprising tyranny of the original author over the style of a translation and the relative invisibility of the translator (Rybicki, "Burrowing" and "The Great Mystery"; Rybicki and Heydel). In his careful and thorough 2012 study, "The Great Mystery of the (Almost) Invisible Translator: Stylometry in Translation," Rybicki begins with an examination of nine of his own translations of Douglas Coupland and John ie Carré from English into Polish. His initial test shows that bootstrap consensus analysis appropriately groups the novels by original author. This is hardly surprising, but it does suggest already that the translator signal is not as strong as the authorial signal (237). When he expands his testing to translations of sixty-five novels by eleven authors (writing in English, French, and Italian) by twenty translators, the results become more surprising:

> It is interesting to observe that works by individual authors cluster together whether or not each has been translated by the same translator; that, within some authorial clusters, some translator clusters can be observed (as in the Austen translations); that separate clusters of authors translated by the same translator occupy adjacent positions on the graph (the Coupland and le Carré translations by Rybicki); finally, that the three translations of the individual volumes of the same book series cluster by volume rather than by translator (for Tolkien in Polish).
>
> *("The Great Mystery" 238–9)*

Although the dominance of the stylistic signal of the original author of the translations is the most striking result of this test, it is fascinating that the strength of the signals of individual texts demonstrated in Chapter 2 is confirmed, even through the process of translation. The glimpses of the elusive translator in this analysis, however, show that the translator's signal can sometimes break through. The pattern of authorial dominance is broken more substantially when Rybicki tests multiple translations of a Polish trilogy, but broken in an especially revealing way. The translations group by text for two of the translators, but not the third—a translator whose work is so "adaptative, modernized and explicative" that his translation of this trilogy is sometimes identified as an adaptation rather than a translation ("The Great Mystery" 241).

One of the strengths of Rybicki's work is his inclusion of large numbers of analyses from multiple genres and from multiple languages in multiple directions, and three further tests deserve mention here. When he turns to Polish translations of seventy thrillers by American authors, the authorial signal continues to show through the translations, even where thrillers by different authors share the same translator ("The Great Mystery" 243). In a test of French translations of English novels, the original author's signal again dominates, with the exception of two early anonymous abridged translations. In the reverse case of English translations by thirty translators of forty-two novels by seven French authors, the grouping by original author sometimes fails, but

> in none of these cases is this caused by translations of a single translator grouping together. In fact, works by the two translators who translated more than one author in this corpus, Ives (Daudet; Sand) and Wormeley (Balzac; Daudet), share their branch with at least one other novel by the author of the original.
>
> *("The Great Mystery" 243–4)*

Translation Style and Authorial Style

In a characteristically perceptive and illuminating discussion, John F. Burrows explores literary translation, comparing fifteen translations of Juvenal's Tenth Satire into English (in prose and verse, dating from 1646 to 1967) to verse samples by twenty-five English Restoration poets. He argues that "comparisons among several English versions of any much translated text give a sharper focus to many suggestive points of style. Such intra-language comparisons are likely to be of special interest when the translators themselves are authors of distinction" (Burrows 677). In this case, the translators include important poets like Henry Vaughn, Thomas Shadwell, Thomas Sheridan, Samuel Johnson, and John Dryden.

Burrows's discussion is relevant to the examination of the durability of style especially because his initial findings show that, when the poets' verse samples are tested against their translations of Juvenal's Tenth Satire, not all of the translations are correctly attributed to their translators. This result is further corroboration of the relative invisibility of the translator, though Burrows's emphasis is different. He focuses instead on the idea that some translators (especially Dryden) are able to suppress their own styles when translating, while others color their translations with their own personal styles (especially Johnson). Much the same phenomenon is seen among actors. Some show a remarkable ability to transform themselves into a character (Meryl Streep's performance as an elderly Rabbi in the 2003 HBO miniseries *Angels in America* comes to mind). Others always seem recognizably themselves, with performances that show a narrower range (Tom Cruise or Harrison Ford, for example). As Burrows puts it,

> The identifiability of the translator of a text that originates in a foreign language makes for subtle attributional problems in which different levels of stylistic versatility and different ideas of translation and imitation have a bearing.
> *(679)*

I will address the identifiability of the translator intensively later in this chapter, but I turn now to a series of tests of just how well computational methods can identify the style of the original author of a translation.

The Invisible Translator Revisited: A Case Study of Five Russian Authors and Their English Translators

> Once when I was translating [Turgenev's] *The Sportsman's Sketches*, I gave the first draft of six of the stories to the Russian revolutionary leader, Stepniak, to read over. I had put, as I always did, alternative words above the line, whenever I was in some doubt of the right word. Well, when I had finished all the stories in the volume, I asked Stepniak for my manuscript, but he declared he had given it back to me. However, I could not remember his doing so, and it was nowhere to be found. So I translated the six stories again. When I had done this Stepniak found my first translation among his papers and returned it, so I compared the two translations to choose the best passages from each. To my surprise I found they were identical; I had hesitated in the same places, over the same words, and had written the same possible alternatives above the line in the same places. I concluded that though someone else might do a better version, it was clear that I could not myself. I had done the only version I was capable of.
> *(Garnett 292)*

So far as I know, no one has been able to explain how the style of the original author of a translation can survive the extreme transformation of translation, but these comments by Constance Garnett, the most important early translator of Russian literature, suggest that she felt the push of the original to the extent that her second attempt at the translation of six Turgenev stories was, to her own surprise, identical to the temporarily misplaced first attempt. Rybicki, in addition, reminds us of the significance of content as well as style in translation. After all, he points out, "two translations of the same text into the same language share much more than any other two literary texts written in the same language" ("The Great Mystery" 246). Whatever the cause of the phenomenon, a further investigation of the radical durability of authorial style in the face of translation will round out this study of modes of composition and the durability of style.

Any reasonably valid study of the dominance of original author over the translator depends on the availability of multiple translations of multiple authors to and from the same languages. Without an ample number of translations, it is impossible to test the relative strengths of the stylistic signals of the original author and the translators. I limit myself here to translations into English because my subject is the durability of English style, though Rybicki's work strongly suggests that it is unlikely the results would be different in other pairs of languages. It may seem surprising, but this limitation to translations into English leads to a study of Russian literature because it is represented by such a great number of multiple translations of multiple authors by multiple translators. Out-of-copyright translations of five major Russian authors are plentiful: Chekhov, Dostoevsky, Gogol, Tolstoy, and Turgenev. These include multiple translations by Constance Garnett, Isabel Hapgood, and Aylmer and Louise Maude that are available as electronic texts from *Project Gutenberg* and *Wikisource*, among other sources. The same sources supplied single or small numbers of translations by other early translators.

To perform this case study, I began by collecting all public domain English translations of my five authors that I could find as electronic texts. After I began my analysis, it became clear that more texts were needed, and I supplemented these nineteenth- and early-twentieth-century translations with more recent ones by Ann Pasternak Slater, Richard Pevear and Larissa Volokhonsky, Andrew R. MacAndrew, Robert Payne, Ronald Meyer, David McDuff, and Jessie Coulson. Electronic texts of some of these modern translations were available in Literature Online; others were created from digital editions purchased for this purpose. My main corpus eventually swelled to 138 English translations by twenty-two translators or translator pairs (in a few cases a translator is part of more than one pair). This corpus contains twenty translations of Chekhov, thirty-seven of Dostoevsky, thirty-eight of Gogol, twenty-seven of Tolstoy, and sixteen of Turgenev and includes translations of more than seventy different texts. In several cases, I extracted long individual stories or created composite story collections by extracting some stories from various collections, in order to maximize the number of translation-translator pairs (the need for this procedure will become clear shortly).

As a first step, consider a test of twenty texts or collections of stories by Chekhov translated by five translators or pairs of translators (each text or collection is more than twenty thousand words long). This test gauges the strength of the stylistic signals of the original author, the translator, and each text. The twenty collections were tested using Stylo's bootstrap consensus analysis (Eder et al. 113–15), based on cluster analyses of the six hundred to two thousand most frequent words, in hundred-word increments, with pronouns deleted, culling from ten to twenty percent in ten percent increments, a consensus level of fifty percent, and classic Delta distance. (All bootstrap consensus analyses in this chapter were performed in Stylo.)

The results of these analyses (see Figure 8.1) show that multiple translations of the same text, rather than multiple translations by the same translator, cluster

FIGURE 8.1 Bootstrap consensus analysis of translations of twenty novellas and story collections by Anton Chekhov, based on the six hundred to two thousand most frequent words, with pronouns deleted, culled at ten to twenty percent, classic Delta distance, and a consensus of fifty percent

consistently, suggesting that text identity is a stronger signal than translator identity (on the strength of various signals, see Jockers 79–81). The three translations of "A Boring Story," for example, form a single group, as do the four translations of "4 Stories," the three translations of "11 Stories," and the two translations of "6 Stories," "13 Stories," and "My Life." It is noteworthy, however, that three of Garnett's four translations of texts that are not translated by any of the other translators group together. Thus, in this analysis, as in Rybicki's analyses, it is clear that the stylistic signal of the translator is not entirely irrelevant. Rather, it is just weaker than that of the author and the text.

The next test involves a larger number of texts, and several authors, but limits itself to translations by one translator. It tests the translations by Pevear and Volokhonsky of thirty texts by Chekhov, Dostoevsky, Gogol, and Tolstoy. These translations were tested with bootstrap consensus analysis based on cluster analyses of the six hundred to twelve hundred most frequent words, in increments of one hundred words, with pronouns deleted, and with culling percentages ranging from twenty to thirty percent, in increments of ten percent, a consensus of fifty percent, and Eder's Delta distance. This analysis, shown in Figure 8.2, does not include any multiple translations of the same text, thereby eliminating the stylistic signatures of the individual texts. Nevertheless, it does an excellent job of grouping authors. The style of the original author somehow survives the process of translation as a stronger signal than that of the translator, in spite of the fact that the text now consists of the translator's words rather than the author's.

The strength of the original author's signal in translations can be tested more thoroughly using Stylo's Classify function (Eder et al. 115–17), which, unlike the bootstrap consensus analysis, is optimized for classification. For the first test, the following thirty texts by Chekhov, Dostoevsky, Gogol, Tolstoy, and Turgenev, translated by thirteen translators or translator pairs, were selected as a training set:

- Five Chekhov texts translated by four translators: Garnett, Koteliansky and Cannan, Koteliansky and Murray, and Pevear and Volokhonsky
- Nine Dostoevsky texts translated by seven translators: Coulson, Garnett, McDuff, Maguire, Martin, Meyer, and Pevear and Volokhonsky
- Five Gogol texts translated by four translators: Field, Garnett, Hapgood, and G. Tolstoy
- Seven Tolstoy texts translated by three translators: Garnett, Aylmer and Louise Maude, and Pevear and Volokhonsky
- Four Turgenev texts translated by two translators: Garnett and Hapgood

Forty-seven texts by the same five authors, translated by fifteen translators or translator pairs (eight of which are also found in the training set), comprise the test set:

- Ten Chekhov texts translated by four translators: Garnett, Koteliansky and Cannan, Payne, and Pevear and Volokhonsky
- Thirteen Dostoevsky texts translated by six translators: Garnett, Hogarth, MacAndrew, McDuff, Meyer, and Pevear and Volokhonsky
- Eight Gogol texts translated by three translators: Field, Hapgood, and Underwood and Cline

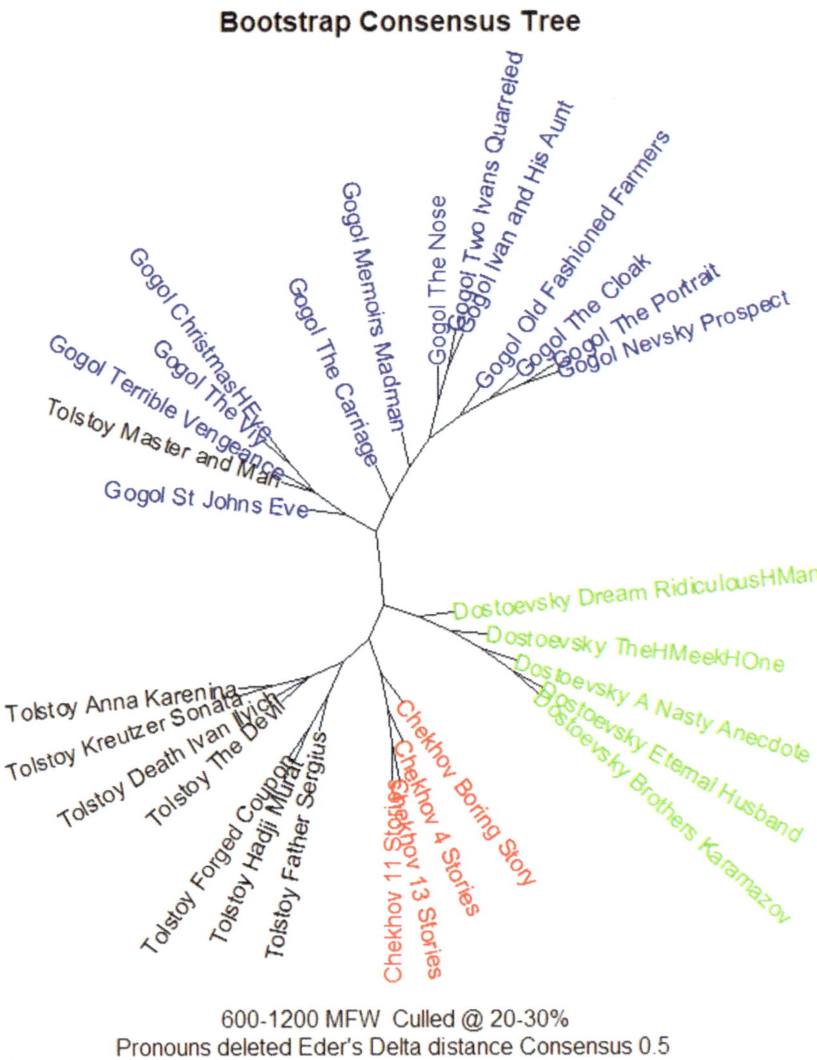

FIGURE 8.2 Bootstrap consensus analysis of thirty translations of Chekhov, Dostoevsky, Gogol, and Tolstoy by Pevear and Volokhonsky, based on the six hundred to twelve hundred most frequent words, with pronouns deleted, culled at twenty to thirty percent, Eder's Delta distance, and a consensus of fifty percent

- Nine Tolstoy texts translated by four translators: Garnett, Aylmer and Louise Maude, Pevear and Volokhonsky, and Slater
- Seven Turgenev texts translated by four translators: Garnett, Hapgood, Hare, and Ralston

Note that, for this test, no translations of the same text appear in both groups, which prevents the signals of individual texts from affecting the analysis. The more difficult task here is thus to attribute a set of test texts, which sometimes include multiple translations of a given text by different translators, to the original authors of a different set of training texts. For example, the test set includes four translations of *The Brothers Karamazov*, by Garnett, MacAndrew, McDuff, and Pevear and Volokhonsky, but this novel does not appear in the training set. The duplicates in the test set seem appropriate, as the training algorithms are not affected by the test texts. Including them also tests the classification methods across multiple translator pairs.

I performed two tests, both based on the one hundred to two thousand most frequent words (with an increment of one hundred words), with forty percent culling and with pronouns deleted. In the test using the NSC method (nearest shrunken centroid), the classification was 94.5 percent accurate, with 888 correct attributions to the original author out of 940. In the test using SVM (support vector machine), the classification was ninety-six percent accurate, with 902 correct attributions to the original author out of 940. Similar testing based on word and character n-grams was generally less accurate, except for one SVM analysis based on the four hundred to two thousand most frequent word two-grams, with ten percent culling. (For an early argument for the effectiveness of the analysis of n-grams, there called "sequences," see Hoover, "Frequent Sequences.") This analysis was 99.1 percent accurate, with 792 correct attributions to the original author out of 799. These results would be very strong even on texts that had not been translated, and they are nothing short of astonishing on translations.

A second and much stricter test involves thirty-three training texts by the same five authors involved in the previous test, translated by five translators or translator pairs:

- Six Chekhov texts by two translators: Garnett, and Pevear and Volokhonsky
- Seven Dostoevsky texts by two translators: Garnett and McDuff
- Ten Gogol texts by two translators: Field and Hapgood
- Six Tolstoy texts by two translators: Garnett, and Pevear and Volokhonsky
- Four Turgenev texts by one translator: Garnett

The test set contains forty-four texts by the same authors, translated by seventeen translators or translator pairs (three of which are also found in the training set):

- Five Chekhov texts by three translators: Koteliansky and Cannan, Koteliansky and Murray, and Payne
- Fourteen Dostoevsky texts by six translators: Coulson, Hogarth, Maguire, Martin, Meyer, and Pevear and Volokhonsky
- Ten Gogol texts by four translators: Garnett, Hogarth, Tolstoy, and Underwood and Cline

- Eight Tolstoy texts by two translators: Aylmer and Louise Maude and Slater
- Seven Turgenev texts by four translators: Hapgood, Hare, Hogarth, and Ralston

For this test, as for the previous one, no translations of the same text appear in both groups, which prevents the signals of individual texts from affecting the analysis. (The fact that this and the previous test involve very similar numbers of texts is coincidental; many, but not all, of the texts in the first test are included in the second.) But here there is an additional restriction: the texts have been chosen so that, if an author-translator pair appears in the training set, that pair is not allowed to appear in the test set. For example, Constance Garnett appears as a translator of Chekhov in the training set, so she does not appear as a translator of Chekhov in the test set. She does, however, appear in the test set as a translator of Gogol. In this analysis, multiple translations of the same text are again allowed in the test set; for example, translations of "The Death of Ivan Ilych" by Aylmer and Louise Maude and by Slater appear in the Tolstoy test set; therefore, neither of these translators or translator pairs is included as a translator of Tolstoy in the training set. Thus the task is to attribute a set of test texts to their original authors when the translators of the training texts by that author are different from the translators of the test texts by that author and when no individual text appears in both the training and test set.

Successful attribution in this difficult test requires, for example, that the language used by Garnett in her translations of Dostoevsky's *A Raw Youth*, "Polzunkov," and *The Double*, and by McDuff in his translation of *The Brothers Karamazov*, "Mr. Prokharchin," *The House of The Dead*, and *The Landlady* be so similar to the language used by six other translators of a set of fourteen *different* Dostoevsky texts that those fourteen texts are attributed to him. Because the task is so difficult, the attributions in this test (using the same settings as the previous test, except that culling was set at ten percent) are naturally less accurate. Nonetheless, NSC classification is still 85.2 percent accurate, with 750 correct attributions to the original author out of 880, and SVM classification is 87.5 percent accurate, with 770 correct attributions to the original author out of 880. The results of SVM, though not NSC, can be improved by running the analysis based on a narrower range of the most frequent words. For example, an analysis based on the six hundred to one thousand most frequent words has an accuracy rate of 92.3 percent, with 202 correct attributions to the original author out of 220.

As with the previous test, using word or character n-grams is less accurate overall; however, also as before, a few analyses based on word two-grams produce even stronger results. For example, NSC classification based on the four hundred to two thousand most frequent word two-grams is 88.6 percent accurate, with 663 correct attributions to the original author out of 748, and a few results within this analysis are ninety percent accurate, as are even fewer SVM analyses (which are much weaker overall for word two-grams than for words).

These results seem almost incredible. I must emphasize again that the original author of a set of English translations by one group of translators is usually correctly identified as the author of a different set of that author's texts translated by a different set of translators. The fact that the styles of these authors stubbornly resist even the extreme transformation caused by translation from Russian to English, and do so in spite of being translated by different translators, perhaps makes the absence of any strong effect of a change in mode of composition more comprehensible.

Some Preliminary Thoughts on the Durable Elements of Authorial Style

This study of the durability of style to a change in mode of composition is not the place for a full study of what survives translation or why, but this study of translation has advantages over the authors and scenarios examined in previous chapters. The large number of translations and translators allows for a series of restrictions that would be impossible for the authors studied in previous chapters. For Chekhov, for example, my corpus contains enough translations by Garnett and by Pevear and Volokhonsky so that it is possible to match four translations of Chekhov and four translations of Tolstoy by Garnett with four translations of each by Pevear and Volokhonsky. Crucially, these sixteen translations contain no duplicates, and all are more than twenty thousand words long. If the same amount of text from each of the sixteen translations is used, a brief investigation into the durability of the styles of Chekhov and Tolstoy across translations can be based on exactly the same amount of text by each author, each translator, and each text. This is important because it equalizes all the factors and places the emphasis on elements of these authors' styles that remain constant across texts and across translators.

Wide spectrum analysis seems idea for this comparison because of its emphasis on consistency of use, rather than frequency (Hoover, "Text Analysis"). To perform this analysis, I created ten sections of each text. The shortest of the texts is 21,821 words long, so I first divided all of the texts into 2,182-word sections, placing any remainder in a final shorter section. After deleting the short final sections, I selected ten sections at random from the remaining sections of each text, or all ten sections, if there were only ten. The resulting eighty sections for each author were then analyzed by wide spectrum analysis to identify the words used most consistently by each author. The one hundred most distinctively distributed words for each author, those used consistently by Chekhov and avoided consistently by Tolstoy, and those used consistently by Tolstoy and avoided consistently by Chekhov, are shown below.

Chekhov's one hundred most distinctive words (present tense verbs in bold type):

> perhaps, cold, God, doctor, sky, somewhere, **am**, morning, big, thoughts, reason, someone, sick, years, dear, probably, **feel**, remembered, till, **sit**, five, low, dark, minute, nature, wind, earth, darkness, smell, trees, usually,

instance, motionless, **cannot**, ago, **knows**, **goes**, ill, **wants**, sea, ordinary, people, work, study, excuse, warm, **don't**, **can't**, soul, read, bed, **remember**, hat, hour, **stand**, softly, heavy, breath, muttered, **begins**, lights, decent, day, every, angry, nor, covered, shoulders, **thank**, lord, **begin**, **beg**, incomprehensible, **takes**, seen, serious, home, night, thinking, silence, pale, friends, free, **laugh**, interesting, grew, green, forehead, philosophy, life, **understand**, dinner, strange, small, yourself, **become**, spoke, fall, reading, quiet

Tolstoy's one hundred most distinctive words (past tense verbs in bold type):

added, making, words, **brought**, **decided**, those, **replied**, matter, especially, officer, **shouted**, handsome, reply, husband, against, fact, therefore, steps, **understood**, **seized**, act, **kept**, horse, others, precisely, count, **fell**, several, hold, pointing, persons, **invited**, hand, **knew**, **wanted**, order, completely, wish, meanwhile, **gathered**, **summoned**, doing, **happened**, **rose**, **remained**, **couldn't**, prince, son, bring, simple, police, **promised**, clean, decision, **went**, any, done, impossible, smiling, obviously, certain, further, contrary, despite, glancing, ball, chief, growing, **ceased**, troops, cloak, unconsciously, special, giving, **expected**, lads, ah, **met**, themselves, mistress, **wouldn't**, **killed**, husband's, tsar, cavalry, arrival, coming, quite, taking, **set**, during, calm, sometimes, few, **reached**, **entered**, **jumped**, significance, **dropped**, forward

One striking characteristic of these lists is the predominance of present tense over past tense verbs in the Chekhov list and of past tense over present tense verbs in the Tolstoy list. Other imbalances can be seen in the larger number of nouns and adjectives in Chekhov and the prevalence of *-ing* verbs in Tolstoy. The Chekhov list is also much more concrete than the Tolstoy list, a tendency that is even stronger among the two hundred most distinctive words.[1] The military vocabulary in the Tolstoy list (*officer*, *horse*, *troops*, *killed*, *cavalry*, *and*, *in context*, *tsar*, *lads*) is perhaps to be expected, but remember that *War and Peace* accounts for only one-eighth of the total amount of text by Tolstoy. In contrast, words related to mental processes seem much more prevalent in Chekhov's list than in Tolstoy's. Observations like these would need more careful examination and discussion in any attempt to understand the durability of style across translation, but features like these are of a kind that would seem intuitively likely to survive translation, and they recall Rybicki's comment about the importance of content. But it is time to return to the question of translator invisibility.

Revealing the Translator's Style

Given the demonstration of the durability of style in the face of changes in mode of composition in previous chapters, it may seem paradoxical that the translator's style seems so nearly invisible. As we have seen, however, this invisibility is only partial, as is revealed by some examples of texts grouping by translator instead of author in some tests. In his discussion of translations of Juvenal, Burrows notes that some authors are not correctly identified as the most likely author (out of twenty-five) of their translation of Juvenal's Tenth Satire and that Dryden, who ranks only second, ranks even lower for some of his other translations (683–7). However, when the comparison is reversed, asking which translation of the Tenth Satire is most like each author, all except Dryden's are correctly attributed, and Dryden's is essentially tied for likeliest (687).

Another of Rybicki's investigations involves a fascinating circumstance in which the translator becomes visible: a single text translated partly by one translator and partly by another. When Anna Kołyszko, the first Polish translator of Virginia Woolf's *Night and Day*, died before completing her translation, it was completed by Magda Heydel (Rybicki and Heydel 709). A series of analyses shows that, in spite of the fact that Heydel also edited the part of the novel translated by Kołyszko, bootstrap consensus analysis was able to pinpoint the change in translator. These results were then confirmed by Heydel herself (710–13).

These suggestive examples of the partial visibility of the style of the translator can be extended more systematically by a classification test that filters out the signals of the original authors of some of the Russian translations tested earlier. This test again removes duplicate texts from the training and test sets and avoids duplicate translators for the same authors in the training and test sets. The crucial additional restriction is that it avoids including duplicate original authors in the training and test sets.

The training set for this test contains six translations of Tolstoy by Garnett and five translations of Dostoevsky by Pevear and Volokhonsky:

- Garnett translations of Tolstoy: *Anna Karenina*, *Family Happiness*, "Polikushka," "The Death of Ivan Ilych," "Two Hussars," and parts eleven and twelve of *War and Peace*[2]
- Pevear and Volokhonsky translations of Dostoevsky: "A Nasty Anecdote," *The Brothers Karamazov*, "The Dream of a Ridiculous Man," *The Eternal Husband*, and "The Meek One"

The test set contains thirty-three translations by Garnett and by Pevear and Volokhonsky:

- Garnett: ten translations of Chekhov, one of Goncharov, and nine of Turgenev (too few translations of Goncharov were available to include him in the main study)
- Pevear and Volokhonsky: thirteen translations of Gogol

This test treats Garnett as the author of her Tolstoy translations and Pevear and Volokhonsky as the author of their Dostoevsky translations. The classification test asks whether or not Garnett is also the author of her translations of Chekhov,

Goncharov, and Turgenev and whether or not Pevear and Volokhonsky are also the author of their translations of Gogol. The testing shows that, when the signals of the original author and text are neutralized, the translator suddenly becomes startlingly visible again. On these tests, based on the two hundred to two thousand most frequent words (with an increment of one hundred words), with fifty percent culling and with pronouns deleted, NSC classification is 82.8% accurate, with 519 correct attributions to the correct translator out of 627, and SVM classification is 94.9% accurate, with 595 correct attributions to the correct translator out of 627. A few selected other strong results are as follows:

- NSC based on the four hundred to two thousand most frequent word two-grams, ten percent culling: 486 of 561 (86.6% accurate)
- NSC based on the one thousand to two thousand most frequent word three-grams, forty percent culling: 224 of 231 (97% accurate)
- SVM based on the four hundred to two thousand most frequent word two-grams, ten percent culling: 505 of 561 (90% accurate)
- SVM based on the one thousand to two thousand most frequent word three-grams, ten percent culling: 336 of 363 (92.6% accurate)

Clearly Garnett's translations of Chekhov, Goncharov, and Turgenev are similar enough to her translations of Tolstoy that she can be identified easily as their "author." Similarly, the translations of Gogol by Pevear and Volokhonsky are similar enough to their translations of Dostoevsky that they can be identified easily as their "author." This is strong confirmation that the translator's stylistic signal is not invisible. Rather, it is simply weaker than that of the original author or the original text. This result seems entirely logical in retrospect: translating another author's text into the translator's language naturally reduces the strength of the translator's own native stylistic signal. Because the translation is not an original text by the translator, the translation is radically constrained by the language of the original author, and the stylistic signal of the original author is durable enough that much of it survives the translation. Yet, the translator's style is also durable. When the other variables are removed, in a neat reversal, the styles of Garnett and of Pevear and Volokhonsky survive even the powerful influence of the styles of the original authors of the training and test texts. The styles of original authors survive the translators' replacement of almost all of their vocabulary, but the styles of translators can be identified in their translations of different original authors in spite of the powerful signals of different original authors, once the effects of those signals are neutralized.

Some Preliminary Thoughts on the Durable Elements of Translators' Styles

A final set of tests can begin to show why it is possible to identify translators' styles across different original authors. As we have seen, wide spectrum analysis is quite effective in identifying the characteristic *translated* vocabularies of the original authors of translations by two different translators. A new set of tests that again eliminates the original author's signal can identify the characteristic vocabulary of Garnett and of Pevear and Volokhonsky. This wide spectrum analysis again treats Garnett as the author of her translations and Pevear and Volokhonsky as the authors of theirs. In this case, the translations of Chekhov and Turgenev by Garnett comprise her "authorial" set, and the translations of Dostoevsky and Tolstoy by Pevear and Volokhonsky comprise their "authorial" set, and the inclusion of two original authors in each set focuses the test on the styles of the translators. An initial wide spectrum analysis produced lists of characteristic vocabulary that contained many proper names. The characteristic list for Garnett also included many British spellings of words that also occur in American spellings in the characteristic list for Pevear and Volokhonsky. Furthermore, Garnett's use of what are now old-fashioned hyphenated forms of words, like *to-day, to-morrow, to-night,* and so forth, also had a significant effect. In a revised analysis, I manually culled out more than four thousand words of these problematic kinds and retested, with the result shown in Figure 8.3.

Considering the proven strength of the author's signal, Figure 8.3 makes an important point. None of the Garnett Ind. Sections or Pevear and Volokhonsky Ind. Sections influenced the selection of characteristic vocabulary that produces the distinction between the two translators, and all but one of these independent texts are by Gogol. Indeed, many of them (in bold) are translations of the same work by both translators. Nevertheless, they are easily placed near the other texts translated by their translators and separate from each other, in spite of the power of the signal of the original author or the power of both the original author and the text itself. Note, for example, the Pevear and Volokhonsky translations of "Christmas Eve" and "Ivan and His Aunt" toward the upper left and the Garnett translation of the same texts to the lower right. The Garnett translation of Goncharov is also appropriately placed, in spite of the fact that no texts by either Gogol or Goncharov influenced the selection of the words that create the distinction between Garnett and Pevear and Volokhonsky.

The forty most distinctively characteristic words for the two translators show some interesting patterns:

Consistently used by Garnett and avoided by Pevear and Volokhonsky:

> *till, fancy, passed, drawing-room, upon, air, flung, answered, muttered, walked, scarcely, cap, sound, slowly, hair, expression, hardly, every, fellow, near, silence, instant, distance, white, low, soft, bent, walking, deal, sky, grew, poor, shoulders, lips, fond, rather, dark, ought, haste, country, black, faint, beside, suppose, window, observed, continually, clever, creature, sank*

Consistently used by Pevear and Volokhonsky and avoided by Garnett:

> *therefore, everyone, precisely, also, finally, I'll, despite, maybe, became, anyone, especially, decided, terribly, you're, having, start, impossible, I'm, unable, obviously, main, I'd, someone, contrary, he's, moment, until, started, order, situation, I've,*

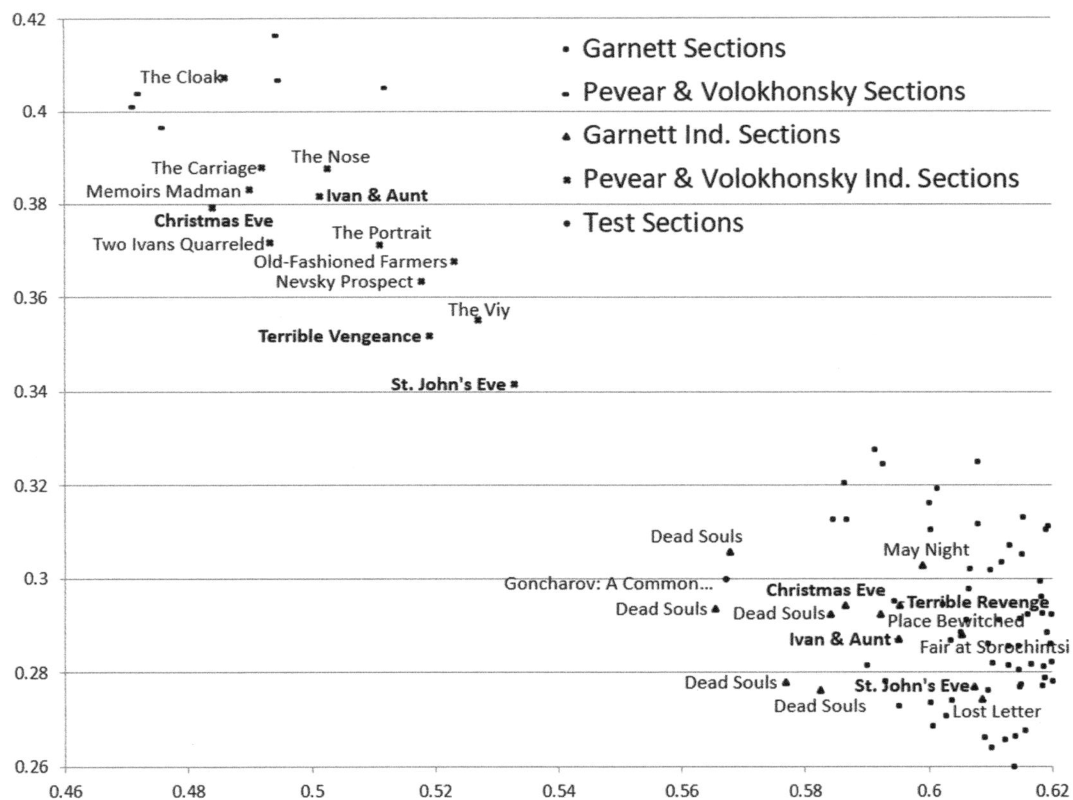

FIGURE 8.3 Wide spectrum analysis of the translator styles of Garnett and Pevear and Volokhonsky, showing the percentage of word types in each text that are characteristic of Garnett (horizontal axis) and Pevear and Volokhonsky (vertical axis)

> *didn't, because, terrible, firmly, front, silently, purpose, earlier, otherwise, immediately, certain, understood, let's, barely, they're, lit, you'll, former, you've*

The words *till* for Garnett and *until* for Pevear and Volokhonsky are a classic authorship pair. Pevear and Volokhonsky also clearly use a less formal style, as is apparent from the large number of contractions among their markers. They also use more *-ly* adverbs, with nine in their list compared to only four for Garnett, and only Pevear and Volokhonsky have indefinite pronouns in their list. By contrast, Garnett's list contains many concrete nouns, while Pevear and Volokhonsky's list contains none. It also contains many more adjectives and full verbs than Pevear and Volokhonsky's. These trends continue far beyond the forty most distinctive words. There is no space here to investigate these differences fully, but this analysis suggests new ways to study the elusive signal of the translator.

Conclusion

The seeming paradox of the invisible translator can be resolved. Although the strength of the original author's signal normally renders the translator's individual style almost invisible, the translators' own signals are quite strong enough to allow the attribution of translations to their translators once the effects of the signals of the text and the original author are eliminated. Given that the stylistic signal of an author normally survives the radical transformation of translation, it seems hardly surprising that a mere change in mode of composition fails to cause a significant change in an author's style. Nevertheless, the fact that translator's styles are consistent enough across the texts of multiple original authors to be correctly identified under appropriate circumstances shows that the translator's signal, though weaker, is also quite durable.

Notes

1. As in Chapter 5, the abstract/concrete indications are based on a set of about forty thousand words tested for human perceptions of concreteness (Brysbaert et al.). Some of the word forms could represent more than one part of speech, so in some dubious cases, I have tested my intuition against a concordance of the Chekhov and Tolstoy texts.
2. The only Garnett translation of *War and* Peace that I could find was a result of relatively poor optical character recognition; given the extraordinary length of the novel, I edited and corrected only parts eleven and twelve. This resulted, nevertheless, in a sample of nearly eighty thousand words of this translation. I included only these same two parts of the Aylmer and Louise Maude translation in my study for balance.

References

Angels in America. HBO, 2003.

Brysbaert, Marc et al. "Concreteness Ratings for 40 Thousand Generally Known English Word Lemmas." *Behavior Research Methods*, vol. 46, no. 3, 2014, pp. 904–11, doi:10.3758/s13428-013-0403-5.

Burrows, John F. "The Englishing of Juvenal: Computational Stylistics and Translated Texts." *Style*, vol. 36, no. 4, 2002, pp. 677–99.

Eder, Maciej et al. "Stylometry With *R:* A Package for Computational Text Analysis." *R Journal*, vol. 8, no. 1, 2016, pp. 107–21. journal.r-project.org/archive/2016/RJ-2016-007/RJ-2016-007.pdf.

Garnett, Constance. 1947. "'The Art of Translation.' Conversation Recorded in *The Listener*, 30 Jan. 1947." *Translation: Theory and Practice: A Historical Reader*, edited by Daniel Weissbort and Astrabur Eysteinsson. Oxford UP, 2006.

Hoover, David L. "Frequent Word Sequences and Statistical Stylistics." *Literary and Linguistic Computing*, vol. 17, no. 2, 2002, pp. 157–80, doi:10.1093/llc/17.2.157.

———. "Text Analysis." *Literary Studies in the Digital Age: An Evolving Anthology*, edited by Ken Price and Ray Siemens, MLA, 2013. dlsanthology.mla.hcommons.org/textual-analysis.

Jockers, Matt. *Macroanalysis: Digital Methods and Literary History*. U of Illinois P, 2013, doi:10.5406/illinois/9780252037528.001.0001.

Literature Online. ProQuest, LLC, 1996.

Project Gutenberg. Founded by Michael Hart, 1971. www.gutenberg.org.

Rybicki, Jan. "Burrowing Into Translation: Character Idiolects in Henryk Sienkiewicz's Trilogy and Its Two English Translations." *Literary and Linguistic Computing*, vol. 21, no. 1, 2006, pp. 91–103.

———. "The Great Mystery of the (Almost) Invisible Translator: Stylometry in Translation." *Quantitative Methods in Corpus-Based Translation Studies: A Practical Guide to Descriptive Translation Research*, edited by Michael P. Oakes and Meng Ji, John Benjamins, 2012, pp. 231–48.

Rybicki, Jan, and Magda Heydel. "The Stylistics and Stylometry of Collaborative Translation: Woolf's *Night and Day* in Polish." *Literary and Linguistic Computing*, vol. 28, no. 4, 2013, pp. 708–17, doi:10.1093/llc/fqt027.

Venuti, Lawrence. *The Translator's Invisibility: A History of Translation*. 1995. Routledge, 2017, doi:10.4324/9781315098746.

Wikisource contributors. "Main Page." *Wikisource*. Hyperlink. https://en.wikisource.org/wiki/Main_Pageen.wikisource.org/wiki/Main_Page.

9

CONCLUSION

A study of the changes in modes of composition in the works of eleven authors—multiple changes for some of them—has not produced a single conclusive or even very probable example of a substantial or an important change in literary style caused by such a change. This is unquestionably a surprising result. Many of the authors examined here have commented on their own perceptions of how a change in mode changed their writing, and there can be no doubt that, for some of them, their changes in mode affected what Kirschenbaum calls their "sense of the text" (see Chapter 1). My concern in this study, however, has been with any detectable change in the texts themselves. Although it remains entirely possible that changes in mode of composition caused some undetectable changes in the styles of some writers, Chapter 2 has shown that it is extremely unlikely that any changes that escape the methods deployed here can be considered important. Critics, too, have suggested, or even confidently asserted, that, in cases like that of Henry James, a change in mode of composition led to a radical transformation in the author's style.

In hindsight, however, perhaps it should not have been so surprising that changes in the ways writers actually produce the language of their texts have so little effect on that language. In the eighteenth century, after all, Buffon famously pronounced that "Le style c'est l'homme même." And King and Pennebaker have made the link between the style and the person(ality) more concrete and precise.

I began with Thomas Hardy and Walter Scott, both of whom adopted dictation only temporarily, and both of whom produced books that were partly handwritten and partly dictated (Chapter 3). These simplest and most tractable cases avoided any complications that might arise from a chronological drift or trend in the author's career and reduced the number of other relevant variables, eliminating intertextual variations caused by different plots, characters, and settings. They also minimized the possibility of an incremental increase (or decrease) in the effect of the mode change that might result from the process of learning to use the new mode or becoming familiar with it or tired of it.

In spite of these simplifications, even these cases involved complexities related to the relationships among mode of composition, plot, setting, and characters. For Hardy, the possibility of obfuscation arising from his desire to minimize his wife's contribution was an additional complication, as was Scott's desire for anonymity, which prompted him to have his manuscripts transcribed and then destroyed and to have the transcription submitted to the publisher. Nonetheless, a series of analyses of various kinds and based on multiple numbers of the most frequent words, including separate analyses of the dialogue and narration, gave results that are not compatible with any significant effect of the change in mode of composition from handwriting to dictation. The styles of Hardy and Scott are surprisingly durable to the influence of changes in mode of composition.

The same is true of the more complex case of Joseph Conrad, which involves some dubious claims by Conrad himself, as well as by Ford Madox Ford, whose involvement in some of Conrad's works has been questioned. These complications had to be addressed carefully before investigating the possibility of a stylistic effect of Conrad's changes in mode of composition. Had his changes in mode caused changes in style, analyses of the handwritten and dictated portions of the novels in sections would have grouped them by mode of composition. Yet that simply never happened consistently or regularly. Although Conrad mused about the possibility that dictation might have changed his style, there is no significant evidence that it did.

Investigating the essentially permanent changes in mode of composition of William Faulkner and Booth Tarkington in Chapter 4 presented some new challenges, some of which affected many of the other cases investigated in later chapters. Most notably, identifying the possibility of stylistic changes caused by the change in mode of composition had to take into account the possibility of a gradual chronological drift in these authors' styles. Clear evidence that the styles of both Faulkner and Tarkington show such a drift required special care to assure that any mode effect could be distinguished from that drift. Faulkner's penchant for including and reworking material that he had written by hand much earlier into later typewritten or partially typewritten novels also complicated his case.

Tarkington's is the simpler of the two cases. Although his style showed a chronological drift, progressively decreasing the span of time surrounding his change in mode made clear that no important shift took place in the year he began dictating. This confirms that the chronological changes in his style could not have been a result of the change in mode. Furthermore, he, like Hardy, Scott, and Conrad, changed mode within a single text, in this case *Young Mrs. Greeley*. For Tarkington, we even have the complete holograph manuscript of novel, the first five chapters in Tarkington's handwriting and the remaining twelve chapters in Elizabeth Trotter's handwriting, taken from Tarkington's Dictation. Separate classification tests of the handwritten and dictated parts of the novel, in which handwritten texts that precede and dictated texts that follow *Young Mrs. Greeley* were used as the texts of known mode, did a poor job of identifying the modes of the two parts. Bootstrap consensus analyses also failed spectacularly in grouping the handwritten or dictated sections of the novel with handwritten or dictated texts written just before and after it. The only reasonable conclusion is that, although Tarkington's style shows a chronological drift over his career, it resisted the effects of a change in mode of composition that he described as the hardest thing he ever did. It even seems possible that the change to dictation stabilized his style to some extent.

The enormous amount of manuscript material that exists for Faulkner's work and the huge amount of critical attention he has received made it possible to disentangle the question of a mode effect from the discernable chronological drift in his style over the period in which the change of mode took place. They also allowed for the secure identification of the portions of his typewritten novels that include or were closely based upon earlier, handwritten work. Once these refinements were made, analyses of *The Hamlet* (either as a whole or in handwritten and dictated parts) along with the preceding handwritten and the following typewritten novels failed to suggest any stylistic change that might have resulted from Faulkner's change in mode of composition. These results were confirmed in analyses of sections of *The Hamlet*, none of which suggested that the typed sections were distinct in style from the rest of the novel.

The four writers discussed in Chapter 5, Arthur C. Clarke, Octavia E. Butler, Stanley Elkin, and Ian McEwan, also changed their modes of composition more or less permanently. The shapes of the careers of Clarke and Butler and the circumstances of their changes in mode required that the analysis focus on the change in mode of composition from typing to word processing within a single novel, simplifying the analysis and making these cases similar, except for the permanency of the change in mode, to the cases of Hardy, Scott, and Conrad.

For Clarke, the relevant novel is *2010: Odyssey Two*, the first quarter of which was typed on an electric typewriter and the rest on a word processor. Several kinds of analysis of the novel in chapters and in sections of equal size based on multiple numbers of frequent words, word sequences, and character n-grams of various lengths produced no evidence of a stylistic change caused by the change in mode of composition. Some analyses produced chaotic results, but even those that produced fairly consistent results never suggested that the first quarter of the novel was stylistically different from the last three quarters. Clarke's change in mode of composition created no measurable difference in his style, in spite of his enthusiasm over the way the word processor eliminated the mechanical drudgery of writing.

The same is true for Butler, who also transitioned from a typewriter (in her case a manual one, rather than an electric one) to a word processor in the process of writing a single novel, *The Parable of the Talents*. There is some doubt about the precise details of Butler's composition process, but there is strong evidence to suggest that the changeover took place after she had written about one-third of the novel. As was true for Clarke, none of the multiple analyses of the novel in chapters or in sections of equal size provided evidence for a change in style caused by her change in mode of composition. There was some relatively consistent evidence that the last third of the novel was stylistically distinct, but external evidence makes a change to word processing before the final third of the novel extremely unlikely. This evidence suggests that the stylistic difference of the end of the novel from the rest has a different cause, perhaps related to a significant plot development that occurs at about this point. However she may have struggled to learn to use the computer and word processing software, there is no significant evidence that her change from a manual typewriter to a word processor significantly affected her style. Instead, her style endured, and her complex process of false starts, rewriting, multiple notes, and fragments and partial drafts simply incorporated the new mode of composition into her writing process, largely replacing typing.

Stanley Elkin also changed his mode of composition while writing one of his novels, *George Mills* (1982), which is thought to be one of the earliest serious novels composed on a word processor. Elkin's oeuvre is such that the novels before and after *George Mills* can be analyzed to look for a mode effect, but doing so reveals no evidence that the handwritten first half of *George Mills* is stylistically similar to the preceding handwritten novels and that the word-processed second half is stylistically similar to the following word-processed novels. None of a series of analyses of *George Mills* by itself provides strong evidence of a local mode effect either. Switching to a word processor may have been the most important event in his writing life, but, despite his claim that any word-processed novel should be perfect (see Chapter 5), Elkin's change in mode of composition is not associated with any significant stylistic revolution.

Like Elkin, Ian McEwan switched from handwriting to word processing, and he, too, explicitly discusses the impact of the switch and is enthusiastic about the effects of the "provisional nature" of electronic text. Unlike Elkin, however, he switched modes between novels. Testing McEwan's first five novels—his first word-processed novel and the two previous and the two following novels—both as whole novels and in sections, shows that the two handwritten novels are distinct in style from the three word-processed novels.

It is unlikely, however, that this clear and significant difference can be attributed to the change in mode of composition. There is a six-year gap between the last handwritten and the first word-processed novel, a gap long enough that a chronological drift might have produced a difference in style. Further study of the characteristic vocabulary of the novels in the two modes casts additional doubt on a mode effect. It is difficult to imagine that changing from handwriting to word processing would cause a decrease in past tense verbs or an increase in abstract nouns. These changes and the different proportions of various topics in the novels in the two modes that are revealed by topic modeling seem more semantic and thematic than stylistic. This accords with some critical commentary on McEwan and with his own comments on his intentional turn away from the darkness and sexual strangeness of his first two novels when he returned to writing novels with his first word-processed novel. McEwan seems, at best, an equivocal and relatively unlikely case of a change in style caused by a change in mode of composition. This conclusion is supported by the fact that many of the authors studied here show significant chronological style variations that cannot be attributed to a change in mode of composition but that none of them show a significant stylistic effect caused by a change in mode.

Henry James's celebrated adoption of dictation in the late 1890s, a date that coincides roughly with the emergence of his rather opaque and convoluted later style, has led to a consensus among many critics that the dictation caused the change in style. As Chapter 6 has shown, however, there was no abrupt shift in his style when he began dictating. Instead, his style shows a strong, continuous, and unidirectional chronological evolution throughout his career—an evolution that began well before he took up dictation and continued long after, as shown by a series of analyses of the novels that precede and follow *What Maisie Knew*, the first novel he partly dictated. This conclusion is confirmed by analyses of his handwritten and dictated letters and by analysis of *What Maisie Knew* in chapters and sections and analyses of the dialogue and narration taken separately. Almost paradoxically, this steady progressive change in James's style shows durability in the face of his change in mode of composition—a durability of change.

The complex case of Stephen King rounded out this study of the durability of literary style in the face of changes in mode of composition (Chapter 7). King's case is complex for a number of unrelated reasons. He wrote by hand until he got his first typewriter at age eleven, and he was an early adopter of word processing in 1981, at the age of thirty-four. Yet he wrote two novels by hand much later: *Bag of Bones* (1998) and *Dreamcatcher* (2001). Further complications are King's well-known tendency to blur genre boundaries and to write in multiple genres and his well-documented abuse of alcohol and cocaine over much of his early career. All of these issues had the potential to mask or exaggerate any effects of his changes in mode of composition.

Teasing apart the multiple variables required special limitations and adjustments of methods, as well as careful attention to which texts were appropriate to include in the various analyses. The surprising results of multiple analyses of multiple texts and sets of texts, analyses based on multiple variables and methods, showed that King's disdain for genre labels was reflected in the fact that his novels showed almost no tendency to group consistently by genre. Building on this evidence allowed novels from multiple genres to be included in later analyses that addressed his alcohol and drug use. Those analyses showed that, quite surprisingly, his style was durable even in the face of the obvious mental effects of alcohol and drugs: there was no detectable difference between the styles of his novels written while he was drinking heavily and using cocaine and those written after he became sober.

After these possibly confounding effects were dealt with, the possible effects of King's changes in mode of composition on his style could be safely investigated. Analyses of King's two handwritten novels (one written under the influence of Oxycontin) that interrupt a series of word-processed novels problematically suggested the possibility of a minor effect of this change in mode on his style. This possibility was rendered less probable by a final series of analyses that showed that King's major change in mode of composition from typing to word processing had no significant or consistent effect on his style. Thus, Stephen's style was surprisingly durable in the face of his abuse of alcohol and drugs and his recovery from that abuse, and it was also durable in the face of changes in mode of composition.

Chapter 8 looked at the durability of style from a very different point of view. Demonstrating that the original author's stylistic signature remains identifiable in translations by multiple translators suggests that the durability of authorial style to changes in mode of composition should have been less surprising than it initially seemed. The astonishing results of multiple analyses show that the original author's style can be detected even when different sets of known texts and test texts by an author have been translated by different translators. This kind of radical durability of authorial style helps to make its resistance to changes in mode of composition more comprehensible. The fact that translators' styles can be recovered if the effect of the original authors' styles is eliminated also shows that even the rather extreme limitation of translating a text from a foreign language cannot completely erase a writer's (here the translator's) style.

This study obviously does not prove that a change in mode of composition never changes an author's style. Some of the cases investigated here show the possibility of minor and localized effects, and other authors might show greater effects. Additional testing using other sophisticated authorship attribution methods might even be able to demonstrate some additional mode effects in the authors I have studied. My conclusion is not that nothing happens when authors change how they write their texts but rather that nothing *dramatic* happens and that literary style is surprisingly durable in the face of such changes.

In spite of that durability, it is well known that the styles of writers like Henry James underwent major, largely unidirectional changes, and I have shown that the styles of Conrad, Tarkington, and King, and, to a lesser extent, Faulkner, show substantial chronological variation. Although some authorship attribution practitioners assume that the styles of all authors except those with very short careers vary significantly and directionally so that their early and late texts will be distinguishable computationally, that assumption seems dubious. Willa Cather's novels and novellas from throughout the twenty-seven years of her career, for example, show some consistent similarities and differences, but no consistent chronological drift. We lack any explanation of such changes, and I have not attempted to provide any here, though Blackmur's suggestion that the elaborateness of James's late style is related to his expression of extreme subtleties of meaning and feeling seems compelling (see Chapter 6).

Is it generally true, as it is for the authors studied here, that authorial style is also resistant to illness, pain, blindness, time pressure, financial difficulties, and even to alcohol and drug use and translation? If so, this has serious implications for the study of bona fide and verifiable examples of substantial variations in authors' styles, such as those associated with chronological style evolution, with the onset of dementia or mental illness, and with tour-de-force stylistic experiments. It seems that we will be forced to search for explanations in the (socially constructed) personalities, mental functioning, and intentions of the authors themselves. In future work, I hope to begin that search by examining the extent to which literary style is affected by profound personal experiences, such as trauma, religious or political conversion, and incarceration.

BIBLIOGRAPHY

ABBYY FineReader 14 Standard. ABBYY Production, LLC, 2017.

Ahmad, Suleiman M. "Emma Hardy and the Ms. of *a Pair of Blue Eyes*." *Notes and Queries*, vol. 26, no. 4, 1979, pp. 320–2, doi:10.1093/nq/26-4-320.

Alcott, Lousia May. *Behind a Mask: The Unknown Thrillers of Louisa May Alcott*. Edited by Madeleine B. Stern, William Morrow, 1975. archive.org/details/behindmaskunkno00alco.

———. *A Modern Cinderella: Or, The Little Old Shoe, And Other Stories*. Hurst, 1910. www.gutenberg.org/files/3806/3806-h/3806-h.htm.

———. *Plots and Counterplots: More Unknown Thrillers of Louisa May Alcott*. Edited by Madeleine B. Stern, William Morrow, 1976. archive.org/details/plotscounterplot00alco.

Alexander, J. H., editor. *The Bride of Lammermoor*. 1995. The Edinburgh Edition of the Waverley Novels, vol. 7 [A], Edinburgh UP, 2017, doi:10.1093/actrade/9780748605712.book.1.

———. *A Legend of the Wars of Montrose*. 1995. The Edinburgh Edition of the Waverley Novels, vol. 7 [B], Edinburgh UP, 2017, doi:10.1093/actrade/9780748605729.book.1.

Angels in America. HBO, 2003.

Antonia, Alexis et al. "Language Chunking, Data Sparseness, and the Value of a Long Marker List: Explorations With Word N-grams and Authorial Attribution." *Literary and Linguistic Computing*, vol. 29, no. 2, 2014, pp. 147–63, doi:10.1093/llc/fqt028.

The Arthur Conan Doyle Encyclopedia. www.arthur-conan-doyle.com/index.php?title=Main_Page; www.arthur-conan-doyle.com/index.php/Pastiches_&_Parodies.

Atwood, Margaret. *The Handmaid's Tale*. Fawcett Chrest, 1987.

Bailey, Peter J. "'A Hat Where There Never Was a Hat': Stanley Elkin's Fifteenth Interview." *Review of Contemporary Fiction*, vol. 15, no. 2, 1995, pp. 15–26.

Balossi, Giuseppina. *A Corpus Linguistic Approach to Literary Language and Characterization: Virginia Woolf's The Waves*. John Benjamins, 2014, doi:10.1075/lal.18.

Barron, Mark. "Tarkington Still Writes for Stage in Maine Retreat: Hoosier Author, Nearing 70, Busy Rewriting an Earlier Play." *The Washington Post*, 10 July 1938, p. TT2.

Barron's BookNotes: "The Turn of the Screw." Barron's Educational Series, Inc., 1986. www.pinkmonkey.com/booknotes/barrons/turnscr2.asp.

Barthes, Roland. "The Death of the Author." *The Death and Resurrection of the Author?* edited by William Irwin, Greenwood Press, 2002, pp. 3–7. Originally published in *Aspen*, vol. 5–6, no. 3, 1967. www.ubu.com/aspen/aspen5and6/threeEssays.html#barthes.

Beahm, George. *The Stephen King Companion: Four Decades of Fear From the Master of Horror.* Palgrave Macmillan, 2015.

———. *Stephen King From A to Z: An Encyclopedia of His Life and Work.* Andrews McMeel Publishing, 1998. archive.org/details/stephenkingfromt00beah.

Bensen, E. F. *As We Were: A Victorian Peep Show.* Longmans, Green and Co., 1930. archive.org/details/aswewere030125mbp.

Bethany [Nowviskie]. "The Turn of the Screw." *The Ivanhoe Game*, 2002. speculative-computing.org/greymatter/ivanhoe/roles/archives/00000019.htm.

Biber, Douglas. *Variation Across Speech and Writing.* Cambridge UP, 1988, doi:10.1017/CBO9780511621024.

Binongo, José Nilo G. "Joaquin's *Joaquinesquerie, Joaquinesquerie's* Joaquin: A Statistical Expression of a Filipino Writer's Style." *Literary and Linguistic Computing*, vol. 9, no. 4, 1994, pp. 267–79, doi:10.1093/llc/9.4.267.

Binongo, José Nilo G., and M. W. A. Smith. "The Application of Principal Component Analysis to Stylometry." *Literary and Linguistic Computing*, vol. 14, no. 4, 1999, pp. 445–65, doi:10.1093/llc/14.4.445.

Blei, David. "Probabilistic Topic Models." *Communications of the ACM*, vol. 55, no. 4, 2012, pp. 77–84, doi:10.1145/2133806.2133826.

"Blindness Menaces Booth Tarkington: Is Writing Furiously to Finish Several Works, Author Refuses to Rest on Order of Eye Specialist." *Boston Daily Globe*, 27 Oct. 1927, p. 1.

Blotner, Joseph. *Faulkner: A Biography.* UP of Mississippi, 2005. muse.jhu.edu.

Blotner, Joseph, and Noel Polk, editors. *William Faulkner: Novels 1936–1940.* Library of America, 1990.

———. *William Faulkner: Novels 1942–1954.* Library of America, 1994.

Blotner, Joseph et al., editors. *William Faulkner Manuscripts.* 25 vols., Garland, 1986–87.

"Booth Tarkington Better: Author to Leave Johns Hopkins Hospital on Monday." *New York Times*, 6 Apr. 1930, p. 6.

"Booth Tarkington Cheered by First Eye Operation: Recovering From Operation." *New York Herald Tribune*, 29 Jan. 1929, p. 6.

Booth Tarkington Papers, 1812–1956. Manuscripts Division, Department of Rare Books and Special Collections, Princeton University Library.

"Booth Tarkington Still Writes at 71 Although Half Blind: Famous Indiana Author Painfully at Work on His Autobiography, Producing 1000 to 2000 Words Daily." *Los Angeles Times*, 16 Feb. 1941, p. 9.

Bosanquet, Theodora. *Henry James at Work. 1924.* Edited by Lyall H. Powers, U of Michigan P, 2006. muse.jhu.edu/book/7215.

Brice, Xavier. "Ford Madox Ford and the Composition of *Nostromo*." *The Conradian*, vol. 29, no. 2, 2004, pp. 75–95. www.jstor.org/stable/20873529.

Brownlee, Jason. *Weka Machine Learning Mini-Course.* 2016. machinelearningmastery.com/applied-machine-learning-weka-mini-course.

Brysbaert, Marc et al. "Concreteness Ratings for 40 Thousand Generally Known English Word Lemmas." *Behavior Research Methods*, vol. 46, no. 3, 2014, pp. 904–11, doi:10.3758/s13428-013-0403-5.

Burrows, John F. "All the Way Through: Testing for Authorship in Different Frequency Strata." *Literary and Linguistic Computing*, vol. 22, no. 1, 2006, pp. 27–47, doi:10.1093/llc/fqi067.

———. *Computation into Criticism*. Clarendon Press, 1987.

———. "'Delta': A Measure of Stylistic Difference and a Guide to Likely Authorship." *Literary and Linguistic Computing*, vol. 17, no. 3, 2002, pp. 267–87, doi:10.1093/llc/17.3.267.

———. "The Englishing of Juvenal: Computational Stylistics and Translated Texts." *Style*, vol. 36, no. 4, 2002, pp. 677–99.

———. "Never Say Always Again: Reflections on the Numbers Game." *Text and Genre in Reconstruction. Effects of Digitalization on Ideas, Behaviours, Products and Institutions*, edited by Willard McCarty, Open Book Publishers, 2010, pp. 13–36. books.openedition.org/obp/646.

———. "Not Unless You Ask Nicely: The Interpretative Nexus Between Analysis and Information." *Literary and Linguistic Computing*, vol. 7, no. 2, 1992, pp. 91–109, doi:10.1093/llc/7.2.91.

———. "A Second Opinion on 'Shakespeare and Authorship Studies in the Twenty-First Century'." *Shakespeare Quarterly*, vol. 63, no. 3, 2012, pp. 355–92, doi:10.1353/shq.2012.0038.

———. "Who Wrote *Shamela?* Verifying the Authorship of a Parodic Text." *Literary and Linguistic Computing*, vol. 20, no. 4, 2005, pp. 437–50, doi:10.1093/llc/fqi049.

Burrows, John F., and Hugh Craig. "Authors and Characters." *English Studies*, vol. 93, no. 3, 2012, pp. 292–309, doi:10.1080/0013838X.2012.668786.

Butler, Octavia E. "Birth of a Writer." *Essence*, vol. 20, no. 1, 1989, p. 74+.

Calvin, Ritch. "An Octavia E. Butler Bibliography (1976–2008)." *Utopian Studies*, vol. 19, no. 3, Octavia Butler Special Issue, 2008, pp. 485–516. www.jstor.org/stable/20719922.

Cameron, Sharon. *Thinking in Henry James*. U of Chicago P, 1989. archive.org/details/thinkinginhenryj0000came/.

Campbell, Sarah. "The Man Who Talked Like a Book, Wrote Like He Spoke." *Interval(le)s*, II.2–III.1, 2008–09, pp. 164–73. labos.ulg.ac.be/cipa/wp-content/uploads/sites/22/2015/07/18_campbell.pdf.

Canavan, Gerry. "'There's Nothing New/Under The Sun,/But There Are New Suns': Recovering Octavia E. Butler's Lost Parables." *Los Angeles Review of Books*, 9 June 2014. lareviewofbooks.org/article/theres-nothing-new-sun-new-suns-recovering-octavia-e-butlers-lost-parables.

Cappello, Mary. *Awkward: A Detour*. Bellevue Literary Press, 2007. archive.org/details/awkward00mary.

Casebeer, Edwin F. "Stephen King's Canon: The Art of Balance." *A Dark Night's Dreaming: Contemporary American Horror Fiction*, edited by Tony Magistrale and Michael A. Morrison, U of South Carolina P, 1996, pp. 42–54. archive.org/details/darknightsdreami0000magi.

Cather, Willa. *O Pioneers!* U of Nebraska P, 2003.

Chatman, Seymour Benjamin. "Parody and Style." *Poetics Today*, vol. 22, no. 1, 2001, pp. 25–39. muse.jhu.edu/article/27848.

Christensen, Peter G. "The Escape From the Curse of History in Stanley Elkin's *George Mills*." *Review of Contemporary Fiction*, vol. 15, no. 2, 1995, pp. 79–91.

Clement, Ross, and David Sharp. "Ngram and Bayesian Classification of Documents." *Literary and Linguistic Computing*, vol. 18, no. v4, 2003, pp. 423–47, doi:10.1093/llc/18.4.423.

Conrad, Joseph. *The Collected Letters of Joseph Conrad*. Vol. 3, edited by Frederic Karl and Laurence Davies. Cambridge UP, 1988. books.google.com/books?id=zJBklzxB5BEC.

———. *The Collected Letters of Joseph Conrad*. Vol. 5, edited by Frederic Karl and Laurence Davies. Cambridge UP, 1996. archive.org/details/collectedletters0005conr/mode/2up.

———. *The Collected Letters of Joseph Conrad*. Vol. 7, edited by Laurence Davies and J. H. Stape. Cambridge UP, 2005. books.google.com/books?id=UVzMFTPFP9MC.

———. *Nostromo: A Tale of the Seaboard*. Oxford World's Classics, edited by Jacques Berthoud, and Mara Kalnins, Oxford UP, 2009.

———. *Nostromo: A Tale of the Seaboard*. The World's Classics, edited by Keith Carabine, Oxford UP, 1984. archive.org/details/nostromotaleofse00conr_0.

———. *A Personal Record*. The Cambridge Edition of the Works of Joseph Conrad, edited by Zdzisław Najder and J. H. Stape, Cambridge UP, 2008, doi:10.1017/CBO9781107341012.

———. *The Secret Agent: A Simple Tale*. The Cambridge Edition of the Works of Joseph Conrad, edited by Bruce Harkness and S. W. Reid, Cambridge UP, 1990. books.google.com/books?id=kp9uRMboUDMC.

———. *The Shadow-Line: A Confession*. The Cambridge Edition of the Works of Joseph Conrad, edited by J. H. Stape and Allan H. Simmons, introduction and explanatory notes by Owen Knowles, Cambridge UP, 2013. books.google.com/books?id=uocPAQAAQBAJ.

———. *The Shadow-Line: A Confession*. Oxford World's Classics, edited with an introduction and notes by Jeremy Hawthorn, Oxford UP, 2003. books.google.com/books?id=o4ceZwmWHGIC.

———. *Youth, Heart of Darkness, The End of the Tether*. The Cambridge Edition of the Works of Joseph Conrad, edited by Owen Knowles, Cambridge UP, 2010. books.google.com/books?id=Kle9WnHV_IsC.

Considine, Austin. "How a *Walking Dead* Guru Brought *Creepshow* Back to Life." *New York Times*, 26 Sept. 2019. www.nytimes.com/2019/09/26/arts/television/creepshow-reboot-greg-nicotero.html.

Craig, Hugh. "Authorial Attribution and Computational Stylistics: If You Can Tell Authors Apart, Have You Learned Anything About Them?" *Literary and Linguistic Computing*, vol. 14, no. 1, 1999, pp. 103–13, doi:10.1093/llc/14.1.103.

Craig, Hugh, and Alexis Antonia. "Six Authors and the *Saturday Review*: A Quantitative Approach to Style." *Victorian Periodicals Review*, vol. 48, no. 1, 2015, pp. 67–86, doi:10.1353/vpr.2015.0004.

Craig, Hugh, and Arthur Kinney, editors. *Shakespeare, Computers, and the Mystery of Authorship*. Cambridge UP, 2009, doi:10.1017/CBO9780511605437.014.

Crane, Joan St. C. "Manuscript of *Mosquitoes* at Virginia." *Faulkner Newsletter and Yoknapatawpha Review*, vol. 8, no. 1, 1988, pp. 1, 3. egrove.olemiss.edu/cgi/viewcontent.cgi?article=1114&context=faulkner_nl.

Curley-Egan, James. "The Master's Voice: A Close Reading of James." *PMLA*, vol. 133, no. 5, 2018, pp. 1251–8, doi:10.1632/pmla.2018.133.5.1251.

Dougherty, David C. *Shouting Down the Silence: A Biography of Stanley Elkin*. U of Illinois P, 2010. muse.jhu.edu/book/18460.

Early, James. *The Making of Go Down, Moses*. Southern Methodist UP, 1972. archive.org/details/makingofgodownmo0000earl.

Edel, Leon. *Henry James: The Treacherous Years, 1895–1901*. Lippincott, 1969. archive.org/details/henryjamestreach00edel.

Eder, Maciej. "Rolling Stylometry." *Digital Scholarship in the Humanities*, vol. 31, no. 3, 2016, pp. 457–69, doi:10.1093/llc/fqv010.

———. "Visualization in Stylometry: Cluster Analysis Using Networks." *Digital Scholarship in the Humanities*, vol. 32, no. 1, 2017, pp. 50–64, doi:10.1093/llc/fqv061.

Eder, Maciej et al. "Stylometry with *R:* A Package for Computational Text Analysis." *R Journal*, vol. 8, no. 1, 2016, pp. 107–21. journal.r-project.org/archive/2016/RJ-2016-007/RJ-2016-007.pdf.

Eiselein, Gregory K., and Anne Phillips, editors. *Louisa May Alcott Encyclopedia*. Greenwood Press, 2001.

Elkin, Stanley. *Stanley Elkin Papers (MSS039), 1943–2013*. Washington University Libraries, Department of Special Collections, 2013. archon.wulib.wustl.edu/index.php?p=collections/findingaid&id=654&q=elkin&rootcontentid=1139248.

Elliott, Jack. "Whole Genre Sequencing." *Digital Scholarship in the Humanities*, vol. 32, no. 1, 2017, pp. 65–79, doi:10.1093/llc/fqv034.

Evert, Stefan et al. "Understanding and Explaining Delta Measures for Authorship Attribution." *Digital Scholarship in the Humanities*, vol. 32, suppl. 2, 2017, pp. ii4–ii16, doi:10.1093/llc/fqx023.

Fargnoli, A. Nicholas et al. *Critical Companion to William Faulkner*. Facts on File, 2008. books.google.com/books?id=dQca8cin24gC&q.

Farrell, John. *The Varieties of Authorial Intention: Literary Theory Beyond the Intentional Fallacy*. Palgrave Macmillan, 2017, doi:10.1007/978-3-319-48977-3.

———. "Why Literature Professors Turned Against Authors—Or Did They?" *Los Angeles Review of Books*, 13 Jan. 2019. lareviewofbooks.org/article/why-literature-professors-turned-against-authors-or-did-they.

Faulkner, William. Local and UVA Communities, Tape 1, 30 May 1957. *Faulkner at Virginia*, created by Stephen Railton and Michael Plunkett. Rector and Visitors of the University of Virginia, 2010. faulkner.lib.virginia.edu/display/wfaudio18_1.html#wfaudio18_1.1.

Fernandez, Henry. "Stephen King, One of the Richest Authors, Still Out to Scare You." *FOXBusiness*, 17 Aug. 2019. www.foxbusiness.com/media/stephen-king-richest-horror-authors.

Flatley, Jonathan. "Reading Into Henry James." *Criticism*, vol. 46, no. 1, Special Issue: Materia Media, 2004, pp. 103–23. www.jstor.org/stable/23127340.

Ford, Ford Madox. *It Was the Nightingale*. J. B. Lippincott Company, 1933. archive.org/details/itwasnightingale0000ford_p1m1.

———. *The Good Soldier: A Tale of Passion*. Oxford World's Classics, edited by Thomas C. Moser, Oxford UP, 1990.

Foucault, Michel. "What Is an Author." *The Death and Resurrection of the Author?* edited by William Irwin, Greenwood Press, 2002, pp. 9–22. Originally published as "Qu'est-ce qu'un Auteur?" *Bulletin de la Societe Française de Philosophie*, vol. 63, no. 3, 1969, pp. 73–104.

Frank, Eibe et al. *The WEKA Workbench*. Online Appendix, *Data Mining: Practical Machine Learning Tools and Techniques*. 4th ed., Morgan Kaufmann, 2016. www.cs.waikato.ac.nz/ml/weka/index.html.

Fry, Joan. "'Congratulations! You've Just Won $295,000': An Interview With Octavia E. Butler." *Poets and Writers*, vol. 25, no. 2, 1 Mar. 1997, pp. 58–69. www.joanfry.com/congratulations-youve-just-won-295000.

Garnett, Constance. 1947. "'The Art of Translation.' Conversation Recorded in *The Listener*, 30 Jan. 1947." *Translation: Theory and Practice: A Historical Reader*, edited by Daniel Weissbort and Astrabur Eysteinsson. Oxford UP, 2006.

Garrard, Peter et al. "The Effects of Very Early Alzheimer's Disease on the Characteristics of Writing by a Renowned Author." *Brain*, vol. 128, no. 2, 2005, pp. 250–60.

Goldstone, Andrew, and Ted Underwood. "The Quiet Transformations of Literary Studies: What Thirteen Thousand Scholars Could Tell Us." *New Literary History*, vol. 45, no. 3, 2014, pp. 359–84, doi:10.1353/nlh.2014.0025.

goodreads. www.goodreads.com.

Gottlieb, Robert. "The Rise and Fall of Booth Tarkington: How a Candidate for the Great American Novelist Dwindled Into America's Most Distinguished Hack." *The Newyorker*. 4 Nov. 2019. www.newyorker.com/magazine/2019/11/11/the-rise-and-fall-of-booth-tarkington.

Govan, Sandra Y., and Octavia E. Butler. "Going to See the Woman: A Visit With Octavia E. Butler." *Obsidian III*, vol. 6, no. 2; vol. 7, no. 1, 2005–06, pp. 14–39. www.jstor.org/stable/44511659.

Graham, Shawn et al. "Getting Started With Topic Modeling and *MALLET*." *The Programming Historian*, vol. 1, 2012. programminghistorian.org/en/lessons/topic-modeling-and-mallet.

"*The Green Mile* (novel)." *Wikipedia*. en.wikipedia.org/wiki/The_Green_Mile_(novel).

Guillory, John. "The Sokal Affair and the History of Criticism." *Critical Inquiry*, vol. 28, no. 2, 2002, pp. 470–508.

Ha, Vi. LAPL BLOG: On Persistence: Octavia E. Butler and Central, Octavia Lab, Tuesday, 11 June 2019. www.lapl.org/collections-resources/blogs/lapl/persistence-octavia-e-butler-central-library.

Hallet, Richard. "Booth Tarkington: At Sea at Home." *The Christian Science Monitor*, 20 Dec. 1941, p. WM7.

Halperin, John. Review of *The Collected Letters of Joseph Conrad*, Vol. 3, edited by Frederick Karl and Laurence Davies. *Modern Fiction Studies*, vol. 35, no. 4, 1989, pp. 786–8. JSTOR. www.jstor.org/stable/26283401.

Hardy, Florence Emily. *The Early Life of Thomas Hardy*. Palgrave Macmillan, 1928. archive.org/details/earlylifeofthoma00hard.

Hartley, James et al. "Speaking Versus Typing: A Case-study of the Effects of Using Voice-Recognition Software on Academic Correspondence." *British Journal of Educational Technology*, vol. 34, no. 1, 2003, pp. 5–16, doi.org/10.1111/1467-8535.d01-2.

Harvey, David Dow. *Ford Madox Ford, 1873–1939: Bibliography of Works and Criticism*. Princeton UP, 1962.

Heim, Michael. *Electric Language: A Philosophical Study of Word Processing*. Yale UP, 1987. archive.org/details/electriclanguage00heim.

Heller, Karen. "Meet the Writers Who Still Sell Millions of Books. Actually, Hundreds of Millions." *The Washington Post*, 20 Dec. 2016. www.washingtonpost.com/lifestyle/style/meet-the-elite-group-of-authors-who-sell-100-million-books-or-350-million/2016/12/20/db3c6a66-bb0f-11e6-94ac-3d324840106c_story.html.

"Henry James." *Wikipedia*. en.wikipedia.org/wiki/Henry_James.

Herrmann, J. Berenike et al. "Revisiting Style, a Key Concept in Literary Studies." *Journal of Literary Theory*, vol. 9, no. 1, 2015, pp. 25–52.

Higashiyama, Y. et al. "The Neural Basis of Typewriting: A Functional MRI Study." *PLoS One*, vol. 10, no. 7, 2015, pp. 1–20, doi:10.1371/journal.pone.0134131.

Hirst, Graeme, and Vanessa Wei Feng. "Changes in Style in Authors With Alzheimer's Disease." *English Studies*, vol. 93, no. 3, 2012, pp. 357–70, doi:10.1080/0013838X.2012.668789.

Hoffman, Arthur S., editor. *Fiction Writers on Fiction Writing: Advice, Opinions and a Statement of Their Own Working Methods by More Than One Hundred Writers*. Bobbs-Merrill, 1923. archive.org/details/fictionwritersonO0indi.

Holmes, David I. "Authorship Attribution." *Computers and the Humanities*, vol. 28, no. 2, 1994, pp. 87–106, doi:10.1007/BF01830689.

Honeycutt, Lee. "Literacy and the Writing Voice: The Intersection of Culture and Technology in Dictation." *Journal of Business and Technical Communication*, vol. 18, no. 3, 2004, pp. 294–327, doi:10.1177/1050651904264105.

———. "Researching the Use of Voice Recognition Writing Software." *Computers and Composition*, vol. 20, no. 1, 2003, pp. 77–95, doi:10.1016/S8755-4615(02)00174-3.

Hoover, David L. "Argument, Evidence, and the Limits of Digital Literary Studies." *Debates in the Digital Humanities: 2016*, edited by Matthew Gold, U of Minnesota P, 2016, pp. 230–50. dhdebates.gc.cuny.edu/read/untitled/section/70f5261e-e268-4f56-928f-0c4ea30d254d.

———. "CaSTAing Breadth Upon the Waters." CaSTA 2006: Breadth of Text—A Joint Computer Science and Humanities Computing Conference, U of New Brunswick. Fredericton, NB, Canada, 13 Oct. 2006.

———. "A Conversation Among Himselves: Change and the Styles of Henry James." *Style in Fiction International Symposium*, Lancaster University, 11 Mar. 2006.

———. "Cora Crane's Contribution to Stephen Crane's Posthumous Fiction." *DH2015: Global Digital Humanities*, U of Western Sydney, 2 July 2015.

———. "Corpus Stylistics, Stylometry, and the Styles of Henry James." *Style*, vol. 41, no. 2, 2007, pp. 174–203.

———. "The End of the Irrelevant Text: Electronic Texts, Linguistics, and Literary Theory." *Digital Humanities Quarterly*, vol. 1, no. 2, 2007. www.digitalhumanities.org/dhq/vol/1/2/000012/000012.html.

———. *Excel Text-Analysis Tools*. 2019. wp.nyu.edu/exceltextanalysis.

———. "Frequent Word Sequences and Statistical Stylistics." *Literary and Linguistic Computing*, vol. 17, no. 2, 2002, pp. 157–80, doi:10.1093/llc/17.2.157.

———. "Hot-Air Textuality: Literature After Jerome McGann." *Text Technology*, vol. 14, no. 2, 2005, pp. 71–103.

———. *Language and Style in the Inheritors*. UP of America, 1999. archive.org/details/languagestyleint00hoov.

———. "Literary Style, Chronology, and Vocabulary: Problems of Stylistics and Classification." Joint Workshop on Data Analysis and Research in the Humanities. Digital Humanities and CSNA, Urbana-Champaign, 8 June 2007.

———. "Making Waves: Algorithmic Criticism Revisited." *Digital Humanities 2014*, Lausanne: EPFL-UNIL, 10 June 2014, pp. 202–4.

———. "Metaphors We May Not Live By." *International Journal of Literary Linguistics*, vol. 5, no. 1, 2016, pp. 1–16, doi.org/10.15462/ijll.v5i1.27.

———. "The Microanalysis of Style Variation." *Digital Scholarship in the Humanities*, vol. 32, suppl. 2, 2017, pp. ii17–ii30, doi.org/10.1093/llc/fqx022.

———. "Mind-Style." *The Bloomsbury Companion to Stylistics*, edited by Violeta Sotirova, Bloomsbury Academic, 2016, pp. 325–40.

———. "Modes of Composition in Henry James: Dictation, Style, and *What Maisie Knew*." *Digital Humanities 2009*, Maryland Institute for Technology in the Humanities, pp. 145–8.

———. "Modes of Composition in Henry James: Dictation, Style, and *What Maisie Knew*." *Henry James Review*, vol. 35, no. 3, 2014, pp. 257–77, doi:10.1353/hjr.2014.0024.

———. "Modes of Composition in Three Authors." *Digital Humanities 2011*, Stanford University Library, 2011, pp. 152–5.

———. "Multivariate Analysis and the Study of Style Variation." *Literary and Linguistic Computing*, vol. 18, no. 4, 2003, pp. 341–60, doi:10.1093/llc/18.4.341.

———. "Simulations and Difficult Problems." *Digital Scholarship in the Humanities*, vol. 34, no. 4, 2019, pp. 874–92, doi.org/10.1093/llc/fqz034.

———. "Some Approaches to Corpus Stylistics." *Stylistics: Past, Present and Future*, edited by Yu Dongmin, Shanghai Foreign Language Education Press, 2010, pp. 40–63.

———. "Statistical Stylistics and Authorship Attribution: An Empirical Investigation." *Literary and Linguistic Computing*, vol. 16, no. 4, 2001, pp. 421–44, doi:10.1093/llc/16.4.421.

———. "Style Evolution in Henry James: Fiction, Short Fiction, Non-fiction, Drama." MLA Convention, San Francisco, 27 Dec. 2008.

———. "Stylometry, Chronology, and the Styles of Henry James." *Digital Humanities 2006*, Centre de Recherche Cultures Anglophones et Technologies de l'Information, 2006, pp. 78–80. www.allc-ach2006.colloques.paris-sorbonne.fr/DHs.pdf.

———. "Text Analysis." *Literary Studies in the Digital Age: An Evolving Anthology*, edited by Ken Price and Ray Siemens, MLA, 2013. dlsanthology.mla.hcommons.org/textual-analysis.

———. "Text-Analysis Tools in Excel." *Digital Humanities for Literary Studies: Theories, Methods, and Practices*, edited by James O'Sullivan, Texas A and MUP, forthcoming.

———. "*The Tutor's Story:* A Case Study of Mixed Authorship." *English Studies*, vol. 93, no. 3, 2012, pp. 324–39, doi:10.1080/0013838X.2012.668791.

Hoover, David L. et al. *Digital Literary Studies: Corpus Approaches to Poetry, Prose, and Drama*. Routledge, 2014.

Horowitz, Floyd R. *The Uncollected Henry James*. Garroll and Graf, 2004.

Hosking, Patrick, and David Wighton. "The 50 Greatest British Writers Since 1945." *The Times* [London], 5 Jan. 2008. www.thetimes.co.uk/article/the-50-greatest-british-writers-since-1945-ws3g69xrf90.

"Ian McEwan, the Art of Fiction No. 173." Interviewed by Adam Begley. *The Paris Review*, Issue 162, Summer 2002. www.theparisreview.org/interviews/393/ian-mcewan-the-art-of-fiction-no-173-ian-mcewan.

Ian McEwan Papers. Harry Ransom Center, the University of Texas at Austin, 2014.

Ingersoll, Earl. "Margaret Atwood's *The Handmaid's Tale:* Echoes of Orwell." *Journal of the Fantastic in the Arts*, vol. 5, no. 4 (20), 1993, pp. 64–72. www.jstor.org/stable/43308174.

Ireland, Ken. *Thomas Hardy, Time and Narrative: A Narratological Approach to His Novels*. Palgrave Macmillan, 2014.

Irwin, William, editor. *The Death and Resurrection of the Author?* Greenwood Press, 2002.

"J. G. Ballard, The Art of Fiction No. 85." Interviewed by Thomas Frick, *The Paris Review*, vol. 94, 1984. theparisreview.org/interviews/2929/the-art-of-fiction-no-85-j-g-ballard.

James, Henry. *The Ambassadors*. Norton Critical Editions. 2nd ed., edited by S. P. Rosenbaum, Norton, 1994.

———. *The American*. Norton Critical Editions, edited by James W. Tuttleton, Norton, 1978. archive.org/details/americanauthorit0000jame.

———. *The American*. Scribner, 1907. archive.org/details/theamerican02jameuoft.

———. *The Art of the Novel*. Edited by R. P. Blackmur, Scribner, 1934. archive.org/details/artofnovel00jame.

———. *The Complete Notebooks of Henry James*. Edited by Leon Edel and Lyall H. Powers, Oxford UP, 1987. archive.org/details/completenotebook00henr.

———. *The Letters of Henry James*. Vol. 1, edited by Percy Lubbock, Palgrave Macmillan, 1920. archive.org/details/lettersofhenryja01jamerich.

———. *Views and Reviews*. Introduction by Le Roy Phillips, Hall, 1908. www.gutenberg.org/files/37424/37424-h/37424-h.htm.

———. *What Maisie Knew*. New York: Stone, 1897. ia331316.us.archive.org/0/items/whatmaisieknew00jamerich/whatmaisieknew00jamerich_djvu.txt.

Jameson, Fredric. *Postmodernism, or, the Cultural Logic of Late Capitalism*. Duke UP, 1992, doi:10.1215/9780822378419.

Jean-Aubry, Gérard. *The Sea Dreamer: A Definitive Biography of Joseph Cornrad*. Translated by Helen Sebba, Doubleday, 1957. archive.org/details/seadreamerdefini0000jean.

Jockers, Matt. *Macroanalysis: Digital Methods and Literary History*. U of Illinois P, 2013, doi:10.5406/illinois/9780252037528.001.0001.

Jockers, Matt et al. "Reassessing Authorship of the *Book of Mormon* Using Delta and Nearest Shrunken Centroid Classification." *Literary and Linguistic Computing*, vol. 23, no. 4, 2008, pp. 465–91, doi:10.1093/llc/fqn040.

Jordan, Ellen et al. "The Brontë Sisters and the *Christian Remembrancer:* A Pilot Study in the Use of the 'Burrows Method' to Identify the Authorship of Unsigned Articles in the Nineteenth-Century Periodical Press." *Victorian Periodicals Review*, vol. 39, no. 1, 2006, pp. 21–45, doi:10.1353/vpr.2006.0024.

Juola, Patrick. "Authorship Attribution." *Foundations and Trends in Information Retrieval*, vol. 1, no. 3, 2008, pp. 233–334, doi:10.1561/1500000005.

———. "*JGAAP:* A System for Comparative Evaluation of Authorship Attribution." *Journal of the Chicago Colloquium on Digital Humanities and Computer Science*, vol. 1, no. 1, 2009, pp. 1–5, doi:10.6082/M1N29V4Z.

Juxta. Applied Research in Patacriticism, U of Virginia. www.juxtasoftware.org.

Karl, Frederick R. *Joseph Conrad: The Three Lives, a Biography*. Farrar, Straus and Giroux, 1979. archive.org/details/josephconradthre00karl.

———. "The Significance of the Revisions in the Early Versions of *Nostromo*." *Modern Fiction Studies*, vol. 5, no. 2, 1959, pp. 129–44. www.jstor.org/stable/26277114.

———. *William Faulkner, American Writer: A Biography*. Weidenfeld and Nicolson, 1989. archive.org/details/williamfaulknera0000karl.

Kenny, Anthony. *The Computation of Style*. Pergamon Press, 1982, doi:10.1016/C2009-0-10976-5.

Kibler, James E. Review of "The Making of *Sartoris:* A Description and Discussion of the Manuscript and Composite Typescript of William Faulkner's Third Novel" by Stephen Neal Dennis. *The Mississippi Quarterly*, vol. 24, no. 3, 1971, pp. 315–19.

———. "A Study of the Text of William Faulkner's *The Hamlet*." PhD dissertation, U of South Carolina, 1970.

King, Laura A., and James W. Pennebaker. "Linguistic Styles: Language Use as an Individual Difference." *Journal of Personality and Social Psychology*, vol. 77, no. 6, 2000, pp. 1296–312, doi:10.1037//0022-3514.77.6.1296.

King, Stephen. *Bag of Bones*. Scribner, 1998.

———. "The Blue-Collar King: An Interview with Stephen King." Interviewed by Angela S. Allan. *Los Angeles Review of Books*, 25 Oct. 2015. lareviewofbooks.org/article/the-blue-collar-king-an-interview-with-stephen-king.

———. "The Cannibals." Unpublished Works—A to Z, 2019. www.stephenking.com/library/unpublished/cannibals_the.html.

———. *Carrie*. Doubleday, 1974.

———. *Cell*. Scribner, 2006.

———. *Christine*. Scribner, 1983.
———. *The Colorado Kid*. Simon and Schuster, 2005.
———. *Cujo*. Scribner, 1981.
———. *Cycle of the Werewolf*. Land of Enchantment, 1983.
———. *The Dark Half*. Scribner, 1989.
———. *The Dark Tower II: The Drawing of the Three*. Donald M. Grant Publisher, Inc., 1987.
———. *The Dead Zone*. Scribner, 1979.
———. *Desperation*. Scribner, 1996.
———. "Digging Up Stories With Stephen King." Interviewed by Wallace Stroby, *Writer's Digest*, 16 Sept. 1991. wallacestroby.com/writersonwriting_king.html.
———. *The Drawing of the Three*. Signet, 2003.
———. *Dreamcatcher*. Scribner, 2001.
———. *Duma Key*. Scribner, 2008.
———. *The Eyes of the Dragon*. Philtrum Press, 1984.
———. *Firestarter*. Scribner, 1980.
———. *From a Buick 8*. Scribner, 2002.
———. *Gerald's Game*. Scribner, 1992.
———. *The Girl Who Loved Tom Gordon*. Scribner, 1999.
———. *The Green Mile*. 1996. Orion, 1998.
———. *The Gunslinger*. Donald M. Grant, 1982.
———. *Hearts in Atlantis*. Scribner, 1999.
———. *Insomnia*. Scribner, 1994.
———. *It*. Scribner, 1986.
———. *Lisey's Story*. Scribner, 2006.
———. *Misery*. Scribner, 1987.
———. *Needful Things*. Scribner, 1992.
———. *On Writing: A Memoir of the Craft*. Scribner, 2000. archive.org/details/onwritingmemoir000king.
———. *Pet Sematary*. Scribner, 1983.
———. "The Politics of Limited Editions." *The Truth Inside the Lie: A Blog About Stephen King . . . Mostly*, by Bryant Burnett. thetruthinsidethelie.blogspot.com/2017/10/a-guided-tour-of-kingdom-chronological_26.html.
———. *The Regulators*. Hodder and Staughton, 1996 (as Richard Bachman).
———. *Rose Madder*. Signet, 1995.
———. *'Salem's Lot*. Doubleday, 1975.
———. *The Shinning*. Doubleday, 1977.
———. *Thinner*. Scribner, 1984 (as Richard Bachman).
———. *Skeleton Crew*. Signet, 1985.
———. *Song of Susannah*. Scribner, 2004.
———. *The Stand*. Doubleday, 1978.
———. *The Stand*. Doubleday, 1990.
———. "Stephen King, the Art of Fiction No. 189." *Paris Review*, vol. 48, no. 178, 2006. www.theparisreview.org/interviews/5653/stephen-king-the-art-of-fiction-no-189-stephen-king.
———. "The Stephen King Interview." *The Guardian*, 14 Sept. 2000.
———. "Stephen King on His Longest Novels: *The Stand*." Podcast, interviewed by Gilbert Cruz, 6 Nov. 2009. pdl-stream.timeinc.net/time/audio/2009/thestand_dl.mp3.

———. "Stephen King: *Playboy* Interview (1983)." Interviewed by Eric Norden, *Playboy*, vol. 30, no. 6, June 1983. scrapsfromtheloft.com/2018/03/08/stephen-king-playboy-interview-1983.

———. "Stephen King: The *Rolling Stone* Interview." *Rolling Stone*, 31 Oct. 2014. www.rollingstone.com/culture/culture-features/stephen-king-the-rolling-stone-interview-191529.

———. *The Tommyknockers*. Scribner, 1987.

———. *The Two Dead Girls*. Scribner, 1995.

King, Stephen, and Peter Straub. *The Black House*. Random House, 2001.

———. *The Talisman*. Ballantine, 1984.

Kirschenbaum, Matthew G. "Technology Changes How Authors Write, but the Big Impact Isn't on Their Style." *The New Republic*, 26 July 2016. theconversation.com/technology-changes-how-authors-write-but-the-big-impact-isnt-on-their-style-61955.

———. *Track Changes: A Literary History of Word Processing*. Belknap Press, 2016.

Kittler, Friedrich A. *Discourse Networks 1800/1900*. Stanford UP, 1990.

———. *Gramophone, Film, Typewriter*. Stanford UP, 1999.

Knowles, Owen, and Gene M. Moore, editors. *Oxford Reader's Companion to Conrad*. Oxford UP, 2011.

Kopf, Dan. "The Guinness Brewer Who Revolutionized Statistics." *Pricenomics*, 11 Dec. 2015. priceonomics.com/the-guinness-brewer-who-revolutionized-statistics.

Kunitz, Stanley. "Booth Tarkington." *Living Authors*. 1931. Edited by Dilly Tante, pseud. [Stanley Kunitz], H. W. Wilson, 1935, pp. 398–400. archive.org/details/in.ernet.dli.2015.260813.

Layne, Bethany. "'Henry Would Never Know He Hadn't Written It Himself': The Implications of 'Dictation' for Jamesian Style." *The Henry James Review*, vol. 35, no. 3, 2014, pp. 248–56, doi:10.1353/hjr.2014.0039.

Le, X. et al. "Longitudinal Detection of Dementia Through Lexical and Syntactic Changes in Writing: A Case Study of Three British Novelists." *Literary and Linguist Computing*, vol. 26, no. 4, 2011, pp. 435–61.

Leech, Geoffrey, and Michael Short. *Style in Fiction*. 2nd ed. Addison-Wesley, 2007.

Lockhart, John G. *Memoirs of the Life of Sir Walter Scott, Bart.* Vol. 1, Carey, Lea, and Blanchard, 1837. archive.org/details/memoirslifesirw01lockgoog/mode/2up.

———. *Memoirs of the Life of Sir Walter Scott, Bart.* Vol. 2, Carey, Lea, and Blanchard, 1837. archive.org/details/memoirslifesirw83lockgoog/mode/2up.

Love, Harold. *Attributing Authorship: An Introduction*. Cambridge UP, 2002, doi:10.1017/CBO9780511483165.

M. L. Parrish Collection of Victorian Novelists. Department of Rare Books and Special Collections, Princeton University Library.

MacDonald, A. B. "Tarkington, Nearly Blind. Hunts Whale: Doesn't Catch Creatures. Just Watches Them—Forbidden to Write, He Dictates Work." *The Hartford Courant*, 17 Sept. 1934, p. 15.

MacDougall, Sarah. "Authors Struggle to Get Down to Work: Homer Croy Takes off His Shoes, Will Irwin Starts at 5 A. M., Booth Tarkington Dons Bathrobe, Anne Parrish Seeks Garage." *The Hartford Courant*, 6 Feb. 1927, p. 5.

Magistrale, Tony. *Stephen King, the Second Decade, Danse Macabre to the Dark Half*. Twayne Publishers, 1992. archive.org/details/stephenking00tony.

Mandelbaum, Paul, editor. *First Words: Earliest Writing From Favorite Contemporary Authors*. Algonquin Books of Chapel Hill, 1993.

Manford, Alan. "Emma Hardy's Helping Hand." *Critical Essays on Thomas Hardy: The Novels*, edited by Dale Kramer, assisted by Nancy Marck, G. K. Hall, 1990, pp. 100–21.

———. "Who Wrote Thomas Hardy's Novels? A Survey of Emma Hardy's Contribution to the Manuscripts of Her Husband's Novels." *The Thomas Hardy Journal*, vol. 6, no. 2, 1990, pp. 84–97.

Mangen, Anne, and Jean-Luc Velay. *Digitizing Literacy: Reflections on the Haptics of Writing, Advances in Haptics*, edited by Mehrdad Hosseini Zadeh, InTech, 2010.

Mayberry, Susanah. *My Amiable Uncle: Recollections About Booth Tarkington*. Purdue UP, 1983. archive.org/details/myamiableunclere00mayb.

McAleer, Neil. *Arthur C. Clarke: The Authorized Biography*. Contemporary Books, 1992.

Mcdowell, Edwin. "Faulkner Manuscript Is Bought." *New York Times*, 10 Oct. 1987.

McCallum, Andrew Kachites. "*MALLET*: A Machine Learning for Language Toolkit." 2002. mallet.cs.umass.edu.

McLuhan, Eric, and Frank Zingrone. *Essential McLuhan*. House of Anansi, 1995. epdf.pub/essential-mcluhan.html.

McLuhan, Marshall. *Understanding Media: The Extensions of Man*. Gingko Press, 2013.

McWilliam, Fiona. "Louisa May Alcott's 'My Contraband' and Discourse on Contraband Slaves in Popular Print Culture." *Studies in American Fiction*, vol. 42, no. 1, 2015, pp. 51–84, doi:10.1353/saf.2015.0001.

Meeks, Elijah, and Scott Weingart. "The Digital Humanities Contribution to Topic Modeling." *Journal of Digital Humanities*, vol. 2, no. 1, 2012. journalofdigitalhumanities.org/2-1/dh-contribution-to-topic-modeling.

Meixner, John A. *Ford Madox Ford's Novels: A Critical Study*. U of Minnesota P, 1962. muse.jhu.edu/book/31799.

Meriwether, James B. *The Literary Career of William Faulkner: A Bibliographical Study*. Princeton University Library, 1961. archive.org/details/literarycar00meri.

Meriwether, James B., and Michael Millgate, editors. *Lion in the Garden: Interviews With William Faulkner 1926–1962*. U of Nebraska P, 1968. archive.org/details/lioningardeninte00meri.

Millgate, Jane. *Walter Scott: The Making of the Novelist*. 1987. U of Toronto P, 2015, doi:10.3138/9781442683211.

Millgate, Michael. *The Achievement of William Faulkner*. U of Nebraska P, 1963. archive.org/details/achievementofwil0000mill_m1x2.

———. *Thomas Hardy: A Biography Revisited*. Oxford UP, 2006.

Minitab Release 19, Minitab, Inc., State College, PA, 2019.

Mizener, Arthur. *The Saddest Story: A Biography of Ford Madox Ford*. Bodley Head, 1971. archive.org/details/saddeststorybiog00mize.

Moore, Gene M. *A Descriptive Location Register of Joseph Conrad's Literary Manuscripts*. 2016. www.josephconradsociety.org/02MSS_register.pdf.

Morehouse, Ward. "Tarkington Ill at Home: Noted Author Delayed From Leaving on Summer Trip to Maine Coast." *Los Angeles Times*, 30 May 1936, p. 10.

Morey, John H. "Joseph Conrad and Ford Madox Ford: A Study in Collaboration." Unpublished PhD dissertation, Cornell University, 1960.

The Morgan Library and Museum, New York, NY.

"Mrs. Tarkington Denies: Novelist's Wife Says He Is Not to Undergo Eye Operation Soon." *New York Times*, 13 Dec. 1928, p. 26.

Najder, Zdzisław. *Joseph Conrad: A Life*. Translated by Halina Najder, Camden House, 2007.

Newman, Dan. *The Dragon Naturally Speaking Guide*. 2nd ed. Waveside Publishing, 2000. lib.store.yahoo.net/lib/sayican/onlinebook.html.

Novick, Sheldon M. *Henry James: The Mature Master*. Random House, 2007. archive.org/details/henryjamesmature00novi.

Nyqvist, Sanna. "Authorship and Authenticity in Sherlock Holmes Pastiches." *Transformative Works and Cultures*, vol. 23, 2017, doi:10.3983/twc.2017.0834.

O'Brien, Robert Lincoln. "Machinery and English Style." *Atlantic Monthly*, vol. 94, 1 Oct. 1904, pp. 464–72.

Octavia E. Butler Papers. The Huntington Library, San Marino, CA.

Ozick, Cynthia. *Dictation: A Quartet*. Houghton Mifflin, 2008.

Patterson, Mark. "Racial Sacrifice and Citizenship: The Construction of Masculinity in Louisa May Alcott's 'The Brothers'." *Studies in American Fiction*, vol. 25, no. 2, 1997, pp. 147–66, doi:10.1353/saf.1997.0000.

Perec, Georges. *La Disparition: Roman*. Denoël, 1969.

Peschel, Bill. *Sherlock Holmes Victorian Parodies and Pastiches: 1888–1899*. Peschel Press, 2015. peschelpress.com/sherlock-holmes-victorian-parodies-and-pastiches-1888-1899.

Pizer, Donald. "'John Boyle's Conclusion': An Unpublished Middle Border Story by Hamlin Garland." *American Literature*, vol. 31, no. 1, 1959, pp. 59–75. www.jstor.org/stable/2922652.

Polk, Noel. *Children of the Dark House: Text and Context in Faulkner*. UP of Mississippi, 1998. archive.org/details/childrenofdarkho0000polk.

Project Gutenberg. Founded by Michael Hart, 1971. www.gutenberg.org.

Purdy, Richard Little. *Thomas Hardy: A Bibliographical Study*. Oxford UP, 1954. archive.org/details/thomashardybibli0000purd.

Queen, Ellery, editor. *The Misadventures of Sherlock Holmes*. Little, Brown, 1944. archive.org/details/scriblio_test_044.

R Core Team. "*R*: A Language and Environment for Statistical Computing." *R* Foundation for Statistical Computing, Vienna, Austria, 2019. www.R-project.org.

Ramsay, Stephen. *Reading Machines: Toward an Algorithmic Criticism*. U of Illinois P, 2011, doi:10.5406/illinois/9780252036415.001.0001.

Reynolds, Margaret, and Jonathan Noakes. *Ian McEwan: The Essential Guide*. Vintage, 2002. books.google.com/books/about/Ian_McEwan.html?id=cXkh1vk3TzwC.

Rhody, Lisa M. "Topic Modeling and Figurative Language." *Journal of Digital Humanities*, vol. 2, no. 1, 2012. journalofdigitalhumanities.org/2-1/topic-modeling-and-figurative-language-by-lisa-m-rhody.

Rogak, Lisa. *Haunted Heart: The Life and Times of Stephen King*. St. Martins, 2008. archive.org/details/isbn_9780312377328.

Rolls, Albert. *Stephen King: A Biography*. Greenwood Press, 2008.

Romero, George A. *Creepshow*. Creepshow Films Inc., 12 Nov. 1982.

Rostenberg, Leona. "Some Anonymous and Pseudonymous Thrillers of Louisa M. Alcott." *The Papers of the Bibliographical Society of America*, vol. 37, no. 2, 1943, pp. 131–40, doi:10.1086/pbsa.37.2.24293383.

Rothman, Joshua. "What Stephen King Isn't." *The New Yorker*, 11 Oct. 2013. www.newyorker.com/books/page-turner/what-stephen-king-isnt.

Rothstein, Edward. "Undo Influence: Stephen King Began Using a Word Processor in 1981. Toni Morrison Writes Longhand. Does It Matter?" *The Wall Street Journal*, 10 June 2016.

Roux, Franck-Emmanuel et al. "The Neural Basis for Writing From Dictation in the Temporoparietal Cortex." *Cortex*, vol. 50, 2014, pp. 64–75, doi:10.1016/j.cortex.2013.09.012.

Russell, Bertrand. "An Outline of Intellectual Rubbish." *Unpopular Essays*, Allen and Unwin, 1921, pp. 95–145.

Russell, Natalie M. "Finding Aid." *Octavia E. Butler Papers*, the Huntington Library, San Marino, CA, 2013. oac.cdlib.org/findaid/ark:/13030/c8hm5br8/entire_text.

Russo, Dorothy Ritter, and Thelma L. Sullivan. *A Bibliography of Booth Tarkington: 1869–1946*. Indiana Historical Society, 1949. archive.org/details/biblibo00russ/.

Rybicki, Jan. "Burrowing Into Translation: Character Idiolects in Henryk Sienkiewicz's Trilogy and Its Two English Translations." *Literary and Linguistic Computing*, vol. 21, no. 1, 2006, pp. 91–103.

———. "The Great Mystery of the (Almost) Invisible Translator: Stylometry in Translation." *Quantitative Methods in Corpus-based Translation Studies: A Practical Guide to Descriptive Translation Research*, edited by Michael P. Oakes and Meng Ji, John Benjamins, 2012, pp. 231–48.

Rybicki, Jan, and Maciej Eder. "Deeper Delta Across Genres and Languages: Do We Really Need the Most Frequent Words?" *Literary and Linguistic Computing*, vol. 26, no. 3, 2011, pp. 315–21, doi:10.1093/llc/fqr031.

Rybicki, Jan, and Magda Heydel. "The Stylistics and Stylometry of Collaborative Translation: Woolf's *Night and Day* in Polish." *Literary and Linguistic Computing*, vol. 28, no. 4, 2013, pp. 708–17, doi:10.1093/llc/fqt027.

Rybicki, Jan et al. "Collaborative Authorship: Conrad, Ford, and Rolling Delta." *Literary and Linguistic Computing*, vol. 29, no. 3, 2014, pp. 422–31, doi:10.1093/llc/fqu016.

Salztman, Arthur M. "Stanley Elkin: An Introduction." *Review of Contemporary Fiction*, vol. 15, no. 2, 1995, pp. 7–14.

Samway, Patrick H. S. J. *Faulkner's Intruder in the Dust: A Critical Study of the Typescripts*. Whitston Publishing Company, 1980. archive.org/details/faulknersintrude0000samw.

Sanyal, Shourjya. "How a Brewer in Guinness Factory Secretly Discovered A Statistical Method." *Forbes*, 8 Jan. 2019. www.forbes.com/sites/shourjyasanyal/2019/01/08/how-a-brewer-in-guinness-factory-secretly-discovered-a-statistical-method/#29584cd5172f.

Schilleman, Matthew. "Typewriter Psyche: Henry James's Mechanical Mind." *Journal of Modern Literature*, vol. 36, no. 3, 2013, pp. 14–30, doi:10.2979/jmodelite.36.3.14.

Schmidt, Benjamin M. "Words Alone: Dismantling Topic Models in the Humanities." *Journal of Digital Humanities*, vol. 2, no. 1, 2012. journalofdigitalhumanities.org/2-1/words-alone-by-benjamin-m-schmidt.

Schmidt, Michael. *The Novel: A Biography*. Harvard UP, 2014.

Self, Will. "My Writing Day." *The Guardian*, 18 June 2016.

Seltzer, Mark. *Bodies and Machines*. Routledge, 1992.

———. "The Graphic Unconscious: A Response." *New Literary History*, vol. 26, no. 1, 1995, pp. 21–8. www.jstor.org/stable/20057262.

Short, R. W. "The Sentence Structure of Henry James." *American Literature*, vol. 18, no. 2, 1946, pp. 71–88.

Sigelman, Lee, and William Jacoby. "The Not-So-Simple Art of Imitation: Pastiche, Literary Style, and Raymond Chandler." *Computers and the Humanities*, vol. 30, 1996, pp. 11–28, doi:10.1007/BF00054025.

Simpson, M. J. *Hitchhiker: A Biography of Douglas Adams*. Justin, Charles and Co., 2005. archive.org/details/hitchhikerbiogra00simp.

Sinclair, John. *Reading Concordances: An Introduction*. Pearson Longman, 2003.

Smith, Stephanie A. "Octavia Butler: A Retrospective." *Feminist Studies*, vol. 33, no. 2, 2007, pp. 385–93, doi:10.2307/20459148.

So, Richard Jean, and Andrew Piper. "How Has the MFA Changed the Contemporary Novel?" *The Atlantic*, 6 Mar. 2016. www.theatlantic.com/entertainment/archive/2016/03/mfa-creative-writing/462483/.

Somers, Harold, and Fiona Tweedie. "Authorship Attribution and Pastiche." *Computers and the Humanities*, vol. 37, 2003, pp. 407–29, doi:10.1023/A:1025786724466.

Spignesi, Stephen. *Stephen King, American Master: A Creepy Corpus of Facts About Stephen King and His Work*. Permuted Press, 2018.

"Stephen King, the Art of Fiction No. 189." Interviewed by Nathaniel Rich and Christopher Lehmann-Haupt, *Paris Review*, vol. 48, no. 178, 2006. www.theparisreview.org/interviews/5653/stephen-king-the-art-of-fiction-no-189-stephen-king.

Strengell, Heidi. *Dissecting Stephen King: From the Gothic to Literary Naturalism*. U of Wisconsin P, 2005. archive.org/details/dissectingstephe0000stre.

Sudol, Ronald A. "The Accumulative Rhetoric of Word Processing." *College English*, vol. 53, no. 8, 1991, pp. 920–32, doi:10.2307/377699.

Sutherland, John. "The McEwan Problem." *Independent on Sunday*, 2 Sept. 2007. www.independent.co.uk/voices/commentators/john-sutherland-the-mcewan-problem-401145.html.

Sutherland, Kathryn. "Made in Scotland: 'The Edinburgh Edition of the Waverley Novels'." *Text*, vol. 14, 2002, pp. 305–23. www.jstor.org/stable/30228002.

"Tarkington Blind; May Regain Sight: Writer, Who Will Be Operated On, Gets 'Thrill' Not Having to See Everything. Helps Him Concentrate He Did More Work in Year Than Ever Before, He Says—His Chief Interest Is Modern Woman." *New York Times*, 28 Mar. 1929, p. 29.

Tarkington, Booth. *Penrod Jashber*. Grosset and Dunlap, 1929. archive.org/details/penrodjashber00tark.

"Tarkington Is Gaining: Author Recovering After Third Eye Operation at Baltimore." *New York Times*, 21 Oct. 1930, p. 4.

Temple, Emily. "The Living Authors With the Most Film Adaptations: An Infographic to Confirm Your Suspicions. . . " Literary Hub, 15 Mar. 2017. lithub.com/the-living-authors-with-the-most-film-adaptations.

Thorp, Margaret Farrand. *Charles Kingsley, 1819–1875, 1937*. Princeton UP, 2015. muse.jhu.edu/book/42948.

Thurschwell, Pamela. *Literature, Technology and Magical Thinking, 1880–1920*. Cambridge UP, 2001, doi:10.1017/CBO9780511484537.

Tracy, Jack, editor. *Sherlock Holmes: The Published Apocrypha, Sir Arthur Conan Doyle and Associated Hands*. Houghton Mifflin, 1980. archive.org/details/sherlockholmespu00doyl.

Tristman, Richard. "Tragic Soliloquy, Stand-up Spiel." *New England Review*, vol. 27, no. 4, 2006, pp. 36–40. www.jstor.org/stable/40244882.

Tulloch, Graham, editor. *Ivanhoe*. 1998. The Edinburgh Edition of the Waverley Novels, vol. 8, Edinburgh UP, 2017, doi:10.1093/actrade/9780748605736.book.1.

van Dalen-Oskam, Karina, and Joris van Zundert. "Delta for Middle Dutch: Author and Copyist Distinction in *Walewein*." *Literary and Linguistic Computing*, vol. 22, no. 3, 2007, pp. 345–62, doi:10.1093/llc/fqm012.

Venuti, Lawrence. *The Translator's Invisibility: A History of Translation*. 1995. Routledge, 2017, doi:10.4324/9781315098746.

Vericat, Fabio L. "Her Master's Voice: Dictation, the Typewriter, and Henry James's Trouble With the Speech of American Women." *South Atlantic Review*, vol. 80, no. 1–2, 2015, pp. 1–23. www.jstor.org/stable/soutatlarevi.80.1-2.1.

Vickers, Brian. "The Misuse of Function Words in Shakespeare Authorship Studies." *Göttingen Dialog in Digital Humanities*, 2016. www.etrap.eu/wp-content/uploads/2016/12/2016-11-30-vickers-misuse.pdf.

———. "Shakespeare and Authorship Studies in the Twenty-first Century." *Shakespeare Quarterly*, vol. 62, no. 1, 2011, pp. 106–42, doi:10.1353/shq.2011.0004.

Victorian Women Writers Project. Indiana University Digital Library Program, the Trustees of Indiana University, 2020. purl.dlib.indiana.edu/iudl/vwwp/VAB7166.

Warwick, Claire. "Beauty Is Truth: Multi-sensory Input and the Challenge of Designing Aesthetically Pleasing Digital Resources." *Digital Scholarship in the Humanities*, vol. 32, Suppl._2, 2017, pp. ii135–ii150, doi:10.1093/llc/fqx036.

Weingart, Scott. "Topic Modeling in the Humanities." *The Scottbot Irregular*, 11 Apr. 2013. scottbot.net/tag/topic-modeling.

Weingarten, Paul. "Meeting the Tiger." *Chicago Tribune*, 27 Oct. 1985, p. C10.

Wershler-Henry, Darren. *The Iron Whim: A Fragmented History of Typewriting*. Cornell UP, 2007.

Westerman, Molly. "'Of Skulls or Spirits': The Haunting Space Between Fictional(ized) History and Historical Note." *CLIO: A Journal of Literature, History, and the Philosophy of History*, vol. 35, no. 3, 2006, pp. 369–93, 463.

Wharton, Edith. *A Backward Glance*. Appleton-Century, 1934. archive.org/details/backwardglance030620mbp.

Widdowson, Peter. *On Thomas Hardy: Late Essays and Earlier*. Palgrave Macmillan, 2016.

Wikisource contributors. "Main Page." *Wikisource*. en.wikisource.org/wiki/Main_Page.

Wilde, Alan. "Final Things: More Letters to Mzimmer Humanitas at Hub.Ucsb.Edu." *Review of Contemporary Fiction*, vol. 15, no. 2, 1995, pp. 61–9.

William Faulkner: "Man Working," 1919–1962: A Catalogue of the William Faulkner Collections at the University of Virginia. Compiled by Linton R. Massey, and an introduction by John Cook Wyllie, UP of Virginia, 1968.

Wood, G. A. M., and D. Hewitt, editors. *Redgauntlet*. 1997. The Edinburgh Edition of the Waverley Novels, vol. 17, Edinburgh UP, 2017, doi:10.1093/actrade/9780748605804.book.1.

Wood, James. "Cult of the Master." *Atlantic Monthly*, vol. 291, no. 3, 2003, pp. 102–8.

Wood, Rocky. *Stephen King: A Literary Companion*. McFarland, 2017.

———. *Stephen King: Uncollected, Unpublished*. Revised and Expanded ed. Cemetery Dance Publications, 2010.

Wood, Rocky et al. *Stephen King: Uncollected, Unpublished*. Kanrock Publishing, 2006.

Woodress, James. *Booth Tarkington: Gentleman From Indiana*. J. B. Lippincott Company, 1954. archive.org/details/boothtarkingtong001459mbp.

———. "The Tarkington Papers." *The Princeton University Library Chronicle*, vol. 16, no. 2, 1955, pp. 45–53. www.jstor.org/stable/26402872.

Worden, Ward S. "A Cut Version of *What Maisie Knew*." *American Literature*, vol. 24, no. 4, 1953, pp. 493–504.

———. "Henry James's *What Maisie Knew*: A Comparison with the Plans in the Notebooks." *PMLA*, vol. 68, no. 3, 1953, pp. 371–83.

Worldcat. OCLC Online Computer Library Center, Inc. www.worldcat.org.

INDEX

Note: Numbers in *italics* indicate a figure and numbers in **bold** indicate a table on the corresponding page.

For Product Safety Concerns and Information please contact our EU representative GPSR@taylorandfrancis.com Taylor & Francis Verlag GmbH, Kaufingerstraße 24, 80331 München, Germany

Batch number: 10726019

Printed by Printforce, the Netherlands